CLEAN ECONOMY NOW

CHRIS,

THANKS FOR ALL YOU DO FOR EZ
— AND FOR OUR PLANET!

BEST,

Bob Keefe

4/12/24

CLEAN ECONOMY NOW

Stories from the Frontlines of an American Business Revolution

BOB KEEFE

ROWMAN & LITTLEFIELD
Lanham • Boulder • New York • London

Published by Rowman & Littlefield
An imprint of The Rowman & Littlefield Publishing Group, Inc.
4501 Forbes Boulevard, Suite 200, Lanham, Maryland 20706
www.rowman.com

86-90 Paul Street, London EC2A 4NE

British Library Cataloguing in Publication Information Available

Library of Congress Cataloging-in-Publication Data
Names: Keefe, Bob, 1966- author.
Title: Clean economy now: stories from the frontlines of an American business revolution / Bob Keefe.
Description: Lanham: Rowman & Littlefield, [2024] | Includes bibliographical references and index.
Identifiers: LCCN 2023048153 (print) | LCCN 2023048154 (ebook) | ISBN 9781538183045 (cloth; alk. paper) | ISBN 9781538183052 (ebook)
Subjects: LCSH: Clean energy industries—United States. | Sustainable development—United States. | Energy policy—Environmental aspects—United States.
Classification: LCC HD9502.C543 U654 2024 (print) | LCC HD9502.C543 (ebook) | DDC 333.79/4—dc23/eng/20231018
LC record available at https://lccn.loc.gov/2023048153
LC ebook record available at https://lccn.loc.gov/2023048154

♾️™ The paper used in this publication meets the minimum requirements of American National Standard for Information Sciences—Permanence of Paper for Printed Library Materials, ANSI/NISO Z39.48-1992.

For Nicole Lederer, for all she's done to make the economic case for our planet, and all she's done for me. And for Larry Orr, champion of entrepreneurs, environment—and life.

Contents

Contents

FOREWORD

Arnold Schwarzenegger

WHEN I RAN FOR OFFICE IN 2003 IN CALIFORNIA AND TOLD PEOPLE I'D be a green governor, many didn't believe it. More empty campaign promises, they thought.

Who could blame them?

After all, I drove a Hummer, went around blowing things up in movies, and I was a Republican.

But what we managed to do in California during my seven years as governor proved that their worries were misplaced.

Our historic Global Warming Solutions Act cut climate pollution by 25 percent and became a model for the world. Our renewable energy policies replaced coal and gas with wind and solar and led to a million solar roofs across the state. Our groundbreaking clean vehicle standards didn't just make our air cleaner; they led other states and the federal government to follow and led automakers to develop hybrid and electric vehicles that are now on the way to dominating the auto market. Even Hummers are now going electric.

Despite what all the naysayers predicted, California's economy didn't collapse. We didn't kill the auto industry. We didn't go back to reading by candlelight and warming our food with fire. To the contrary, we created more than 500,000 clean energy jobs in California. We sparked the creation of companies like Tesla and Sunrun. And today, solar and wind are the cheapest power available—not just in California, but in just about every part of the country.

We showed in California that building a clean economy isn't a Democrat or a Republican thing to do, it's the right thing to do. We showed that we could have the best and toughest environmental laws and still have the best and strongest economy in the country. We showed that when government works, good policies can send the right signals to businesses to invest, innovate, and expand.

Finally, Washington, D.C., is beginning to catch up. The federal government has started to see the importance of growing the clean economy nationwide. It's been a long time coming, but—just as we saw in California—the benefits can rack up quickly.

As Bob Keefe details in *Clean Economy NOW*, we are on the cusp of a business revolution in America like we haven't seen in generations. We can lead the world in the most important economic transition in history. The only thing that can stop it is us.

Companies are now investing billions of dollars in new factories to build solar panels, batteries, electric vehicles, and wind turbines, all of which put millions of Americans to work. It's not just happening in California anymore, either. The clean economy is now also being built in Georgia and South Carolina, Texas and Michigan, New York and New Mexico, and every other state as well. In just one year, more than two hundred companies announced $80 billion in clean energy projects, creating 70,000 new jobs. That's simply fantastic.

When I think about how far America has come in building a cleaner economy, I can't help but smile.

It's hard to imagine we can fail, but make no mistake: We can.

If we do, it won't be a failure of innovation or of business. It will be a failure by us to come together to keep this great progress going. It will be a failure by us to put aside our ideologies and political divisions and our complacency.

It will be a failure by us to act.

There are no more excuses. We now have the technology for clean energy, electric vehicles, and energy efficiency. We now have the policy, both at the state and federal level. And we certainly have the need. As nature continues to warn us, we are in an emergency, and this emergency demands action. Lives depend on it. So do businesses and our economies.

At the USC Schwarzenegger Institute, we believe it's time to stop bickering over what we know is happening or who's to blame and end the attempts to roll back policies we can see are working. It is the time to come together—as Republicans and Democrats, businesspeople and environmentalists.

I founded the USC Schwarzenegger Institute in 2012 to advance post-partisanship and find solutions to some of the most pressing issues we face, like air pollution and environmental destruction. Today, we continue to lead initiatives that will clean up our communities, ramp up renewable energy, and build a more sustainable future. We must continue to build. Build more clean energy. Build more electric vehicles. Build more transmission lines. Build better. Build cleaner. Build faster.

My whole life has been about reaching goals that to others seemed impossible. I wanted to be a professional bodybuilder and become the best in the world. I wanted to succeed in business, and I made my first million in real estate. I wanted to be a movie star, and I made more than fifty-five movies. I wanted to be governor of California—a green Republican governor who helped our environment and our economy—and I was.

However, the challenge of air pollution and climate change can't be bench-pressed away or edited out. With record heat, wildfires, storms, drought, and flooding dominating the headlines and partisan politics continuing to get in our way, reaching the goals we need to reach to leave a better planet for our children can seem impossible.

But it's not.

We just have to seize this opportunity to keep moving forward and stop others from taking us backward. We're making real progress, and the future is brighter than ever.

The time for action, the time for progress, the time for a clean economy is *now*.

ACKNOWLEDGMENTS

Writing is a solitary business.

Yet you can't write anything like this alone. At least I can't. I was fortunate to have a small army of supporters who helped make this book a reality. I strung the words together, but they helped me find them, sharpen them, and bring them to life. I am forever grateful.

Thanks to Jon Sisk and the team at Rowman & Littlefield for realizing the impact we made with my previous book, *Climatenomics*, and for having the foresight for a follow-up. Neither *Climatenomics* nor *Clean Economy Now* could have happened without Jon and the team.

Ed Chen, my friend, mentor, fellow ex-journo, and ex-boss, kindly came out of retirement to try and make my work better, as he has done for years. From Europe, Jeff Benzak, who understands the importance of good storytelling, was good enough to channel his inner Robert Gottlieb and lend his editing prowess and perspective.

Arnold Schwarzenegger deserves the thanks from all of us for his climate leadership during his time as California's governor, and for continuing to help focus the world's attention on climate policy and action through his Schwarzenegger Institute and his annual Austrian climate conference. I'm extremely grateful to Governor Schwarzenegger for providing the foreword for this book. I first met Arnold as a journalist when I covered the West for Cox Newspapers and he shocked the world with his successful campaign to become California's governor during the zany recall election of 2003. Like with everything he does, Governor Schwarzenegger surprised everybody and anybody who doubted him or his abilities, going on to pass and sign into law what was the country's most important climate legislation before the Biden administration came along two decades later. As a staunch Republican, Governor Schwarzenegger also is proof that climate action isn't—and shouldn't be—a partisan issue. Special thanks to Conyers Davis at the Schwarzenegger Institute for his help and his support of me and E2 over the years, and to former state Senator Fran Pavley for connecting us from the beginning.

Few people were more supportive of this endeavor than the amazing Sandra Purohit, who in her wisdom encouraged me to pick up the pen again even as the ink from *Climatenomics* was still drying. Much of the data in the pages that follow comes thanks to Jeff Slyfield and Michael Timberlake and the boys at BW Research Partnership, who did the hard and unsung work of number crunching and analysis that allows me and others to tell this story to the world. I also owe a ton of thanks to others at E2 and the Natural Resources Defense Council (NRDC), including Bob Deans, Ed Yoon, Rob Perks, Alex Adams, Gail Parson, Zach Amittay, Rachel Fakhry, Manish Bapna, Christy Goldfuss, and others who supported me and the work that resulted in this book, reviewed drafts, and helped make it better. Thanks to eagle-eyed environmentalists and dear friends Charles Smith and Liz Ramos, for taking time to read and provide edits, and to Todd Gossett—Kings Mountain boy, veteran, electric Mini Cooper driver, and fellow Tar Heel—for keeping me straight about history, his hometown, and much more.

My greatest professional pleasures typically have involved picking up a notepad, hitting the road, and meeting interesting people. For this adventure, I connected with many.

They included businesspeople on the front lines of this revolution. Michael Rucker, Ariel Fan, and Jon Carson helped me understand the wind, EV charging, and solar industries. Scott Moskowitz and Lisa Nash taught me about solar panel manufacturing. Colleen Campbell and Jason Peace helped me better understand the battery business. Sarah Degnan and Ellen Lenny-Pessagno helped explain the lithium business to me, while Laura Berland, Vikram Ayer, and Matthew Bright helped educate me on carbon capture. Ajulo Othow, Tonya Hicks, Devin Hampton, and others gave me insight into equity—or rather the lack of it in clean energy—and why we must do better in America's next economic transition. Thanks also to Tom Soto, who understands the clean economy, equity, and California's Latino story better than anybody, for taking time out of his busy schedule for me and this book.

Along with the businesspeople behind this economic revolution are the current and previous policymakers who made it happen and helped me understand how we got here. I'm especially grateful to Kate Gordon, who has spent a lifetime advancing clean energy policy at the state and federal level and who understands the risky business of climate inaction like few others. Dave Foster, my fellow tracker of clean energy employment, helped explain how recent federal climate policies translate into investments and jobs. Bob Inglis, who did the right thing even when it cost him his job, helped show all of us what happens when politics gets ahead of common sense on climate action, and that there shouldn't be anything political or partisan about creating jobs and driving economic growth. And I owe a special, heartfelt thanks to Gina McCarthy, a hero for all of us who work for a better environment, for always making time to help me and E2 over the years, most recently during my reporting for this book.

I am grateful always to Nicole Lederer for her support and her vision. It's partly because of Nicole that there is a business movement for the environment today. And it's largely because of her that I'm lucky enough to do the work I do every day.

Finally, the solitary business of writing meant countless hours away from family. For all the support I got from others, nothing matches the love and support I've been lucky enough to receive from my beautiful daughters, and—as always—from Tammie.

Thanks, pal.

Carlsbad, California

August 2023

CHAPTER I

Revolution

THE BATTLE OF KINGS MOUNTAIN ISN'T THE BEST-KNOWN FIGHT OF the American Revolutionary War. The brutal hand-to-hand skirmish on the footprint-shaped mountain near the the border of South and North Carolina on October 7, 1780, lasted but an hour or so, a mere moment in a war that went on for eight years. Even so, what happened at Kings Mountain that day is widely considered a turning point in the American Revolution, a time and place when the future of America forever changed.

British general Charles Lord Cornwallis was on the move that autumn of 1780. He had just resoundingly routed Patriots in coastal Charleston in one of America's worst defeats of the Revolution and then marched on to Camden, South Carolina, in the middle of the state, where he did the same. Now, his long line of redcoats was headed north, seemingly well on the way to gaining control of the Carolinas and edging closer to completing Britain's Southern Campaign. As he mustered his troops, Cornwallis dispatched Major Patrick "Bulldog" Ferguson to the foothills of the Carolinas to defend the flank of the British army as it made its way along the edge of the Appalachians and up to Virginia.

From a 1,200-foot ridge along Kings Mountain, Ferguson controlled a commanding perspective. What he didn't see, however, was a guerrilla contingent of nine hundred "over-mountain men" who had stealthily crept through thick brush and pine trees and surrounded the base of the big hill. At about 3 p.m. on October 7, they rushed up the mountain, screaming, shouting, and shooting with skills honed from years of hunting deer and turkey along those same ridgelines. Surprised and terrified

I

by the caterwauling that echoed across the hillside, and unable to match the locals' marksmanship, Ferguson responded desperately with a series of bloody bayonet charges, resulting in savage combat that pitted brother against brother and neighbor against neighbor in a horrific harbinger of the fighting that would sweep the South a century later in the Civil War. When the smoke cleared and the screaming finally subsided, Ferguson and more than 150 British Loyalists lay dead, alongside just twenty-eight American Patriots. It was one of the worst defeats for the British in the Revolutionary War and a critical turning point that ultimately led to Cornwallis's eventual surrender at Yorktown one year later. Thomas Jefferson would refer to the Battle of Kings Mountain as "the turn of the tide of success" in the war. General George Washington would call the Patriots at Kings Mountain "proof of the spirit and resources of the country."[1]

Nearly 250 years later, the town of Kings Mountain, North Carolina, is once again on the front lines of an American revolution—an economic revolution, one of a size and scope that may be unparalleled in American history and driven by the existential battle of our time: The battle against climate change.

A few miles from the historic battlefield, off Holiday Inn Drive and Interstate 85, Albemarle Corp. is planning to restart a World War II–era lithium mine left dormant for nearly forty years. If it is successful, it would be the first mine of its kind in the United States, annually producing an estimated 50,000 metric tons of lithium,[2] the core material used in electric vehicle (EV) batteries. Kings Mountain could produce enough raw material to power 1 million EVs every year, filling a critical missing link in the American supply chain for lithium-ion batteries and significantly boosting the country's attempt to become a legitimate contender in a global market led by Chile and Australia and dominated by China.[3] As of 2023, there was only one company producing lithium in America— Albemarle, at a separate operation in Nevada where it produces the white powder by evaporating bromide extracted from below the hot desert sand. Albemarle's Silver Peak operation supplies about five thousand tons of lithium each year to Tesla and other battery makers—about 5 percent of what it plans to produce in North Carolina, and a miniscule amount compared to what's needed to supply the EV market.

Restarting the North Carolina mine would inject hundreds of millions of dollars into the economy and create three hundred full-time jobs. It would also once again make Kings Mountain a unique and pivotal player in America's future.

"It's extremely strategic for the U.S.—not just the Southeastern U.S., not just the Eastern half of the U.S.—*the* U.S.," Eric Norris, president of Albemarle's energy storage business, told Kings Mountain residents at a standing-room-only town hall meeting in March 2022. Norris made the thirty-five-mile drive from Albemarle's headquarters in Charlotte in his EV a few hours earlier, parking among a sea of gas-powered pickup trucks and other vehicles outside City Hall. "This is a significant resource that can really help drive some independence for the U.S. when it comes to building electric vehicles," he said.[4]

The Kings Mountain mine is only part of Albemarle's ambitious plans. In Charlotte, it is building a $180 million materials research and technology center, creating another two hundred jobs. Just across the border in rural Chester County, South Carolina, it is investing another $1.3 billion into a massive lithium processing plant that will be the biggest of its kind, a "mega-flex" facility that can process lithium produced by hard rock mining at Kings Mountain, brine removal in Nevada or from "black mass," the powdery mix of valuable metals extracted from recycled batteries.[5]

Albemarle's projects have the potential to revitalize a region that's been searching to reestablish its economic identity ever since the local textile industry left for Asia and other parts of the world a generation earlier. As Republican South Carolina Governor Henry McMaster said in announcing the lithium processing plant on his side of the state line, the company's plans are "positively electric."

Developments like these are electrifying states across the country, turbocharging a business revolution the likes of which America hasn't seen in generations. Centuries-old US industries are being disrupted and resurrected, with all the consequences that come with it. States and communities left behind by previous economic transitions are suddenly at the forefront of the global clean energy economy. And now that dollars, jobs, and economic growth are involved, many Americans—regardless of their political persuasions or geography—are being forced to reconsider the way they think about climate change and clean energy.

In one single year, between the summers of 2022 and 2023, private companies announced a mind-boggling $86 billion in US investments in 210 major clean energy and clean transportation factories and other projects. Collectively, those projects promise to create more than 70,000 new jobs across thirty-nine states[6] and reset the playing field in the fastest-growing segment of the global economy.[7] By the end of 2023, companies were planning or building more than 265 major clean energy projects in America, representing $108 billion in private-sector investments.

In a country where just a few years ago it didn't make much business sense to open new solar panel factories because of high costs and uncertain demand, businesses from around the globe are now opening or planning to open nearly fifty solar panel and equipment factories in the United States, getting America back into an industry it ceded to Asian manufacturers years ago. Domestic and foreign automobile manufacturers and their suppliers, from pioneers like Ford, GM, and Volkswagen to upstarts like Rivian and VinFast, are building more than one hundred new mega-factories—in some cases even creating whole new cities—that will employ hundreds of thousands of workers and help shift American drivers from the gas vehicles we've relied on for a century to electric cars, trucks, and buses. New battery, offshore wind, clean hydrogen, carbon sequestration—and as Albemarle illustrates, lithium production—projects are suddenly putting America at the forefront of industries in which we didn't even compete a few years ago, but also forcing the country to make hard new environmental and social choices.

Like past business revolutions, the clean economy revolution is creating a new generation of business winners and losers, billionaires, and bankruptcies. Businesspeople who understand what's happening will reap the benefits. Those who fail to act—and act quickly—will fail.

The clean economy is now.

And it's happening at a speed, and in ways and places that few could've predicted.

Two hours east of Kings Mountain, in an area where cotton was once king and local mills along the Deep River once produced uniforms for Confederate soldiers, Japan's biggest automaker is building a nearly $14 billion factory where more than five thousand workers will produce batteries for hybrid and electric vehicles.[8] By 2025, Toyota expects to produce enough battery packs at its factory near the town of Liberty, North Carolina, to power 1.2 million EVs per year. The factory will create as many as 2,100 jobs that promise to pay $62,000 annually on average—about 60 percent better than the $38,000 average salary in surrounding Randolph County.[9]

In the Canadian border town of Massena, New York, where one of America's first hydroelectric plants began producing electricity in 1900, Air Products and Chemicals, Inc., is building a new kind of power plant. In October 2022, the company announced a $500 million investment to build a new ninety-employee plant to separate hydrogen from water—using renewable energy to do it—to produce "green" hydrogen fuel that can power big industrial plants as well as heavy-duty trucks and cargo ships like those that ply the mighty St. Lawrence River nearby. It's one of at least two such plants that eighty-year-old industrial gas and chemical company Air Products is building.[10]

In Newton, Iowa, TPI Composites announced in November 2022 that it would reopen a wind turbine blade factory it closed a year earlier, restoring hundreds of local jobs it previously eliminated amid uncertainty about the future of clean energy in America.[11] While TPI makes wind turbine blades in the middle of the country, a century-old marine services company that got its start shuttling supplies by rowboat to ships anchored in San Francisco Bay is turning a former coal-fired power plant in Salem, Massachusetts, into a shipping terminal that will supply the new-to-America business of offshore wind. The terminal is expected to employ more than eight hundred local workers and revitalize a waterfront that last saw its heyday in the 1700s, back when Salem was known not just for its witch trials but also as one of the country's biggest and busiest seaports. Crowley Maritime Corporation is planning a similar offshore wind terminal on another ocean on the other side of the country, in California's Humboldt Bay, not far from where developers are planning what could be America's first floating offshore wind farm.

In Iberia Parish, Louisiana, best known as the birthplace of Tabasco hot sauce, a new kind of industry is heating up. The biggest US-based solar company is building a $1.1 billion factory in the heart of Cajun country that will employ about seven hundred local workers. The investment by Arizona-based First Solar, Inc., is part of a massive $4 billion company expansion plan that also includes new operations in Alabama, Ohio, and California.[12] It's not just US companies building new solar panel factories in America. Companies from Asia that have dominated the industry for decades are now investing in America and creating jobs here instead of overseas. The world's biggest solar panel maker, China-based LONGi Green Energy Technology, is teaming up with Chicago-based clean energy developer Invenergy to build a $600-million, 850-employee solar panel factory in the town of Pataskala, Ohio, east of Columbus.[13] Korean solar panel company Hanwha Qcells, meanwhile, is building new factories as fast as it can in rural Georgia. Qcells opened its first US factory in Dalton, north of Atlanta, in 2019. But with solar energy expected to grow exponentially in the United States in coming years, it realized it can't come close to meeting expected demand with one factory. So in 2022, Qcells announced a second factory in Dalton to triple its production.[14] Eight months later, it announced a third factory there, along with another new factory in nearby Cartersville that will make solar ingots and wafers that are the building blocks of solar panels. In all, the company plans to employ four thousand workers at its plants in Cartersville and in Dalton, which is part of the congressional district represented by Republican US Rep. Marjorie Taylor Greene, a conservative firebrand who has said global warming and carbon pollution are healthy and suggested expanding solar and wind energy will force Americans to give up air-conditioning, household appliances, and lights.[15]

The economic boom in his state made another conservative Georgia Republican, Governor Brian Kemp, a big supporter of clean energy. In addition to becoming the country's biggest producer of solar panels, Kemp declared at his 2022 inauguration that he wants Georgia to be "the electric mobility capital of America"[16]—a once unfathomable idea that now looks very likely.

The dramatic growth in the clean energy economy occurring across America is only the start. By 2032, an estimated $3 trillion in public- and private-sector investment is expected to flow into clean energy–related manufacturing, green hydrogen, and carbon-capture projects in the United States, an eyepopping amount equivalent to the gross domestic product (GDP) of Canada or Italy.[17] Behind those record investments and inside those factories and other businesses are American workers. More than 1.5 million new jobs in clean energy, clean vehicles, and energy efficiency are expected to be created by 2030 because of America's new clean economy boom. That's 1.5 million good-paying careers for assembly line workers, electricians, installers, scientists, and engineers that wouldn't exist otherwise.[18]

If projections are right, wind energy in America will double by 2030. Solar energy will triple. Battery storage will increase by a factor of nine. And the number of EVs on the road will increase twenty-six-fold. Very few industries will ever see that sort of growth rate in that amount of time.[19]

The foundation of this new economy has been coming together brick by brick for some time. From 2009 to 2019, the price of solar and wind power and lithium-ion batteries fell by as much as 90 percent, making clean energy more affordable for businesses and consumers. By 2022, utility-scale solar and wind was the cheapest power available in just about every part of America. Private-sector investments in clean energy and climate-tech companies have been steadily growing. Globally, investments in low-carbon businesses eclipsed the trillion-dollar mark for the first time in 2022, totaling $1.1 trillion, according to BloombergNEF.[20] Consumer demand also increased as EVs and renewable energy have become cheaper and more commonplace and Americans continue to understand—and suffer from—climate-related disasters and their connection with emissions from fossil fuels. More than 75 percent of Americans surveyed by the Pew Research Center in June 2023 said they wanted more renewable energy.[21] About 70 percent of Americans polled by Consumer Reports in July 2022 expressed at least some degree of interest in buying or leasing an EV.[22] After the Earth experienced its hottest summer in history in 2023, when record heat engulfed the continental United States for weeks, the majority of Americans said they were fearful that climate change would have "a significant negative effect" on the globe during their lifetimes.[23] Before the end of that miserably hot summer, the Hawaiian island of Maui was on fire, with nearly one hundred people perishing in the nation's worst wildfire in at least a century.

Along with public demand, what dramatically ramped the clean economy from a slow build to a bona fide boom was the arrival in Washington of a committed architect with a set of detailed plans, a big budget, and enough experience in policy and politics to know how the government can uniquely send the market signals businesses need to invest and expand.

In 2020, President Joe Biden was elected with the promise that he would finally take decisive action to address climate change and its growing impacts that are being increasingly felt with wildfires, floods, hurricanes, and other disasters that hit new record highs the year he took office. The new president's climate and clean energy goals were bold by any measure. He promised the world that the United States would reduce its greenhouse gas emissions by 50 percent or more by 2030. To do it, he pledged to transition the nation's electricity sector to 100 percent clean energy by 2035. He established a goal to increase the number of electric and other zero-emission vehicles on the road from about 2 percent to 100 percent by 2050. To reduce energy waste, he promised to help consumers and businesses dramatically improve the efficiency of their homes and office buildings, starting with a decree to reduce greenhouse gas emissions to zero in all federal buildings by 2045.

And then he set about to pass federal policies to make it happen.

The explosion in clean energy jobs, manufacturing, and products we're now seeing is a direct result of three pieces of Biden administration legislation passed in 2021–2022: The bipartisan Infrastructure Investment and Jobs Act, the Inflation Reduction Act (IRA) and the CHIPS (Creating Helpful Incentives to Produce Semiconductors) and Science Act. Together, this triple play of policy will invest an estimated

$1.65 trillion into the US economy over ten years through direct federal investments and tax credits, representing the biggest combined investment into clean energy, climate solutions, and technology in the history of America, if not the world.[24] Atop these foundational legislative building blocks, the Biden administration layered other key clean energy policies, including clean air standards requiring carmakers to increase the number of electric and other zero-emissions vehicles they sell; new regulations for utilities to reduce carbon emissions at their power plants and requirements for the federal government—the biggest purchaser of goods in the world—to purchase more EVs for its fleets and more renewable energy for its buildings. The federal government isn't working alone, either. State and local governments also are leading the charge in the clean economy revolution, passing groundbreaking policies in recent years requiring carmakers to build cleaner vehicles if they want to sell them in their states; approving new standards to eliminate fossil fuels for heating and cooling in buildings and new codes that require builders to include solar panels and high-efficiency HVAC (heating, ventilation, and air-conditioning) systems in homes in some states. These policies are creating new markets for businesses, new jobs for workers, and new savings for consumers.

"It's really kind of basic," President Biden told attendees at an event in Milwaukee, Wisconsin, marking the first anniversary of his signing of the IRA. "We just decided to invest in America again."[25]

America's historic climate and clean energy investments, of course, are not just about creating jobs or spurring economic growth. They're about reducing greenhouse gas emissions to slow the pace of climate change that is exacerbating drought, flooding, heat waves, wildfires, and other weather-related disasters that are battering our economy and civilization as we know it. By deploying more clean energy and clean vehicles, the IRA alone is expected to reduce US greenhouse gas emissions by about 40 percent. That would be one big step toward the Biden administration's pledge to the world to cut US emissions by 50–52 percent by 2030, and one giant leap in humankind's attempt to avoid the worst impacts of climate change. New federal vehicle and power plant standards, coupled with state regulations and continued improvements in technology, are the country's best bet to reduce those emissions even more.

It will be years before we know whether the government's landmark policies will produce the environmental benefits they're intended to produce. What we do know is that they're already producing economic benefits in ways we've not seen in generations.

Not long ago, shifting to a clean economy meant pain and cost. Now, it means opportunity, profit, and savings. The fact that companies and consumers can get tax credits for buying solar panels or EVs means more businesses for companies like First Solar, Ford, and Albemarle. More business means more need to expand and hire new workers. Federal investments in battery, semiconductor, and energy-efficiency research and development mean jump-starting innovation at both established clean energy companies and start-ups that previously may have been stuck in the financial valley of death because of a lack of access to capital. And making it cheaper through tax credits and rebates for consumers and businesses to buy more energy-efficient heat pump HVAC systems, water heaters, stoves, and other appliances not only will drive retail sales, manufacturing, and construction industry growth; it will also save consumers money on every monthly power bill that can be reinvested into other parts of the economy.

Building a clean economy now in America is important for other reasons too. It's important for national security. It's important to help improve the treatment of workers and ensure we don't cause more environmental degradation. And it's important for restoring American leadership and making the country competitive again in some of the biggest and most important economic opportunities in the world.[26]

Consider the business of batteries.

If we are going to drive EVs, store energy after dark or when the wind isn't blowing, and wean ourselves off the fossil fuels that are exacerbating climate change, we need batteries. When Oxford and later University of Texas engineering professor John Goodenough and a small team of scientists created the world's first working lithium-ion batteries in 1980, they never imagined the demand for their product the world is now facing.[27] Like so many other modern-day technologies that have their roots in American innovation, China eventually overtook the business, controlling nearly 80 percent of the global market for lithium-ion batteries by 2023. Six of the top ten manufacturers of EV batteries in 2023 were based in China; three were based in Korea and one was from Japan. With the notable exception of Tesla, few companies were building batteries at scale in America.

By the end of 2023, though, an unexpected thing happened. On the heels of the new federal policies and investments, North America became the fastest-growing market for battery production in the world. In the year following the passage of the IRA, companies announced more than thirty U.S. battery factories and related projects.

General Motors teamed up with LG Energy, Samsung, and others to announce new battery factories in Michigan, Ohio, and Tennessee, investing billions of dollars and creating thousands of jobs. BMW and Volkswagen started new battery plants in South Carolina. Hyundai announced new battery plants in Georgia. Ford teamed up with two of the world's biggest battery makers—Korea's SK On to announce a new factory in Tennessee, and China's Contemporary Amperex Technology Co., or CATL for short, to build a much-scrutinized plant in Michigan. Newcomers also announced they were coming to America, including Norway's FREYR Battery, which announced a $1.7 billion, seven-hundred-dred-employee factory in rural Newnan, Georgia, south of Atlanta, that will make batteries for renewable energy storage.

"In the battery space at least, and probably in others as well, China had a 10–15 year head start on us," said Jason Peace, a senior vice president of FREYR who is responsible for its new Georgia factory.[28] "A lot of the materials we rely on are almost entirely produced in China today. So we're excited about the IRA not only for its impacts on us, but on the supply chain" in America. In August 2023, FREYR announced it wasn't just opening a new factory in Georgia; it announced it was moving its entire company to the United States.

The ramifications of America's newfound strength in batteries are huge. According to the International Energy Agency, more than 75 percent of all lithium-ion batteries are manufactured in China, and about half of all raw materials used to make those batteries—lithium, cobalt, graphite, and manganese—are processed there.[29] So if China remains unchecked in its domination of the battery business, it essentially becomes the equivalent of Saudi Arabia or the Middle East for the next generation of automobiles. If Chinese factories shut down or are otherwise impacted, as we learned during the COVID-19 pandemic and subsequent global supply chain meltdown, it turns off the main spigot for the battery supply chain for the rest of the world. As auto companies in America and every other country shift to all-electric vehicles, and as batteries become an ever increasingly important part of America's electric grid (and its national security), American companies and consumers become increasingly beholden to China for their battery packs—unless the United States gets back in the game. In one indication of just how important batteries are to the country's national security, the Department of Defense in September 2023 announced a $90 million grant to Albemarle to help jump-start its Kings Mountain lithium mine.

Building battery production from the ground up in America is important in other ways too. Part of the reason China leads the world in production of lithium-ion batteries is because it can produce them cheaply through its documented use of forced labor and its lax environmental practices.[30] In other countries involved in the battery business, including Chile and Argentina, home to some of the world's biggest reserves of lithium and cobalt, and the Democratic Republic of Congo, the world's biggest source of cobalt, unchecked mining companies and poor government oversight for health, safety, and environmental regulations have led to human rights violations (including the alleged use of child labor in Congo) and damage to local watersheds and communities. Producing batteries in America, especially when the federal government is involved and tax dollars are in the mix, means U.S. regulators can help ensure that lithium mining and battery manufacturing is done as sustainably as possible, that environmental safeguards protecting air and water are enforced, and that workers receive fair wages. The battery business is so important for energy, national security, and other reasons that the Department of Energy is planning to award $7 billion in grants made possible by the bipartisan infrastructure law to fund battery research and development projects that can help America regain a foothold in the global market. The first $2.8 billion in grants were awarded to twenty cutting-edge companies in October 2022, and are in addition to tax breaks and other credits that are flowing to battery companies.

The battery projects funded through the grants are intended to be geographically and technologically diverse. They also illustrate how the infrastructure law can help improve economic conditions and bring new opportunities to states and communities nationwide, including coal communities, low-income communities, and communities of color, in both blue Democratic states and deep red Republican states. In Western Kentucky—the traditional heart of America's coal industry—Ascend Elements received $316 million in Department of Energy grants to build the nation's first commercial battery cathode factory of its kind, alongside a lithium-ion battery recycling plant where workers and robots will separate cathodes from spent batteries for use in new ones. The operation will create an estimated 130 jobs in Christian County (adjacent to much-memorialized Muhlenberg County, home of Kentucky's first commercial coal mine), a place where unemployment hit a record 18 percent in 2020. In rural St. Gabriel, Louisiana, a predominantly African American community where two state prisons dominate the region's economy and workforce, the government is investing $100 million to help build the nation's first lithium hexafluorophosphate processing plant, creating an estimated eighty new jobs. In Lancaster, Ohio, Cirba Solutions received a Department of Energy grant to also help solve the problem of what to do with old lithium-ion batteries after they're spent. With $75 million in Department of Energy funding and an additional $107 million investment of its own, Cirba plans to expand its Ohio battery recycling plant and hire 150 workers to collect and disassemble tens of thousands of used lithium-ion batteries, extracting and recycling enough materials and components to power two hundred thousand new electric car batteries per year. Cirba also is opening battery recycling plants in Arizona and South Carolina.

And in Kings Mountain, the Department of Energy agreed to invest nearly $150 million to help Albemarle reopen its mine and train people for the jobs it will create. Since there hasn't been an operating lithium mine at the site in four decades, there aren't many people left in the region—or anyplace in America—with experience in how to do the work. The federal grant will invest $8 million for workforce training programs, including $5 million to start a lithium processing training program in nearby Cleveland Community College; $1.5 million to expand an engineering program at N.C. State University and another $1.5 million to support a new minerals research program at Virginia Tech. To receive the federal grants, Albemarle pledged to invest $225 million of its own money. Similarly, in exchange for Albemarle's $180 million investment in its new battery materials technology center near its Charlotte headquarters, the state of North Carolina ponied up nearly $13 million in state tax breaks and incentives. Given that the high-tech research center is expected to create two hundred new jobs paying an average of $94,000 annually—well above the state median wage—state officials are betting it's a pretty good investment. "Reducing carbon emissions is good for our environment—and great for our economy," North Carolina Governor Roy Cooper said in announcing the Charlotte battery innovation park and the state's investment in it.[31]

Of course, mining isn't an environmentally friendly business. You can't extract minerals from the Earth without negatively impacting it. For nearly four decades, the original mine pit at Kings Mountain has been a quiet country lake, filled with rainwater accumulated over the years and home to little more than fish, turtles, and waterfowl.

The lithium Albemarle now wants to extract is in the old open pit that has been filling with water from rain over the past two decades. The water in the pit will be pumped out and slowly discharged in nearby Kings Creek in preparation for the new mine to get started. Albemarle says it is intent on mitigating any negative impacts of emptying the pit and will be required to meet environmental and other laws in doing so. While most of the new mine will essentially fit inside the old mine pit, the overall operations will expand, forcing the relocation of a section of the scenic Kings Mountain Gateway Trail, a local treasure that will be rerouted and expanded before mining starts up.

As more mining operations like Kings Mountain start popping up around the country to meet the demand for critical materials for batteries, solar panels, and other clean energy products, lessons from the past show the government needs to have better oversight. Remarkably, federal mining laws have barely changed since they were written in 1872. "It's long past time to update our ancient mining laws," said senior White House advisor John Podesta.[32] "Suffice it to say that even though the memoirs of Ulysses S. Grant are still on recommended reading lists, mining legislation he signed 150 years ago is a little out of date."

Still, mining today isn't what it used to be, said Fernando Rodriguez, Albemarle's director of mining at Kings Mountain. The mine, he said, will be the cleanest he's ever worked at—and he's worked at quite a few. Rodriguez started in the mining industry in the 1990s. He worked in mines extracting gold, silver, copper, lithium, and other materials in places stretching from Armenia to Peru before he joined Albemarle in August 2022. "This isn't my first rodeo," Rodriguez said as we bounced along a dirt road in a white, electric-powered Ford F-150 Lightning truck one afternoon.[33] A blue heron landed in a tree hanging over the mine-pit-turned-lake beside him. Up on the hill, on the other side of a chain-link fence, the first of the late afternoon walkers and joggers on the Gateway Trail were getting their steps in. Rodriguez's electric pickup truck is a small part of Albemarle's attempt to make its mining operation as environmentally friendly as possible. In addition to a fleet of F-150 Lighting trucks and Teslas that shuttle workers around the site, Albemarle wants every vehicle and piece of equipment at the mine to be powered by electricity and batteries, though Rodriguez acknowledges it may be a while before the battery-powered versions of heavy equipment used in mining are even commercially available.

Even if it can reduce the use of fossil fuels and limit the loss of biodiversity at its mines, other environmental impacts can't be avoided at Kings Mountain or any other mine. Clean energy operations can be dirty, whether it's mining or producing lithium for batteries, polysilicon for solar panels, or steel for wind turbines and automobiles. But it's important to note that mining minerals for clean energy products is far less harmful to the environment than fossil fuels. For starters, producing the minerals required for clean energy—lithium, cobalt, nickel, silica, to name a few—requires far less mining than fossil fuels in the first place. In 2021, the world strip-mined, blasted, and dug up nearly eight billion tons of coal just to burn it up in power plants. By 2040, the International Energy Agency estimates all the minerals needed for EVs, solar panels, and other clean energy goods that will power our economy for decades will be less than thirty million tons.[34] Include oil drilling and gas fracking, and the disparities are even greater. By some estimates, the amount of fossil fuels that are mined and extracted in a single year is 535 times more than the amount of raw materials required to supply EV companies, and solar panel, battery, and wind turbine makers. The real differences, however, come after the mining is done. The emissions and other environmental damage done by clean energy minerals extraction are tiny compared to those created by the burning of fossil fuels, according to research from the Massachusetts Institute of Technology.[35] Add up all the greenhouse gas emissions tied to an EV over its lifetime—the mining, the manufacturing, the charging—and it's still about a quarter the amount of carbon dioxide produced by a gas-powered vehicle, other studies show.[36]

Of course, American industry has a long history of environmental disasters, from the Cuyahoga River to Love Canal. The country's record for environmental justice and equity isn't great either. Just look at where petroleum refineries, power plants, and coal mines are located today. Or consider the impacts of the interstate highway system on inner-city communities. Or count how many Teslas and solar panels you see in communities of color and low- and middle-income areas.

Almost certainly, there will also be failures during this clean economy revolution, and they will cost taxpayers. Rare is the major government-led program that doesn't have failures. The construction of the transcontinental railroad was replete with instances of money-skimming and failed ventures that ultimately cost the government and taxpayers.[37] When President Kennedy announced plans to go to the moon, a majority of Americans were against it, considering it a waste of money and time with no real lasting benefit for the people back here on Earth. As poet-musician Gil Scott-Heron chanted in his 1970s anthem, the billions spent putting "Whitey on the Moon" could've instead been spent addressing poverty and other social ills plaguing the United States.[38] More recently, the name of one failed solar company, Solyndra, became a rallying cry in the

2000s for anybody opposed to government spending on clean energy, because the company failed despite funding from a U.S. Department of Energy loan program.

Yet with history as a lesson, few Americans would suggest that logistical, economic, and social advances created by America's investments in a transcontinental railroad in the 1880s didn't pay off economically and socially. Same for all the government-funded scientific and technological advancements created for man's trip to the moon in the 1960s that now permeate our daily lives, from integrated circuits and accurate weather forecasts to freeze-dried food. Even though Solyndra and a few other risky clean energy projects crashed and burned, the success of the other 98 percent of projects funded by the Department of Energy's Loan Programs Office—including a little start-up called Tesla that received and fully paid back a $465 million government loan—is a big reason why solar and wind are the sources of the cheapest electricity available today and why every automaker now has the technology and market demand to shift to EVs.

The Biden administration and its supporters tend to refer to the Infrastructure Investment and Jobs Act, the IRA, and the CHIPS and Science Act as the biggest, most sweeping climate bills in history. They are, for sure. And if they reduce carbon emissions by the levels they're supposed to, they could be the turning point in our fight against climate change. But in the meantime, they're also a giant step forward for America's economy that will impact virtually every business and investor.

"The global market for clean energy technologies is projected to reach $23 trillion by the end of this decade—at a minimum," said Department of Energy Secretary Jennifer Granholm.[39] "This market could be the most powerful engine for economic growth that the world has ever seen."

It's a market and an economic engine girded by transformational public policy.

Policy that almost didn't happen.

CHAPTER 2

Policy Matters

IT WAS SPRINGTIME IN WASHINGTON, BUT ANY HOPES FOR A NEW beginning on federal climate action had come and gone as quickly as the cherry blossoms.

It had been promising, but also questionable, from the start. Democrats who rode Joe Biden's coattails into Washington now controlled Congress with pent-up ambition that had been building over four years of the Trump administration and a mission to do as much as they could as quickly as they could, especially on climate and clean energy.

In the House, Democratic leadership took the all-encompassing American Jobs Plan that President Biden's staff developed three months after moving into the White House and spun off two separate bills. The Infrastructure Investment and Jobs Act (initially called the INVEST in America Act) would pump trillions into fixing highways and bridges, replacing lead drinking water pipes, and installing a national network of EV chargers, among other things.[1] The second, more contentious bill, the Build Back Better Act, would extend tax breaks for solar and wind projects and EVs and invest billions of dollars in grants and loans for clean energy, clean vehicles, and batteries. To appeal to the most left-leaning Democrats, Build Back Better also included billions more for childcare and education credits and investments and made significant changes to Medicare to reduce prescription drug prices. To pay for it all, Democrats proposed raising taxes on the wealthiest Americans and biggest corporations, going after tax cheats, and reaping new tax revenues from all the new clean energy projects and factories.

Republicans quickly painted the proposals as a liberal tax-and-spend program that would put Americans out of work, decimate the domestic energy industry, and kill democracy. With gas prices rising and Democrats squawking about solar panels and electric cars, Representative Jim Jordan of Ohio took to calling Biden the "New Jimmy Carter."[2] Companies would later announce $6 billion in new solar panel and EV factories and thousands of new jobs in his state thanks to policies Jordan mocked. Powerful Senator John Barrasso of Wyoming billed Build Back Better as an "out-of-control socialist spending spree" that "builds back worse" even though it was enabling the building of one of the biggest wind energy operations in the country in Wyoming.[3] Senator Lindsey Graham, whose home state of South Carolina lured more major clean energy projects and jobs than any state except for Georgia because of the Biden administration's clean energy investments and tax credits, referred to the Democrats' policies as "a spending orgy" that was "paving a path to socialism."[4] And Senate Minority Leader Mitch McConnell declared that he was "100 percent focused" on stopping the Biden administration at every opportunity, even though the administration's proposals would later lead automakers to announce at least four major EV plant expansions and thousands of new jobs in his home state of Kentucky.

Biden, however, understood both political posturing and the political allure of passing policies that drove jobs and investments in the states. Most importantly, he knew the Senate, after more than thirty years of serving in the august chamber. The partisan divide was wider than ever, but the seasoned political warhorse understood that building roads and bridges and taking credit for them with constituents back home was irresistible to just about any politician, regardless of political party. The key, Biden knew, was convincing his fellow politicians that EV charging stations and upgraded power lines should also be considered parts of America's modern-day infrastructure—just like roads or bridges or sewer lines. To make Biden's case, the president dispatched his chief economic advisor, Brian Deese, to Capitol Hill. Smart and affable, Deese cut his political teeth and developed key relationships in Congress while serving as a young staffer in the Obama administration during the Great Recession and later became one of Obama's closest economic advisors. For days that turned into weeks, Deese paraded in and out of congressional offices on the Hill, trying to win them over to the plan, often working alongside White House Chief of Staff Ron Klain, another Obama administration alum who had also served as Biden's chief of staff when he was vice president. On August 10, 2021, their work paid off: The Senate passed Biden's infrastructure bill with nineteen Republicans—including McConnell and Graham—voting with Democrats to approve the biggest infrastructure legislation since President Eisenhower's 1956 Federal-Aid Highway Act.

Getting the Infrastructure Investment and Jobs Act through the Senate was tough. Getting it through the House proved much tougher—not because of Republicans but because of Democrats. Led by progressive House members known as "the Squad"—Representatives Alexandria Ocasio-Cortez, Ilhan Omar, Ayanna Pressley, Cori Bush, Jamaal Bowman, and Rashida Tlaib—several Democrats were threatening to vote against the bipartisan infrastructure act. If Democratic leadership chalked up a big victory on infrastructure, they worried, leadership wouldn't be as willing or able to spend more political capital to push as hard for the more socially expansive Build Back Better Act. There was precedent for their concern: The last big climate policy to pass the House, the 2009 Waxman-Markey bill, never got a vote in the Senate because Democratic leadership instead decided to refocus all their political effort and capital on passing President Obama's Affordable Care Act, more commonly referred to as Obamacare.

Then, on November 2, 2021, wavering Democrats got a wake-up call. The party got trounced in several key gubernatorial and House elections in what was quickly seen as a prelude for even bigger Democratic losses in the next congressional election, scheduled for a year later. Driven by fear and fleeting opportunity, Biden and team used the 2021 election scare as leverage with his party, asking congressional Democrats to trust him and warning that if they couldn't even pass the party's signature infrastructure bill that got bipartisan support in the Senate—something that even GOP leader Mitch McConnell supported, for goodness' sake—they should expect voters to give them the boot in the next election. Three days later, on November 5, 2021, the House voted 228–206 to pass the Infrastructure Investment and Jobs Act. All six members of the

Squad lived up to their promise and voted against it, but thirteen Republicans joined in voting for it, giving the infrastructure bill rare bipartisan approval in both chambers of Congress.

Gina McCarthy watched the legislation play out with a sense of relief that had been building up for most of her nearly four decades in public environmental policy work. A former Environmental Protection Agency (EPA) administrator under President Obama, McCarthy was selected by Biden to be the nation's first-ever National Climate Advisor shortly after he took office. As such, she was responsible for the administration's overall climate vision and also coordinating climate policy across every federal agency. For the administration, the infrastructure law was the first piece—but a critical piece—of the administration's overall plan.

"The value of the bipartisan infrastructure law wasn't just that it had money for grid modernization or money for electric vehicle infrastructure," McCarthy said.[5] "The real value was to show people that government was working for them again. That we were actually building things again. It showed that our economy wasn't dead, it was revived, alive and moving. That was the reason why the bipartisan infrastructure law going first was absolutely essential."

Emboldened by their bipartisan win and desperate to hand the president another victory before the Thanksgiving break, Democrats turned to a former Republican from Kentucky to introduce the Build Back Better Act in the House. Eight-term Representative John Yarmuth was chair of the House Budget Committee, which he often used as a platform to highlight the economic costs and opportunities of his priority issues, including childhood education, technology, and climate change. Like Republican Senate Minority Leader Mitch McConnell, Yarmuth was an old-school politician who hailed from Louisville. He got his start in politics working as a legislative aide for moderate Republican Senator Marlow Cook of Kentucky in the 1970s but turned away from the GOP in 1985 during the Ronald Reagan years out of his fear and concern over the rise of the religious right. In presenting the $3.5 trillion Build Back Better Act on the House floor on November 18, 2021, Yarmuth spoke as much about what it would do for public education, health care, and prescription drug costs as it would do for combating climate change and expanding clean energy. The bill, he said, was "the most consequential legislation for American families since the New Deal."[6]

Despite Yarmuth's Republican roots and their fresh bipartisan win on the infrastructure bill, Democratic leaders didn't fool themselves for a minute into thinking they'd get much—if any—Republican support for Build Back Better. It was one thing for GOP lawmakers to support spending taxpayer money on roads and bridges back home. They got what they wanted: brick-and-mortar projects for the folks back home. But there was nothing Republicans wanted in Build Back Better. And the one thing they didn't want for certain was to hand the president another victory before the midterm elections. The fact that climate change was now causing $175 billion in damage annually to roads, bridges, and other U.S. infrastructure, or that clean energy and EVs could make America more competitive internationally and more independent economically, just didn't resonate with the Republican party.[7] So while voting in favor of the infrastructure bill, McConnell and other Republican leaders made it clear the president shouldn't expect the same sort of support for Build Back Better. "Infrastructure is something we needed, unlike all the rest of what they're trying to do," McConnell said during an appearance on a conservative Kentucky podcast.[8]

Once again, it was Biden's party, not the GOP, that was posing the biggest problem for his climate agenda. First, there was the Squad and other progressive House Democrats, who repeated their steadfast pledge to torpedo any climate bill that also didn't include their priority social programs. Then there was an even bigger hurdle: Senator Joe Manchin, the West Virginia Democrat and coal industry millionaire whose support for Build Back Better had been questionable all along. From the moment the legislation was conceived, Manchin expressed concerns it was too big, too sweeping, and too damaging to the fossil fuel industry. His state was the number two producer of coal in America, and the coal industry was still among the state's biggest employers. Through his company Enersystems Inc., which for years bought scrap coal left behind from mining operations and resold it to power plants, Manchin and his family made millions from the coal industry, enough for the senator to afford to drive an $80,000 Maserati Levante and live on a sixty-five-foot houseboat on

Washington, D.C.'s waterfront—both of which became instant targets for climate activists in their attempts to pressure him into supporting Build Back Better.[9]

By late 2021, after months of negotiations, the Biden administration had agreed to cut the cost of Build Back Better in half to appease Manchin. Gone were plans for the government to pay for universal prekindergarten and extend new tax credits for childcare, as well as a proposal to help provide long-term home health care for the elderly and disabled. In were provisions to expand oil and gas leases in the Gulf of Mexico and Alaska and ensure that fossil fuel companies were as entitled to leases on public lands as renewable energy companies—provisions that Manchin had insisted upon.

Still, after nearly six months of negotiation, Manchin continued to publicly express worry about the impacts of the bill on the national debt and inflation, and about the potential economic consequences of the latest strain of the COVID-19 virus that was once again on the rise heading into the holidays. The uncertainty over the senator's position hung over Washington like a tired fog that just wouldn't lift, bogging down everything else on Capitol Hill and leaving environmentalists and climate activists grasping for ideas for what else they could do. The uncertainty cast a pall over a country beleaguered by politics and pandemics that stretched across the Atlantic to Glasgow, Scotland, where the United Nations in November was hosting the COP 26 global climate change conference. President Biden and his team went to the conference with a bold new commitment for the United States to reach zero emissions by 2050, but nobody from the president on down could say how they planned to do it given the uncertainty surrounding Manchin's position. On December 19, 2021, any questions about where Manchin stood were answered. Appearing on Fox News, he dropped the surprise bombshell that he would not support Build Back Better, saying it was too complex, too expensive, and too much for the country to afford. "I've always said . . . if I can't go home and explain it to the people of West Virginia, I can't vote for it," Manchin told Fox News Host Brett Baier. "And I cannot vote to continue with this piece of legislation. I just can't."[10]

Democrats, including President Biden, were dazed and confused. Why would a fellow Democrat go public—on Fox News on a Sunday morning just before Christmas, no less—and announce he was single-handedly killing his party's signature legislation? In a scathing statement the Biden administration later came to regret, the White House accused the senator of going back on his word, saying his decision to vote against Build Back Better was "at odds with his discussions . . . with the President, with White House Staff and with his own public utterances." Frustrated and irate, White House chief of staff Klain, who had led negotiations with Manchin up until that point, didn't hold back. The statement that Klain approved went so far as to suggest Manchin's decision represented "a breach of his commitments to the President and the Senator's colleagues in the House and Senate."[11]

Manchin was furious. He still saw an opportunity to reach an agreement on a smaller, slimmed-down version of the Build Back Better bill. He was willing to go back to the drawing board with the White House and congressional leadership to hammer something out after the holiday break. But after the White House statement hit the airwaves, his demeanor changed. Without naming Klain or others specifically, he blamed the breakdown on the administration and declared he would only negotiate directly with Senate Majority Leader Chuck Schumer from then on. "It's not the president. It's staff. And they drove some things and put some things out that were absolutely inexcusable," Manchin told radio host Hoppy Kercheval on WV MetroNews, the statewide radio network and the senator's preferred media outlet in his home state.

It wouldn't be the last time Manchin would say no to Build Back Better, taking his fellow Democrats, environmentalists, and the watching world on an emotional and political roller-coaster ride toward what seemed like an inevitable tunnel of climate doom looming around every twisted curve. After a cooling-off period over the holidays, discussions between Schumer and Manchin quietly resumed in the new year. Yet within a few weeks, it quickly became clear that Build Back Better wouldn't survive in its current form—or possibly, in any form. In February, the West Virginia senator returned to Washington to pronounce that Build Back Better was dead. "What Build Back Better bill?" Manchin replied facetiously to reporters when asked about it. "I don't know what you all are talking about."[12] By springtime 2022, it appeared that it wasn't just the legislation that was lost to history, so was the president's climate policy writ large—and with it, any chances of averting the worst impacts of climate change. "President Biden's Climate Ambitions Are All but Dead," *Bloomberg News* wrote in April 2022.[13] Lost too, it seemed, was any chance of the United States catching up with global competitors like China in the race to dominate the multitrillion-dollar global clean energy economy.

"Let me tell you, as we went through this, month after month, week after week, hour after hour, the ups and downs were incredible," Senate Majority Leader Schumer said.[14] "On some days we thought we were going to get something real done. On other days we said it won't happen."

At the White House, Biden administration officials were also discouraged, but unconvinced that their ambitions were dead.

"I've known Senator Manchin for a long time," said former national climate advisor McCarthy. "I was not going to lose sleep over Senator Manchin saying he was or wasn't going to do something, because oftentimes that's just posturing, a seat of the pants sort of thing, or a challenge to get more. I felt like it was just constant positioning, not unlike how politics in Washington always is."

Nobody involved with the discussions—Manchin included—wanted to give up. After decades of failed attempts to pass meaningful climate policy, the environmental community and lawmakers had come too tantalizingly close to throwing in the towel again, especially when everything came down to one Democratic senator and with Democrats controlling Congress and the White House. Time mattered for other reasons as well. To pass the bill with a simple majority in the Senate—and with a 50–50 split in the Senate and the vice president as the tiebreaker, there wasn't a chance Democrats could pass it otherwise—it had to be done under a legislative process called budget reconciliation that allows lawmakers to pass high-priority fiscal legislation without the typical requirement of approval by sixty senators. But to meet budget reconciliation rules, Democrats had to pass it before the end of the government's fiscal year—September 30.

Also driving the need for climate action was the climate itself. While Congress dallied, more than 80 percent of the rest of the nation, including almost all 100 percent of the west, was gripped in the worst drought conditions on record, with every hot dry day bringing another threat of catastrophic wildfire.[15] Meanwhile, the South and Midwest that spring were hit by devastating floods that wiped out billions of dollars of property and crops and helped send prices soaring for everything from chicken to cornflakes. By summer, even Manchin's home state of West Virginia was facing some of the worst flooding ever recorded. At one point, almost a foot of rain fell in twelve hours, causing swollen rivers— including the Kanawha River where the Manchins owned a home—to overflow their banks. By the time the flooding stopped, more than one hundred homes and dozens of bridges were washed out and more than twenty people lost their lives in West Virginia and Virginia.

On Capitol Hill, lawmakers pulled out all the stops. Senate Finance Committee Chairman Senator Ron Wyden scrutinized every bit and piece of the legislation that he thought could get Manchin's approval and could also clear his committee, which was tasked with developing the extensive tax code revisions. Senator Tom Carper, chair of the Senate Environment and Public Works Committee, worked directly with Manchin on provisions to limit methane from oil and gas operations, coming away encouraged at the progress and Manchin's demeanor. During a meeting in Silicon Valley with local business leaders, Carper said that despite the uncertainty hanging over Washington, he felt good that the West Virginian would ultimately come around.[16] While the senior-most members of the Senate worked on policy particulars, newer members did what they could do. Freshman Colorado Sen. John Hickenlooper, a former oil and gas industry geologist who shared a bond with Manchin since they both represented states with a history of coal mining, led an effort to keep Manchin at the bargaining table, in part by feeding the West Virginian everything he could showing the proposed legislation wouldn't substantially impact inflation or the national debt. In particular, Hickenlooper pushed economists at the University of Pennsylvania's Wharton School to release an analysis showing how the proposed clean energy investments and tax credits would have a negligible effect on inflation over the next two years, and then begin to reduce inflation after that.[17] In part because of that analysis, and because they knew Manchin hated the moniker Build Back Better, some lawmakers began to float a new name for their policy: the Inflation Reduction Act.

Outside of Congress, other influential voices weighed in too. Billionaire Bill Gates, who first started talking with Manchin about what could be done about climate and energy policy during the Trump years, resurrected discussions with the senator, urging him to think about how investing in clean energy and climate action could drive American innovation.[18] At one point, the Microsoft cofounder even suggested that TerraPower, a modular nuclear reactor company that Gates bankrolled, could build a small nuclear plant in West Virginia, hiring former coal miners and other locals to build and run it.[19] Less than a year later, Gates traveled to West Virginia to meet with Manchin and visit a former coal plant in Kanawha County where such a plant could be built.

Still, Manchin continued to frustrate his fellow Democrats with his whipsaw waffling, waving the prospects of his vote and ultimately, the fate of civilization, back and forth like a tantalizing bone in front of a hungry dog. On July 15, 2022, Manchin once again went back on the Hoppy Kercheval radio show to say he was no longer interested in moving forward with negotiations on legislation that included billions in clean energy and climate investments until data came out showing that July inflation was on the decline—even if waiting for that data meant missing the opportunity to pass the legislation before the deadline for budget reconciliation. Once again, agonized proponents of the legislation were shell-shocked. Back in December, the meme on Washington's social media channels was of Joe Manchin as the Grinch. Seven months later, Twitter, Facebook, and other social media outlets lit up with remade *Peanuts* cartoons showing a Lucy-like Joe Manchin pulling the football away from a befuddled Charlie Brown–like Joe Biden. The Beltway publication *The Hill* called Manchin's latest pronouncement "the FINAL NAIL in the Biden agenda coffin."[20]

Others were less defeatist. One week after Machin appeared on the WV MetroNews radio show to declare he was once again killing the climate and clean energy bill, I was invited in my role as executive director of business advocacy organization E2 to appear on the show. West Virginians had been sold a bill of goods before with past climate proposals that promised instant careers in solar and wind for every out-of-work coal miner, I told host Hoppy Kercheval and his listeners. But the clean energy industry and the jobs that come with it now encompass a lot more than just solar and wind. The clean economy now includes jobs manufacturing batteries and EV parts and high-efficiency heat pumps, water heaters, and other appliances—all of which were a good fit for West Virginia's workforce, and all of which would be boosted by the legislation that Senator Manchin was currently derailing. The biggest area for clean energy jobs is in energy efficiency, and programs in the legislation designed to reduce energy waste could be a boon to local electricians, construction workers, HVAC technicians, and other everyday small businesses and workers. There was no reason West Virginia should once again be left behind by another economic transition—but its senior senator needed to return to the bargaining table.

Unknown to almost anyone, Manchin and Schumer were already secretly at the bargaining table again back in Washington. Over nine days, the two senior senators talked and met secretly together, unbeknown even to members of their staff. Schumer and Manchin didn't tell anyone what they were discussing—not even the president. The two grandfathers discussed what a failed climate bill would mean to their grandchildren and their legacies as lawmakers. Just a month earlier, Schumer's daughter had given birth to his newest granddaughter, named Eleanor, after Eleanor Roosevelt.[21] The future, as well as the legacy of passing what could be the most transformative legislation since Franklin Roosevelt's New Deal, was on the mind of the senator who had represented New York since 1999. Schumer desperately wanted to strike a deal with his colleague from West Virginia.

Manchin had long supported many of the climate provisions of the bill, even when it was still called Build Back Better. He wasn't necessarily against clean energy. But he was against anything that hurt coal and the rest of the fossil fuel industry. That left him in a precarious position. Production tax credits and investment tax credits for wind and solar seemed like a good solution. Clean energy companies couldn't benefit from such credits, after all, unless they made investments (in the case of the investment tax credit) or produced energy (in the case of the production tax credit). Manchin also didn't have a problem with imposing a 15 percent minimum corporate tax and eliminating other tax loopholes to help pay for other investments in clean energy—as long as those investments also included hydrogen, small nuclear reactors, energy storage, and yes, fossil fuels.

He also was generally okay with tax credits for EVs—but only as long as those vehicles, or at least the batteries in them, were predominantly made in America. He was insistent that even if an EV was made in America, it shouldn't run on a battery made in China. To address that issue, Manchin's staff inserted language requiring that at least 40 percent of the lithium and other materials in EV batteries be extracted or processed in the United States and at least 50 percent of the assembly and manufacturing of a battery be done in America for EV buyers to qualify for a full $7,500 tax credit.

What Manchin wouldn't budge on were any provisions that called for production limits or the eventual phaseout of coal or other fossil fuels or that put renewable energy ahead of fossil fuels when it came to leasing on federal lands. There was no way Manchin was going to let the government open up new areas of the Gulf of Mexico to build offshore wind turbines, for instance, if it wasn't also going to open up those areas for offshore oil drilling. As a result, his staff wrote language into the bill that requires that any federal lands or waters used for renewable energy development also be available for oil and gas development.

The final area Manchin was interested in was around permitting for fossil fuel projects—particularly, a single pipeline in his state that was very important to him. For years, Manchin had tried everything he could to get federal approval for a three-hundred-mile natural gas pipeline that would run through West Virginia called the Mountain Valley Pipeline.[22] Coal was still king in West Virginia, but natural gas was growing in importance, thanks to the state's location on the Marcellus Shale formation. If West Virginia had a bigger pipeline, petroleum industry lobbyists told Manchin, it could export more of the natural gas companies that were hydraulically fracking from the Marcellus Shale to other states and other countries. In the Inflation Reduction Act, Manchin's team saw an opportunity to finally get the pipeline approved. Ultimately, they couldn't get permitting language into the bill. Instead, Manchin offered Schumer an ultimatum: He would vote for the IRA, but only if Schumer before the end of the year promised to allow and support a Senate vote on a comprehensive permitting reform bill—one that could clear the way for the Mountain Valley Pipeline.

On July 27, with Washington and the world still in the dark about the secret talks, Manchin and Schumer were ready to announce a deal. But first, they cooked up one other trick play. The Senate that Wednesday was scheduled to vote on another sweeping piece of legislation, the $280 billion CHIPS and Science Act that provides grants and subsidies to support the construction of new semiconductor factories and advance semiconductor research and development—both key to the EV, wind, and solar industries. Senate Republican leadership had said they could support the bill—but only as long as Schumer didn't bring a budget reconciliation bill with climate and clean energy provisions up for a vote. Like most of the rest of Washington and the world, Minority Leader Senator Mitch McConnell and other top Republicans had no idea Schumer and Manchin were close to a deal. For their part, Schumer and Manchin did nothing to lead them to believe otherwise. So shortly after noon, the Senate passed the CHIPS and Science Act, with sixteen Republicans—including McConnell—voting in favor of it.

Four hours later, Manchin and Schumer shocked Capitol Hill and the world, issuing a joint public statement announcing agreement on the IRA. Included in their statement was a link to the 725-page bill and a one-page fact sheet breaking down how it would invest nearly $370 billion into clean energy and $64 billion into extending the Affordable Care Act health program. The new legislation, they declared, would pay for itself—and then some—by raising nearly $740 billion through a combination of a new minimum corporate tax, increased IRS enforcement, and changes to Medicare that would reduce the government's cost for prescription drugs. Ultimately, the senators announced, the bill would reduce the deficit by about $300 billion and the investments in clean energy and climate action would reduce greenhouse gas emissions by 40 percent by

2030. Since some of the biggest components of inflation are energy, fuel, food, and drug costs, the legislation would reduce, not increase the pace of inflation, the senators said.

As soon as they heard about the Manchin-Schumer deal, red-faced Republicans were at first shocked then infuriated that the agreement had been kept secret from them until after Democrats had secured GOP support for the CHIPS Act. "Senators Manchin and Schumer did not draft this 725-page bill in the four hours between the passage of the CHIPS Act and Senator Manchin's press release," Republican Senator John Cornyn of Texas would say later in a heated speech on the Senate floor. "They've been working on this the entire time when they told us it was off the table."

Republican senators weren't the only ones caught off guard by the Manchin-Schumer announcement. Across the country and around the world, journalists dissected every word, trying to get a clue as to how such a secret negotiation could've gotten past them in a town of news leakers like Washington. Climate activists and environmentalists who had resigned themselves to the idea that climate policy had been slowly and painfully strangled to death at the hands of Joe Manchin celebrated and cheered—but also cautiously worried. Even Democratic senators who worked alongside Schumer and Manchin every day were rocked by the unexpected news. "Holy Shit," tweeted Senator Tina Smith of Minnesota. "Stunned, but in a good way. $370B for climate and energy and 40% emissions reduction by 2030. BFD."[23]

It turned out there would be one more surprise hurdle along the tortured path of the IRA. Once again, it came from a Democrat, Senator Kyrsten Sinema of Arizona. Unlike seasoned veterans Manchin and Schumer, Sinema was relatively new to the ways of Washington. But she proved to be just as adept at leveraging her power to get what she wanted in the Democrats' razor-thin control of the Senate. A former social worker, Sinema represented the Tucson area in the U.S. House for six years before winning a Senate seat in November 2018. After she landed an appointment to the Senate Banking Committee's influential Subcommittee on Securities, Insurance, and Investment, she also won the support of the investment industry—and along with it, millions of dollars in campaign contributions. From 2017–2022, Sinema attracted nearly $3 million in campaign funding from the securities and investment industry—about 2.5 times as much as the industry contributed to the chairman of the Senate Banking Committee, Sherrod Brown.[24] No other industry had given more money to Sinema's campaigns.

Sinema's subcommittee had relatively little to do with the IRA—except for in one area, the so-called carried interest tax loophole for hedge fund and private equity managers, law firm partners, and other big earners in the financial services and real estate industries. Along with going after tax cheats and forcing companies to pay a minimum tax rate of 15 percent, Democratic leadership saw the carried interest loophole as a good way to raise revenues to offset the overall costs of the bill. Estimates show the government could've raised about $14 billion in new taxes from the richest financial services executives by eliminating the tax break. Past attempts to eliminate the loophole had widespread bipartisan support. Even former President Donald Trump, who publicly bragged about his own exploitation of tax loopholes in his businesses, claimed he didn't like it. Schumer knew taxing the rich would also help make the overall legislation more appealing to the most liberal members of his party, even if his pinstriped constituents back on Wall Streetdidn't like it. For his part, Manchin had no problem getting rid of the loophole: In 2021, he and Ohio Senator Brown coauthored a bill that would've done just that.[25]

But the financial services industry had a huge problem with the idea of getting rid of the carried interest loophole—and they let their friend Senator Sinema know. Sinema was already on record as being against any attempts to kill the carried interest tax break. Because of her opposition, the House had left it out of previous iterations of what would become the IRA. At a closed meeting of senators that Schumer convened to explain what was in the new agreement that he and Manchin had just reached, Sinema was notably absent, further raising concerns about where she stood on the bill.[26] While saying little publicly, Sinema soon confirmed to Schumer what he and others had feared: That she wouldn't support the IRA if it removed the carried interest loophole for the wealthiest Americans. As with Manchin before, the bill couldn't pass without Sinema.

Democratic leadership and the environmental community, so close to success, were once again in a state of exhausted torment, sick and tired and ready to get off the roller-coaster ride they had been on for more than a year. Some environmental advocacy groups brought in mental health counselors for their emotionally drained employees and organized workshops on preventing burnout.

In the six days after Schumer and Manchin announced their agreement, the two senators and other key Democrats worked tirelessly to win over Sinema. To appease the freshman senator from Arizona, Schumer agreed to remove two elements of the 15 percent corporate minimum tax rate provision, even though doing so reduced the revenues raised by the IRA by $55 billion. The White House and business advocacy organizations pushed hard to show Sinema how approving the bill would lead to big investments in solar, batteries, and other clean energy industries in Arizona. Still, she wouldn't budge.

Finally, on August 3, Schumer acquiesced. He agreed to drop the carried interest provision from the bill. In doing so, the old veteran who had been in Congress for nearly as long as forty-six-year-old Sinema had been alive said he had "no choice" but to give in to the freshman who was nearly three decades his junior.[27]

Four days later, on August 7, after sixteen hours of further debate and votes on amendments, the Senate passed the Inflation Reduction Act with a 51–50 vote, with Vice President Kamala Harris coming from the White House to break the tie between Democrats and Republicans. The following Friday, the House passed the bill 220–207, also along party lines, sending it to an all-too-eager President Biden, who was waiting to sign it. Like a legislative Lazarus, the first major climate bill to ever pass the Senate; the bill that scientists, environmentalists, health-care experts, businesspeople, young people and anyone else who cared about the future of the planet had all but begged for so long; the bill that just about everyone in Washington had thought was dead was now the law of the land.

"To pass such an amazing piece of legislation is one of the greatest legislative feats that has ever occurred," Senator Schumer said. "And it wouldn't have happened without all 50 (Democratic senators), each of whom knew they wouldn't get everything they wanted, and that they had to pull together as a team."[28]

Schumer said even when he and his fellow senators—and seemingly everybody connected with the climate legislation—thought it would fail, "there was one sort of beacon, who always had that optimism, who always propelled it forward, and who always said we can get it done." President Biden, Schumer said, never gave up.

At a White House celebration to mark the passage of the IRA, Biden emphasized how the policy was the biggest and most important climate legislation ever passed. But he also emphasized how many people—not just politicians, but climate and environmental advocates, business leaders, labor unions, economists, and scientists—had worked to get the legislation to the finish line. Never in recent history had such a broad and far-reaching constituency worked together to pass legislation like this.

"You did this," the president said to me shortly after the White House celebration concluded. "No—I really mean it. This only happened because you all kept pushing and pushing and pushing. You didn't give up."

A few minutes later, while walking from the lawn into the East Wing of the White House, I spoke briefly with the man who ultimately decided the fate of the legislation—and with it, the environmental and economic future of America: Senator Joe Manchin. As we walked, I told Manchin what he and others already knew: That none of this would've happened if he had not decided to return to the bargaining table and ultimately vote to approve the most sweeping climate and clean energy package in history.

"It takes a whole team," Manchin said to me. "It takes a whole team."

CHAPTER 3

Modern-Day Triple Play

THE BIDEN ADMINISTRATION'S TRIPLE PLAY OF CLEAN ENERGY, CLIMATE, and technology legislation is invariably compared to some of the biggest and most impactful public policies in American history.

And for good reason.

In terms of size and spending, the climate and clean energy provisions of the IRA add up to about $370 billion. The Infrastructure Investment and Jobs Act (IIJA) will inject another $163 billion into climate and clean energy projects such as EV charging stations and electric school buses. The CHIPS and Science Act includes another $280 billion to build and expand the nation's semiconductor industry, which is critical to building more and better American-made EVs, solar panels, batteries, wind turbines, and just about every other electronic device. The CHIPS Act also included billions for scientific research necessary to fight climate change, including nanotechnology, clean energy, quantum computing, and artificial intelligence, as well as disaster-resilience research and funding to create a new federal office to manage clean-energy innovation. As *The Atlantic* put it, the CHIPS Act is "one of the largest climate bills ever passed."[1]

By comparison, President Kennedy's moonshot program cost about $275 billion (adjusted for inflation to 2022 dollars).[2] The biggest infrastructure project in U.S. history, President Eisenhower's Federal-Aid Highway Act of 1956, cost the equivalent of about $305 billion.[3] The nation's most ambitious social and public works policy, Roosevelt's New Deal, totaled about $793 billion in inflation-adjusted dollars.[4]

"In terms of magnitude, you have to go back to the '50s and early '60s to find a similar approach, a similar magnitude with respect to infrastructure," Brian Deese, the former director of the National Economic Council, told the *New York Times*.[5] "And there is no historic analog on the clean energy side."

Biden administration insiders like to look at three pieces of legislation—the IRA, IIJA, and CHIPS—as symbiotic, part of a whole body of legislation that is at the core of everything the administration does and wants to do when it comes to climate and the economy. As Energy Department leaders like to say, the infrastructure act is the backbone. The CHIPS Act is the brains. And the IRA, the heart and lungs.

"We all love to talk about the IRA—it is the single-biggest climate legislation in the history of this country," said Kate Gordon, former senior advisor to Energy Department Secretary Jennifer Granholm.[6] "But it's really about the whole package. And we've never seen anything like it since the New Deal in terms of the investment in the transformation of our economy."

The Biden administration and congressional Democrats always expected it would take two pieces of legislation—one focused on infrastructure and one focused on clean energy and clean transportation—to meet their climate agenda goals. The CHIPS Act was later deemed necessary when they realized that semiconductor supply shortages could seriously hamstring America's ability to deploy enough EVs, solar panels, or wind turbines to meet their goals.

Just like with the New Deal or the race to the moon, the plan all along was to make it not about climate change, but about jobs, the economy, and building a better, more equitable America. It was a way of talking about climate change that both Biden and the American public could understand, and a strategy that Gina McCarthy—long before she became National Climate Advisor—helped Biden develop as an advisor to his campaign for president.

"It was totally designed—and rightly so—as an economic development strategy," said McCarthy, whose long career in environmental policy included working for five Republican governors, one Democratic governor, and two Democratic presidents.[7]

"The circumstances, if you think about it, really warranted a different approach to climate," she said. "You were coming away from the COVID pandemic. Millions of people had lost their jobs. People were sitting in their homes worried about if they will have food to eat, water to drink or if they will ever be able to go outside again.

"It was a horrid time," she said. "And we had to have a strategy that didn't go, 'Oh, you have to worry about climate on top of all of that.'"

Along with the economic battering from COVID, other economic shocks that followed—including soaring natural gas prices resulting from Russia's invasion of Ukraine and supply chain issues that ground technology, automotive, and other sectors to a standstill—helped make the administration's case for action even with lawmakers who could care less about melting icebergs or polar bears or global warming. Instead of talking about climate change, the message—and the policy—became all about jobs, investments, and economic growth. It became about creating opportunities for new careers, lowering energy bills, and building up the fundamental pillars of America, including manufacturing and global competitiveness. And it became about doing it with equity, and in ways that could help lift Americans from Appalachia to Silicon Valley, from Wall Street to Main Street, and from the poorest neighborhoods in the country.

Like the New Deal, these policies promise to fundamentally change America's economy, pumping overdue federal support into the highest of high-tech research and development programs but also into rural areas, communities of color, and other states, cities, and counties left behind by previous economic and technology transitions.

Like the Interstate Highway System, these programs will touch every state and corner of the country, whether it's with new EV charging stations cropping up every fifty miles along the sides of those highways; new factory towns churning out solar panels and EVs, or new clean energy transmission lines stretching from California to Texas.

Like Kennedy's moonshot, America's climate and clean energy programs also promise to accomplish feats that previously were only hopes and dreams. This time, though, the choice isn't just about something as relatively straightforward as landing on the moon. It's about slowing climate change and disasters like wildfires, drought, and extreme weather that come with it, the biggest of which caused more than $612 billion in damage to the country's economy and prematurely killed more than 1,750 Americans in the five years between 2018–2022 alone, according to NOAA.[8]

As with other transformative policies in America's history, the economic impacts of these programs are poised to far exceed their direct investments. Through tax credits, direct investments, and loans for clean energy and clean transportation projects, the IRA itself is expected to spur about $3 trillion in private-sector investments in renewable energy technology alone, which would be an eightfold return on the government's $370 billion investment.[9] Goldman Sachs predicts that the combination of private and public sector investments could result in America producing twice as much energy from renewables than it did from the fracking and shale gas boom of 2005–2010.[10]

Government investments and incentives are just the kindling to light an economic fire. What matters is what the private sector does, and so far, the private sector, flush with cash, likes what it sees. "The private sector is going to run where the public sector gives signals, gives tax breaks, gives opportunities to them that makes it even more amenable for them to invest," said former climate advisor McCarthy.

For businesses, the incentives to invest in new projects, factories, and equipment are much greater than they appear. Investment bank Credit Suisse (now part of UBS) examined sixty climate and clean energy provisions in the IRA.[11] While these programs add up to about $370 billion in total, the real impact of the legislation could be closer to $800 billion—more than double what the government estimates. What government forecasters underestimate are two things, according to the Credit Suisse report: The expected increased demand for clean energy as the programs get implemented, and the full impacts of the "stackability" of tax credits.

To understand stackability, consider a clean energy company that is building a new wind turbine factory in America. In doing so, it can claim a tax credit of up to 30 percent if its workers are paid prevailing wages and it uses union apprenticeship programs.[12] If it doesn't have the capital on hand to build the factory, that's okay. It can leverage those tax credits, using them essentially as collateral to borrow money from investors. If the company uses domestically made materials to build its turbines—say, steel made in Pennsylvania and electric motors made from domestic materials in Ohio—it can claim an additional 10 percent tax credit. If the company also happens to develop its own wind farms, it can get a tax credit of $30 for every megawatt of energy its new turbines produce. And if that new wind farm is built in an area transitioning from fossil fuels or that historically was bypassed by clean energy development—say, an abandoned coal strip mine or a low-income rural community—the company could get an additional 10 percent tax credit stacked on top of that. The opportunities of stackability don't end there, however. If the energy that the new wind farm produces is used to make hydrogen that in turn can be used to power airplanes or power that steel factory back in Pennsylvania, the company can claim another tax credit of $3 for every kilogram of clean hydrogen it produces.

Some tax credits are designed specifically to revitalize manufacturing in America. The Advanced Energy Project Tax Credit provides tax breaks for companies to build new clean energy product factories, such as those used to make or recycle solar panels, wind turbines, EVs, and batteries or semiconductors, or make existing factories more energy efficient. The separate Advanced Manufacturing Production Credit provides tax breaks for producing such goods. Businesses can get other tax breaks for producing sustainable fuels for vehicles or airplanes; capturing and storing carbon at industrial plants or producing hydrogen.

These tax credits aren't government giveaways. To qualify for the investment tax credit, a company has to *invest* in a factory or solar or wind farm, and the amount of credit depends on how much they're willing to invest. To qualify for the production tax credit, a company has to *produce* clean energy, and the credit is based on how much clean energy they produce. And to claim additional add-on credits, it has to invest in or produce cleaner energy in the parts of America that need jobs and investments the most; it has to employ union labor or at least pay prevailing wages and it has to use domestically made materials to do it. Similarly, grants and loans tied to these policies also require companies to make matching investments.

In other words, for all the focus on the size of the federal investments, it's only a fraction of the overall investment from private industry. The government was never going to be able to address climate change on its own, and federal policies aren't intended to do so. Instead, they're intended to send the market signal, provide the seed funding in some cases, and most importantly, provide visibility to companies and investors to reassure them it's smart to make investments on their own.

"We often say these investments are private-sector led, government-enabled," Department of Energy Secretary Granholm said.[13] Together, government tax credits, grants, loans, and clear policy direction have "made the United States the world's most attractive investment landscape for new energy and decarbonization technologies," she said. "In many cases, it makes the U.S. irresistible."

In its analysis, Credit Suisse notes that the multiplier effect for public-sector investments is typically somewhere between 1.1x to 1.6x—meaning that every $1 in public investments (or tax credits) generates somewhere between $1.10 and $1.60 in private-sector investments. When it comes to loans from the Department of Energy or from government-backed green banks, the multiplier effect is closer to 3.7x.

The tax credits and other investments from America's climate and clean energy programs will make the United States the cheapest place in the world to make solar panels, wind turbines, EVs, and other clean energy goods—even cheaper than China or Mexico, said Credit Suisse analyst Betty Jiang.[14] The ability to make things cheaper here, in turn, means more foreign companies will move here to do it.

"We all knew all of this was coming," Jiang said. "But the missing link until before the (federal climate policies) was that the economics didn't make sense for all of this to happen. For the first time, the economics are all now aligned . . . and it's really turbocharged all of these things."

Solar panel maker Qcells is an example of how the IRA is turbocharging businesses, attracting foreign investments, and transforming local economies.

Founded in Germany, Qcells was acquired in 2012 by the Korean conglomerate Hanwha Group, which consolidated its manufacturing operations in China, Malaysia, and South Korea to reduce costs. Producing millions of solar panels each year, those Asian factories made Qcells one of the biggest makers of solar panels in the world. When the company expanded to the United States in 2019, the Korean company incongruously landed in a place known for making carpet and flooring, in an ultraconservative area where 70 percent of voters in 2020 voted for clean energy opponent Donald Trump and against Joe Biden and his climate agenda.

Located among pine trees and kudzu at the end of a bumpy road in the Carbondale Business Park, Qcells' Dalton, Georgia factory produces 14,000 solar panels every day that are shipped out via nearby Interstate 75 to solar developers and installers around the country.

Qcells picked this area partly because of the skill set of the local labor pool. For more than a century, Dalton was the carpet manufacturing capital of the world. Companies like Shaw Industries and Mohawk Industries still dominate the labor force and have employed generations of local residents, but as jobs at those companies began to decline and move overseas, many locals, especially young people, were looking for something new.

Robert Howey was one of them. A native of nearby Resaca, Georgia, Howey's mother and father both work in the flooring industry in Dalton. So did he after returning home from a tour in the U.S. Navy following high school. But after spending two years in a carpet factory, he didn't get a single promotion and didn't see a future for himself. So when he learned Qcells was hiring, he applied and was hired first as a temporary worker and then full time. Within one and half years, he was promoted—several times.

"I knew if I stayed in the carpet business, I'd never move up," said Howey, who now has one of the busiest jobs at Qcells: Coordinating training for the army of new employees being hired at the factories.[15] "So I left, and I never looked back."

When he told his friends and coworkers at the carpet factory he was leaving to build solar panels for a Korean company, they laughed, Howey recalled. "They said good luck, but it would never last," he said. Other companies had come and gone in Dalton, they reminded him, but flooring was still king, and everybody eventually ended up spending their lives working in the industry. "This time it's different," Howey said. "This time we have the government behind us, and we're going nonstop."

As Howey spoke, Qcells production lines behind him were indeed running nonstop. Working at a solar panel factory is not unlike working at a carpet factory. Inputs go into banks of machines that stretch almost as far as the eye can see and finished products come out. In a carpet mill, it's fabric, string, and chemicals that go in. In a solar panel factory, it's silicon wafers, wires, and glass. At Qcells, the process starts with precision lasers that finely cut silicon cells as thin as human hair. Wires known as fingers and busbars connect the cells in a circuit, and then they're overlaid with white sheets of ethylene vinyl acetate that bind the cells together like tiles on a countertop. Robotic arms and conveyor belts place the packaged cells sandwich-like between two sheets of thin glass, which are then heated and framed with aluminum and blasted with artificial "sunlight" to test their wattage and check their performance. Next, another bank of robots attach junction boxes to the backs of the panels, and then, after each panel is inspected by both humans and machines, robotic forklifts move them and stack them, pausing on the giant factory floor anytime they come close to a human.

Qcells has always considered the Dalton factory just the first block to eventually building a complete solar panel supply chain in America. But it wasn't until the Biden administration announced its climate aspirations, sending a clear market signal to the clean energy business, that the company decided to definitively double down on America. In 2022, the company announced a $204 million agreement to buy controlling interest in REC Silicon, which owned two idled factories in Washington and Montana that made polysilicon, the essential core element used in solar panels and semiconductors. At their peak, the plants together employed more than one thousand workers who made polysilicon and monosilane for solar panel and semiconductor manufacturers in China and other Asian countries. Beginning in 2019, however, REC Silicon shut down the factories amid a trade dispute between the United States and China, and as cheaper supplies of polysilicon became available in China and Europe.[16]

At the time of the purchase, Qcells said it planned to restart the REC Silicon factories in 2023 as part of its overarching plans to build a complete end-to-end solar supply chain in America and hinted at future investments. "Our commitment to the U.S. is more serious than ever before," Qcells CEO Justin Lee said.[17] Eight months later, Lee and Qcells revealed just how serious they were. In January 2023, following the passage of the IRA, the company announced what at the time was the biggest investment in solar manufacturing in US history: A $2.5 billion commitment to expand its existing solar panel factory in Dalton and to build a new factory in nearby Cartersville. Combined, the Qcells factories could help get America back in the global market for solar from the ground floor up. While the company assembles solar panels in Georgia, it traditionally has had to import most of the basic materials from China and other markets. With its new investments, the company will be able to produce polysilicon in Washington and Montana, ship it to its new factory in Cartersville, Georgia, to make ingots, wafers, and cells, and then use those ingredients to make panels. It would be the first time that solar panels will be mass-produced end-to-end in America in a decade, according to Qcells—and never at such a scale. "We are really starting to see a supply chain starting to emerge in the United States for solar products," said Scott Moskowitz, head of market strategy and public affairs at Qcells.[18]

Qcells had its eye on growth in the United States for a long time. But it wouldn't have made the investments it is making today without the passage of federal climate and clean energy policies. The IRA "really changed everything for companies like us," Moskowitz said. Tax credits for manufacturing are part of the reason. But so are the consumer tax credits that are driving demand for solar panels like never before in America. When all its new factories are up and running, Qcells will be able to produce about five times as many panels as it did pre-IRA, but that will still only meet a fraction of the expected demand. "We are going to make 8.5 gigawatts of solar panels a year, but the demand is more like 40," Moskowitz said. "If we had 40 gigawatts of solar panels to sell, we would sell them all."

There's another way America's new climate and clean energy policies are revolutionizing America's economy: Through savings.

Already, utility-scale solar and wind energy is the cheapest energy available in just about every part of the country, with or without government subsidies. At the end of 2021, a megawatt-hour of wind energy sold for as little as $26 (about $9 when subsidies are factored in), while solar power sold for as cheap as $28 ($23 with subsidies), according to investment bank Lazard.[19] By comparison, a megawatt hour from a gas-fired power plant costs about $38 at its cheapest, while electricity from a coal plant costs $61, even with a wide range of fossil fuel subsidies included. By 2023, only one coal-fired power plant in the country—the Dry Fork Station coal plant in Wyoming—was even competitive with clean energy.[20] Even there, it was only about $0.32 per megawatt hour cheaper than local wind energy. After Russia's invasion of Ukraine and a particularly cold winter in parts of the West sent natural gas prices soaring by as much as fourfold in 2023, many gas-fired plants also became even less competitive with wind and solar.

New tax credits and other investments for clean energy projects and production means the cost of wind turbines and solar panels, as well as the electricity they produce, will become even cheaper and more available in every part of the country. New incentives for manufacturers of high-efficiency heat pumps, water heaters, and other energy-efficiency products, coupled with incentives for consumers and businesses to buy them, mean Americans will pay less for their monthly electric bills. And new incentives for EVs will make them cheaper to produce and more attractive for consumers and businesses to buy. That will create tremendous economic savings too, since filling up an EV with electricity in

2022 costs about half as much as filling up an internal combustion engine vehicle with gasoline.[21]

Put all that together and industrial energy and transportation costs alone in America will decrease by about $55 billion on an annual basis compared to business as usual, according to an analysis by Energy Futures Initiative (EFI), a think tank run by former U.S. Department of Energy Secretary Ernie Moniz.[22] At the residential level, EFI estimates that consumers and businesses will see their annual energy costs fall by almost 10 percent because of energy-efficiency improvements spurred by federal climate and clean energy programs.

Money is part of the equation. People are another. To build all those new wind turbines and solar panels and EVs and heat pumps, businesses will have to hire a lot of people. EFI estimates that the IRA alone will create about 1.5 million new jobs—welders, electricians, assembly line workers, HVAC technicians to name a few—by 2030. The BlueGreen Alliance, a collaboration of labor unions and environmental groups, estimates overall employment in clean energy and similar sectors will be closer to 9 million jobs.[23]

Between energy cost savings, new jobs, businesses, factories, and investments, the total impact of new federal climate and clean energy programs will add $240 billion per year to the U.S. GDP, according to EFI estimates. That's like adding the economic equivalent of the state of Kentucky or any of twenty other states to the country's GDP every year. On a per capita basis, it translates to about $6,200 more in real disposable income per year for every American by 2023.[24] That means more opportunities for businesses not just in clean energy, but across the economy.

The way the three pieces of legislation are structured, the investments they're already driving, the jobs they're already creating, "is about as good an outcome as anybody could've imagined," said Dave Foster, an energy and labor expert who cofounded the BlueGreen Alliance and now is senior fellow at EFI.[25] "It's pretty incredible."

And it's happening now.

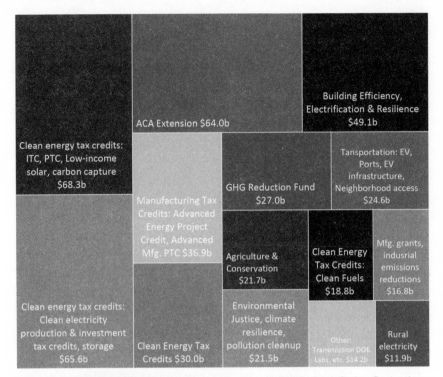

Figure 3.1. Inflation Reduction Act. Passed in August 2022, the Inflation Reduction Act (IRA) includes about $370 billion in tax credits and federal investments in clean energy, energy efficiency, clean transportation and manufacturing.

SOURCE: JOBS, EMISSIONS, AND ECONOMIC GROWTH: WHAT THE INFLATION REDUCTION ACT MEANS FOR WORKING FAMILIES © 2023 ENERGY FUTURES INITIATIVE

Inflation Reduction Act climate and clean energy programs include:

Energy

- Production tax credit for electricity from renewables: $30 per megawatt hour; 5X increase in credit for projects meeting prevailing wage/apprenticeship requirements

- Investment tax credit for new clean energy projects: 6 percent base; up to 30 percent for projects meeting prevailing wage/ apprenticeship requirements

- Advanced energy project credit: 6 percent base; up to 30 percent for projects meeting prevailing wage/apprenticeship requirements

- Zero-emission nuclear power production credit: $15 per megawatt hour for power produced at a qualifying nuclear facility
- Advanced manufacturing production credit: Production tax credit for manufacture of components for solar, wind, batteries, and critical materials
- Clean hydrogen production credit: $3 per kilogram
- Sustainable aviation fuel production credit: $1.75 per gallon

Engines

- Up to $7,500 tax credit for purchase of new EVs
- $4,000 tax credit for purchase of used EVs.
- Commercial clean vehicle credit: Up to 30 percent of the cost of EVs; 15 percent for hybrid-electric vehicles
- Advanced technology vehicle manufacturing loan program: $3 billion available for advanced vehicle factories; loan amounts cannot exceed 80 percent of total costs
- Domestic manufacturing conversion grants: $2 billion to refit existing vehicle factories and supply chains for clean vehicles
- Alternative fuel vehicle refueling property credit: up to $100,000 for businesses to add charging stations at their properties

Efficiency

- Energy-efficiency home improvement credit: Up to 30 percent of costs, with annual credit caps. Includes credits for heat pumps ($2,000), windows ($600), doors ($250).
- Residential clean energy credit: Up to 30 percent for the purchase of battery storage and other clean energy equipment
- New energy-efficient homes credit: $2,500 for new homes meeting Energy Star standards; $5,000 for new zero-energy ready homes
- High-efficiency electric home rebates: $4.5 billion for rebates for energy-efficiency electric appliances including stoves, water heaters, and other products

Innovation/Investment

- Greenhouse Gas Reduction Fund: $27 billion in grants to mobilize financing and leverage private capital for clean energy and climate products, with emphasis on low-income and disadvantaged communities.

- Department of Energy Loan Programs Office: $40 billion in total loan authority, supported by $3.6 billion in credit subsidy for qualifying projects for innovative clean energy technologies.

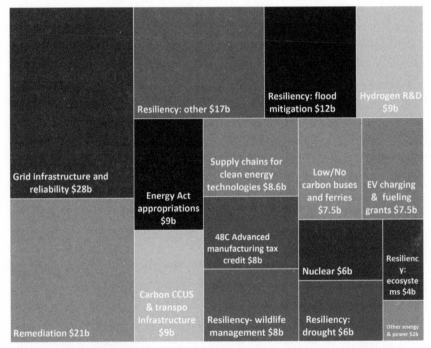

Figure 3.2. Infrastructure Investment and Jobs Act. Passed in November 2021, the $1 trillion Infrastructure Investment and Jobs Act (IIJA) includes $74 billion in clean energy investments and an additional $89 billion on climate impact and resiliency investments.

SOURCE: JOBS, EMISSIONS, AND ECONOMIC GROWTH: WHAT THE INFLATION REDUCTION ACT MEANS FOR WORKING FAMILIES © 2023 ENERGY FUTURES INITIATIVE

Infrastructure Investment and Jobs Act climate and clean energy programs include:

Energy

- Grid reliability and infrastructure: $28 billion
- Miscellaneous energy and power: $2 billion
- Nuclear: $6 billion

Engines

- Public transit: $149 billion
- EV charging and funding grants: $7.5 billion
- Low/no carbon buses and ferries: $7.5 billion
- Carbon capture and storage and transportation infrastructure: $9 billion

Innovation/Investment

- Hydrogen research & development: $9 billion
- Supply chain infrastructure for clean energy technologies: $8.6 billion
- Advanced manufacturing tax credit: $8 billion

CHIPS and Science Act climate and clean energy programs include:

- R&D, commercialization, workforce/economic development investments: $200 billion
- Advanced manufacturing tax credit: $24 billion
- CHIPS for America International Technology Security and Innovation Fund: $0.5 billion
- National Semiconductor Technology Center: $2.5 billion
- Microelectronics R&D center: $0.5 billion
- NIST semiconductor programs: $6 billion
- Public wireless supply chain innovation fund: $1.5 billion

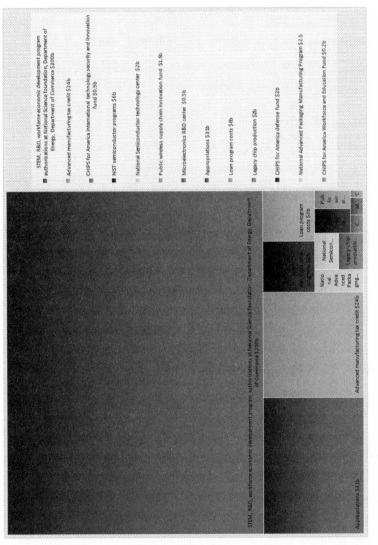

The following legend items appear with the figure:

- STEM, R&D, workforce economic development program authorizations at National Science foundation, Department of Energy, Department of Commerce $200b
- Advanced manufacturing tax credit $24b
- CHIPS for America international technology security and innovation fund $0.5b
- NIST semiconductor programs $6b
- National Semiconductor technology center $2b
- Public wireless supply chain innovation fund $1.5b
- Microelectronics R&D center $0.5b
- Appropriations $33b
- Loan program costs $6b
- Legacy chip production $2b
- CHIPS for America defense fund $2b
- National Advanced Packaging Manufacturing Program $2.5
- CHIPS for America Workforce and Education Fund $0.2b

Figure 3.3. The CHIPS and Science Act. Passed in August 2022, the nearly $280 billion CHIPS and Science Act is designed to advance R&D and manufacturing of semiconductors, which are critical for clean energy, batteries, and electric vehicles.

SOURCE: MCKINSEY & COMPANY. "THE CHIPS AND SCIENCE ACT: HERE'S WHAT'S IN IT."

CHAPTER 4

Energy

"We Need More Electricity"

MICHAEL RUCKER HAS SPENT HIS LIFE IN CLEAN ENERGY.

After graduating from Pomona College and the John Hopkins School of Advanced International Studies in the 1990s, he toyed briefly with the idea of getting into the nonprofit sector while pursuing his real passion at the time, beach volleyball. Instead, the tall and soft-spoken Californian relocated to Washington, D.C., to work on renewable energy and energy-efficiency issues for the utility think tank Edison Electric Institute, and then went to Paris to work for the International Energy Agency. In 1999, Rucker moved into the private sector, working for a company that helps corporations purchase and trade renewable energy certificates. He later went on to work in the wind turbine manufacturing arm of GE and lead development operations for some of the biggest wind developers in the United States, including Clipper Windpower Development and Germany-based Juwi Wind.

From his international work and travels, Rucker knew other countries like Germany and Spain were speeding past the United States on clean energy. Back then, solar and wind generated less than 1 percent of the electricity supply in the United States, while in other countries the market share was nearing double digits and growing fast. Given America's wide-open West, its spirit of innovation and its abundant wind and sunshine, it didn't make sense. America had the resources to tap into more clean energy and lead the world in doing it. But Europe had something America didn't: More favorable government policies for clean energy.

For more than thirty years, the biggest driver of wind energy development in America had been an obscure tax credit created as part of a bipartisan energy bill signed into law in 1992 by Republican President George H. W. Bush. Designed to help lessen America's dependence on oil and diversify the country's energy sector, the Production Tax Credit (PTC) allowed producers of wind or biomass energy to claim a tax credit of a couple of cents for every kilowatt hour of electricity they produced. Compared to other countries—and compared to tax credits provided to fossil fuel companies—the PTC was a pittance. But at least it was something.

It was also incredibly unreliable. Unlike more stable, long-term credits for fossil fuels, some of which have been in place for more than one hundred years, the PTC typically had to be renewed every year.[1] Whether or not it was reinstated depended on political and partisan whims and how much attention the fossil fuel industry felt like paying attention to its pipsqueak competitors, wind and solar. Coal and oil companies are generally quick to push back on anything that challenges their dominance of the U.S. energy market. But as long as renewable energy remained a minuscule part of the nation's energy makeup, and as long as clean energy companies had to claw and fight for the PTC to be renewed every year, the fossil fuel industry didn't worry too much. Sometimes the industry didn't have to worry at all. Since its passage, the PTC lapsed seven times, including three times under the presidency of George W. Bush, the son of the president who created the law in the first place. Since it can take four to eight years to build a wind farm, it got to the point where many investors and developers didn't even consider projects because they knew the PTC would expire or lapse before they could even break ground.

That began to change in 2009. Elected in the middle of the worst recession since the Great Depression, and amid growing concerns over the impacts of climate change, President Barack Obama and then–Vice President Joe Biden began to realize expanding clean energy could help both the economy and the environment. It could create jobs, drive new investments, and help bring the economy out of recession, and it could also reduce greenhouse gas emissions that turbocharge climate change. Just a month after taking office, Obama signed into law the American Recovery and Reinvestment Act (ARRA), which included the nation's biggest investments in clean energy at the time: $90 billion in federal investments into clean energy projects. Encouraged by clean energy business groups and environmentalists, Obama also began considering ways to increase and extend tax credits for clean energy and also scale back tax credits for fossil fuel companies, which were adding up to roughly $20 billion a year, to help level the playing field that had tilted in favor of fossil fuel companies for decades.[2]

The Obama administration's support of clean energy encouraged Rucker and many other clean energy entrepreneurs to have hope again. In 2014, Rucker struck out on his own, cofounding a wind energy operations, maintenance, and construction business called Harvest Energy Services in his home in Boulder, Colorado.

It was a rough start.

"Things were still pretty bleak in project development back then," he said.[3] "The uncertainty with the tax credits made new projects extremely risky. Financing was very hard to come by. Nobody wanted to put up their money."

With little demand for new wind energy development, Rucker shifted into the business of repairing and servicing other companies' wind turbines. Instead of building his wind projects, he found himself in the more humbling and less lucrative business of taking care of other developers' projects. "I really thought I would just be fixing wind turbines for the rest of my career," he said.

In 2015, Rucker's career—and the wind industry in general—changed. After seeing how federal clean energy investments through ARRA were spurring hundreds of clean energy projects across the country in ways that had never been seen in America before, Congress and the Obama administration agreed to extend the PTC for wind not for one year, but for three years. Finally, wind developers and their financiers had some business certainty beyond just twelve months. Later that same year, Rucker started another company, Scout Clean Energy. While Harvest was in the business of repairing turbines and managing wind farms,

Scout was founded to do what Rucker originally thought he'd be doing all along: Develop new wind energy projects.

"It was really policy that started Scout," he said. "We saw the first multiyear extension of the PTC, and suddenly we had the longest visibility we'd ever had—four years. I started Scout to take advantage of that."

Within seven years, Scout had over ninety major projects under development and 1,200 MW of operating wind farms across twenty-four states. The company also branched out beyond wind, adding solar and battery storage to its projects, which gives it the ability to supply its utility customers with electricity around the clock regardless of how hard the wind blows or how bright the sun shines. Scout also announced the biggest hybrid clean energy project of its kind, the 1,150-megawatt Horse Heaven Clean Energy Center in Washington state that will combine solar, wind, and battery storage. The project is expected to create nearly one thousand union-labor construction jobs and contribute more than $250 million in new local tax revenues.

Just as earlier policies drove the creation of Scout Clean Energy and many other solar and wind companies like it, the U.S. government's latest climate and clean energy policies and investments are now driving unprecedented growth for businesses generating clean energy. The result is a fundamental remaking of America's energy system, akin to earlier shifts from whale oil to coal or coal to gas, with all the economic changes that come with it. Clean energy is turning states like Mississippi and Louisiana into the solar powerhouses of tomorrow. It's bringing manufacturing of solar panels and wind turbine parts back to America, with new factories in places like Iowa and Georgia. And it's giving new life to nascent technologies like geothermal energy in America's deserts and offshore wind in American waters off our coastlines.

Part of the reason for the gold rush in clean energy is simple supply and demand. There's a looming surge in demand for electricity, and finally, a realization by governments that new supply must come from clean energy if we're to avert the worst impacts of climate change. Since 2005, the U.S. population has grown about 12 percent. The number of gadgets, tools, and equipment we plug into power outlets has grown exponentially. Remarkably, America's electricity usage has remained relatively flat during that time frame. Chalk that up to improvements in energy efficiency—Energy Star refrigerators and dishwashers; LED lighting; low-voltage semiconductors and other advances.

But that's about to change. As America continues buying more EVs, electric appliances, heat pumps, water heaters, and other devices that get plugged into an outlet, Princeton University estimates that electricity demand in America will be 24 percent higher in 2030 than it was a decade or so earlier.[4] Similarly, consulting firm McKinsey predicts electricity demand will triple by 2050 as automobile drivers shift from gas to EVs, and homeowners and businesses shift away from gas to electricity.[5] For a glimpse at the future, look to California. In the second quarter of 2023, about 25 percent of all new cars sold in the state were electric or zero-emission vehicles, up from just 5 percent a few years earlier. California surpassed its short-term goal of reaching 1.5 million zero-emission vehicles a full two years ahead of schedule, putting it solidly on a path to reach its longer-term goal of 100 percent zero-emission vehicles by 2035.[6] The growth in EVs is good news for the environment. But along with the growth in building electrification, data centers, and high-use computing applications like artificial intelligence and cryptocurrency mining, more EVs mean more electricity is needed. California's Pacific Gas & Electric Co., the nation's biggest utility, forecasts a 70 percent increase in demand for power by 2043.

"I can't emphasize enough: We need more electricity," said Elon Musk, the man who started the EV boom when he took over Tesla.[7] "However much electricity you think you need, more than that is needed." That's not necessarily a bad thing, Musk said, but an opportunity for electricity suppliers who can deliver sustainable energy to meet the demand. "It's a very positive future for producers and distributors of electricity," Musk said. "Really, you couldn't ask for a market that's going to grow in a better way than this."

To meet that market demand, we're going to need a lot more wind turbines, solar farms, and batteries, especially as fossil fuel and nuclear plants are phased out because they cost more to operate, are too old, or are required to comply with new environmental regulations. Princeton predicts U.S. wind energy installations will more than double between

2020–2026, from fifteen gigawatts to nearly forty gigawatts. Solar will grow even faster, increasing more than fivefold, to nearly fifty gigawatts by 2026, according to Princeton.[8]

Federal climate and clean energy policies are jump-starting that growth in clean energy supplies. Under the IRA, the 30 percent PTC for wind projects was extended through 2024. Beginning in 2025, the PTC will be replaced with a technology-agnostic clean energy tax credit of up to 30 percent (or if the developer chooses, a 2.6 cent inflation-adjusted credit per kilowatt hour produced) for low-carbon electricity generation of any kind—wind, solar, geothermal, hydrogen, nuclear or the next technology we don't even know about yet. These new tax credits won't begin phasing out until the year 2032, or until U.S. power sector greenhouse gas emissions decline by 25 percent of 2022 levels, whichever comes first.[9] What that means is that investors and developers who want to build new wind, solar, geothermal, or other clean energy projects have more market visibility than they've ever had: Up to ten years, instead of one year under the old PTC model. It also means there will be a rush by investors and developers to build as many clean energy projects as they can before the tax credits expire or before the United States reaches its greenhouse gas emission reduction goals, whichever comes first.

That rush to build new renewable energy projects started almost immediately following the passage of the IRA. In just the first three months after President Biden signed the legislation, private companies invested more in new wind, solar, battery, and other clean energy projects than they did during all of 2021.[10] By the end of 2022, more than $141 billion in private investments flowed into new clean energy projects and companies in the United States, up 11 percent from the previous year, according to BloombergNEF.[11] Only China saw more investments in clean energy than the United States, attracting $546 billion, or about half of the entire $1.1 trillion invested worldwide.

Following the investments were jobs. In just the first year after the passage of the IRA, developers announced more than eighty major, utility-scale solar, wind, and energy storage projects or new factories to make panels, turbines, batteries, and related equipment. Together these projects created nearly 30,000 new jobs and generated more than $270 billion in investments.[12]

The boom in major solar projects is filtering down to small businesses. What happened at Illinois solar developer Trajectory Energy Partners is illustrative of the impact of the IRA. On a computer-generated map, Trajectory founder and managing partner Jon Carson zoomed in on squares, rectangles, and trapezoids representing project after project that his company had been trying to develop, in some cases over years. New clean energy laws passed by the state of Illinois were driving demand for solar projects. But "before the IRA was passed, they just didn't pencil out," Carson explained.[13] In addition to bringing clean, renewable energy to towns throughout the state, including to many low-income communities that had little choice except to buy their electricity from pollution-belching coal-powered plants, the surge of projects also brought new jobs. Trajectory's workforce doubled in size, from fifteen to thirty employees, not including the hundreds of construction workers, surveyors, lawyers, and other contractors it hires to build its projects.

One of the first major solar projects announced after the IRA was signed into law wasn't in Illinois or California or New York or some other big blue state with renewable-friendly regulations. It was in rural Mississippi. Just a few weeks after President Biden signed the bill into law, clean energy developer Origis USA announced plans for a $200 million solar farm spanning two thousand acres in Clay County, Mississippi, south of Tupelo. The project is expected to create hundreds of construction jobs, generate enough electricity to power nearly 46,000 homes, and put that part of Mississippi, known locally as the "Golden Triangle," on the map as a hot spot for clean energy in the Southeast. "This project is a game changer for Clay County and the Golden Triangle," said public utilities commissioner Brandon Presley, who happens to be a second cousin to a more famous Mississippian named Elvis. "It will create jobs, boost economic development, and show the world that Mississippi is committed to an innovative approach to renewable energy expansion." Presley may have a point. In 2021, Mississippi ranked dead last among states for solar installations. In 2022, it moved up to number twenty-nine, according to the Solar Energy Industries Association (SEIA).[14]

Mississippi's solar boom represents a broader trend of clean energy growth throughout the Southeast, led in large part by Origis. The company was founded in Europe in 2008 and grew quickly with projects in Italy and Greece. In 2012, attracted by those same Obama–era federal policy signals that were attractive to Michael Rucker and other clean energy entrepreneurs, the company relocated its headquarters from Europe to Miami. A year later, it opened one of the biggest solar projects in the Southeast, deploying more than 78,000 solar panels at a sprawling project in rural Georgia that can generate enough power to supply nearly six thousand homes.[15]

In 2016, Origis went farther south, opening a 560-acre solar farm with more than 240,000 panels in the Mississippi town of Sumrall. It was the biggest solar project in the state. And then a few years later, Origis doubled it to create the biggest solar project east of the Mississippi River. Origis's latest investment will once again double its footprint in Mississippi, and now it's turning its attention to other states too. In August 2023, the company announced it had secured a $750 million credit agreement from lenders that will allow it to continue to grow its footprint across the Southeast. Origis CEO Guy Vanderhaegen said the company was "in an unprecedented growth cycle fueled by customer demand and the Inflation Reduction Act."

Other companies are adding solar in the Deep South too. Of the fourteen major solar farms announced in the months following the passage of the IRA, five of them were in the South. Leading the pack were projects in Mississippi, Arkansas, and Louisiana. On the west side of the Mississippi River, power giant Entergy in March 2023 filed a request with the Louisiana Public Service Commission for the biggest energy expansion request in state history. Entergy wants to add three gigawatts of solar power, an amount equivalent to eleven times as much solar power as the state generated at the time.[16] In announcing the plans, Entergy Louisiana president Phillip May touted the jobs and economic investment his company would create by building the huge solar farm but also said it would help Louisiana attract and retain new businesses by ensuring they had access to cheap, renewable clean energy for years ahead. Clean energy has become an economic development tool. See table 4.1.

For states and developers to deploy more clean energy, they first need solar panels, wind turbines, and other equipment to do it. That's coming too. Within months after the passage of the IRA, the only major U.S.-based solar panel company, First Solar, sold out of every single panel it could possibly make—through the year 2025 and much of 2026.[17] To meet demand, First Solar announced it would invest $4 billion to expand its three existing factories in Ohio and build two new factories, in Alabama and in Louisiana in its quest to be the biggest solar panel manufacturer in the Western Hemisphere. In November 2022, First Solar picked Lawrence County, Alabama (population 33,000), a place best known for producing the oak barrels used to make Jack Daniel's whiskey for its first major plant in the Southeast. With an expected workforce of more than seven hundred, First Solar's $1.1 billion Alabama factory will become the region's biggest employer, far outpacing the two-hundred-employee bourbon barrel factory. Nine months later, First Solar said it would build another $1 billion, seven-hundred-employee factory, this one in Iberia Parish, Louisiana, best known as the birthplace of Tabasco hot sauce. First Solar is also building a new factory and research and development center in Perrysburg, Ohio, where it has had a factory since 2002. It will no longer be the only major solar panel factory in that state, however. In March 2023, the largest panel maker in the world, China-based LONGi Solar, announced it was teaming up with Midwest energy company Invenergy to build their massive new factory in Pataskala, Ohio, east of Columbus. LONGi is the biggest of several Chinese solar panel makers that now can make panels cheaper in the United States than they can in China to meet the boom in clean energy in America. The U.S. subsidiary of China's Zhejiang Hounen Photoelectric is building a factory in South Carolina; Jinko Solar is expanding a factory in Florida and JA Solar is building in Arizona.

In the middle of America, it's the wind industry that is blowing new life into the economy. A few months after the passage of the IRA, wind turbine blade manufacturer TPI Composites announced it would reopen its factory in Newton, Iowa, which had closed a year or so earlier.[18] The factory had been the region's biggest employer, providing jobs to as many as seven hundred people before its closure. News of its reopening was

Table 4.1: Renewable Energy and Grid Announcements in Year 1 of Inflation Reduction Act

Company	Type	Jobs	Investment	Location	State
Crowley Wind Services	Wind	800	n/a	Salem	Massachusetts
Crowley Wind Services	Wind	n/a	n/a	Eureka	California
TPI Composites	Wind	n/a	n/a	Newton	Iowa
Regen Fiber	Wind	n/a	n/a	Fairfax	Iowa
Fincantieri Bay Shipbuilding	Wind	n/a	n/a	Sturgeon Bay	Wisconsin
GE Vernova	Wind	n/a	$20,000,000	Pensacola	Florida
Apex Clean Energy	Wind	n/a	$1,450,000,000	Nowata County	Oklahoma
Siemens	Wind	n/a	n/a	Hutchinson	Kansas
Gulf Wind & Shell	Wind	30	$10,000,000	Avondale	Louisiana
Arcosa	Wind	250	$55,000,000	Belen	New Mexico
Flender Corp	Wind	50	n/a	Elgin	Illinois
Orsted	Wind	145	$14,000,000	Sparrows Point	Maryland
GE Vernova	Wind	200	$50,000,000	Schenectady	New York
Fugro	Wind	15	n/a	Norfolk	Virginia
Vestas	Wind	n/a	$40,000,000 (split)	Brighton	Colorado
Vestas	Wind	n/a	$40,000,000 (split)	Windsor	Colorado
First Solar	Solar	n/a	$185,000,000 (split)	Lake Township	Ohio
First Solar	Solar	n/a	$185,000,000 (split)	Perrysburg	Ohio
SPI Energy	Solar	n/a	n/a	McClellan Park	California
Seg Solar	Solar	500	$60,000,000	Houston	Texas
Entergy	Solar	400	n/a	Osceola	Arkansas

Company	Type	Jobs	Investment	City	State
Mission Solar	Solar	n/a	n/a	San Antonio	Texas
Ecoplexus	Solar	n/a	$89,000,000	Silverstreet	South Carolina
Unitil	Solar	n/a	$16,300,000	Kingston	New Hampshire
First Solar	Solar	700	$1,100,000,000	Decatur	Alabama
Stellantis	Solar	10	n/a	n/a	Michigan
JA Solar	Solar	600	$60,000,000	Phoenix	Arizona
QCells	Solar	2,000	2,500,000,000	Cartersville	Georgia
QCells	Solar	510	n/a	Dalton	Georgia
JFK Airport	Solar	n/a	n/a	Queens	New York
May Renewables LLC	Solar	n/a	$70,000,000	Cope	South Carolina
Pine Gate Renewal	Solar	300	$115,000,000	Lucedale	Mississippi
Illuminate USA & Invenergy	Solar	1,000	$600,000,000	Pataskala	Ohio
Bullrock Renewables	Solar	12	n/a	Bristol	Vermont
Hounen Solar	Solar	200	$33,000,000	Orangeburg	South Carolina
Qcells	Solar	160	$147,000,000	Cartersville	Georgia
Toyota	Solar	n/a	$49,000,000	Huntsville	Alabama
Rayzon Solar	Solar	n/a	n/a	Atlanta	Georgia
NewCo. Manufacturing	Solar	250	$100,000,000	St. Louis	Missouri
Jinko Solar	Solar	250	$52,000,000	Jacksonville	Florida
Alliant Energy	Solar	n/a	n/a	Janesville	Wisconsin
Vitro	Solar	130	$93,600,000	Cochranton	Pennsylvania
SEM Wafertech &	Solar	300	$65,900,000	Sumter	South Carolina
Nextracker, MSS Steel	Solar	129	$6,000,000	Memphis	Tennessee
Enel	Solar	900	$1,000,000,000	Inola	Oklahoma

(continued)

Company	Type	Jobs	Investment	Location	State
Canadian Solar	Solar	1,500	$250,000,000	Mesquite	Texas
SolRiver Captial	Solar	n/a	n/a	Canyonville	Oregon
Holcim US	Solar	n/a	n/a	Alpena	Michigan
VSK Energy	Solar	900	$250,000,000	Brighton	Colorado
Enphase & Flex	Solar	600	$20,000,000	West Columbia	South Carolina
First Solar	Solar	n/a	$370,000,000	Perrysburg	Ohio
Heliene	Solar	n/a	$145,000,000	Minneapolis-StP	Minnesota
Meyer Burger	Solar	350	$400,000,000	Colorado Springs	Colorado
Chevron	Geotherm	n/a	n/a	Weepah Hills	Nevada
Berkshire Hathaway Energy	Grid	n/a	$500,000,000	Ravenswood	West Virginia
Hitachi	Grid	n/a	$37,000,000	South Boston	Virginia
ELM	Grid	100	n/a	The Colony	Texas
Nucor	Grid	200	$125,000,000	Decatur	Alabama
ABB	Grid	55	$40,000,000	Albuquerque	New Mexico
Prolec GE USA	Grid	153	$28,500,000	Shreveport	Louisiana
Prysmian Group	Grid	27	$22,500,000	Williamsport	Pennsylvania

SOURCE: E2. "CLEAN ECONOMY WORKS: IRA ONE-YEAR REVIEW." HTTPS://E2.ORG/REPORTS/CLEAN-ECONOMY-WORKS-2023.

the best thing many townspeople had heard in a long time. Shortly after, wind turbine giant Siemens Gamesa announced it was also reopening plants it had shuttered in Fort Madison, Iowa, and in Hutchinson Kansas, thanks to the passage of federal climate policies, providing a shot in the arm for communities suffering from previous plant closures.[19] About one hundred miles north of Siemens Gamesa's Iowa factory, the boom in clean energy is driving another company to figure out what to do with old and broken wind turbine blades. REGEN Fiber in January 2023 announced it would build a new factory in Fairfax, Iowa, where it will recycle used fiberglass wind turbine blades to create fiber that can be mixed in to strengthen pavement and concrete. The factory is expected to recycle as much as thirty thousand tons of shredded turbine blades each year.

To be sure, the clean energy industry continues to find its way. Despite the new government support, rising interest rates, permitting problems and supply chain issues in 2023 sent the cost of wind and solar projects soaring, to the point where many were delayed. But temporary setbacks aside, the IRA and other federal policies will only make clean energy less expensive, according to Jesse Jenkins, head of Princeton University's ZERO Lab and the lab's REPEAT project, which evaluates the impacts of federal energy and climate policies. "The fundamental focus of (federal clean energy policies) is to make clean energy cheap; to make it a better business decision, a better household financial decision for you and I and all the businesses across the country to pick clean options," he said at a speech at Princeton's Center for Policy Research on Energy and the Environment.[20]

Cheap, clean energy is good for consumers, businesses, and anybody else who has to buy it. But cheap energy is not necessarily a good thing for the people and companies that produce it and the equipment needed to generate it. As the marginal costs of power from wind or solar continue to decline, it gets harder for investors and clean energy developers to make back the money it costs to build projects. And as returns to investors get lower, finding money for new projects gets harder.

The paradoxical predicament of cheap energy is felt from the top to the bottom of the clean energy industry. It's shaping how and where companies build solar and wind and also potentially stalling its growth. While federal climate investments convinced Siemens Gamesa to restart those plants in Iowa and Kansas, the company also announced around the same time that it was cutting nearly three thousand jobs in other parts of the globe amid mounting financial losses and declining prices for wind energy. "What we've clearly achieved is that wind power is now cheaper than anything else. But I believe we shouldn't make it too cheap," then–Siemens Gamesa CEO Andreas Nauen told Reuters.[21] "We have probably driven it too far." If wind energy prices continue to fall, Nauen warned, it will impact the industry's ability to build new factories and invest in new technologies.

The low cost of wind energy particularly hurts the potential of offshore wind, one of the most expensive forms of clean energy to develop. The Biden administration has set a goal to build thirty gigawatts of offshore wind by 2030, mainly on the East Coast but also with floating wind turbines in deeper waters off California. New climate and clean energy investments include billions in funding and tax incentives to support new offshore wind projects. The Department of Energy even launched an "offshore windshot" program, including $50 million in prizes and other funding, to encourage companies to figure out ways to lower the costs of floating offshore wind.[22] Even so, plans for several of the most promising offshore wind projects in America in 2023 were shelved or delayed as developers struggled with NIMBY opposition from coastal communities. In July 2023, a Danish wind company got final government approval to build a one-hundred-turbine wind farm more than thirteen miles off the coast of New Jersey that would generate enough clean energy to supply a half-million homes. Yet the project was immediately stalled by lawsuits from beachfront homeowners and small businesses along the New Jersey shore who don't want to see turbines in the distance. Also clouding the future of offshore wind are rising construction costs and lower projected returns as wind energy prices continue to decline. In 2022, financing for offshore wind projects worldwide (outside of China) hit the lowest level in a decade, despite the positive signs and policies from the United States.[23] In one of the most notable indications of the choppy waters surrounding offshore wind, Avangrid Renewables in October 2022 delayed its Commonwealth Wind project off Massachusetts and paid $48 million to terminate power purchase agreements with local utilities that were expecting energy from it beginning in 2023. Avangrid said the previous agreements were priced too low for the company to make money given rising supply chain costs and inflation, and that it would seek to rebid its project at higher prices at another time.[24]

The impacts of cheap clean energy also trickle down to smaller wind energy developers like Michael Rucker and Scout Clean Energy. "The marginal cost of energy is going to be zip at many locations," he said. "That's a great thing for utilities and energy buyers . . . but it's a problem for generators that work independently. If we can't generate enough cash to make money for our investors, we can't develop more projects."

There's an even bigger problem looming for clean energy, however: The grid.

Lower prices and tightening financial markets may be putting a squeeze on clean energy development in America. But the lack of a modern electricity grid is squeezing the majority of clean energy projects quite literally to death.

Nearly 70 percent of the nation's electricity grid was built more than twenty-five years ago. Most of the wires that carry electricity from power plants to our homes and offices were installed back when solar and wind power barely existed in America, never mind modern-day EVs or batteries big enough to power a home throughout the night. Meanwhile, the number of connections to the nation's power grid has increased dramatically, due to population growth and sprawl and also due to the explosion of new clean energy projects across the country. Back when the only companies producing power in any given state were limited to a few major utilities, the U.S. power grid was fairly adequate. But now that there are thousands of solar farms, wind farms, geothermal, and other energy producers across the country, it's not. Through 2020, more than 1,700 clean energy projects were connected to the five primary power grids that provide electricity to about 85 percent of Americans, according to data from Lawrence Berkeley National Lab.[25] But more than four times that many projects—nearly seven thousand in all—were withdrawn by developers in part because they couldn't get approval to connect their projects to the grid quickly enough to make them financially viable, or it became too expensive to do so. For those projects that did ultimately get approved, it took longer than ever. Twenty years ago, it took about two years from the time a clean energy developer requested a connection to the grid to when it could finally flip the switch and start providing power to customers. Between 2011–2021, that wait time for connections was closer to four years.

Researchers at Berkeley Lab estimate that more than 1.4 terawatts of energy projects—mostly solar, wind, and battery storage projects worth a combined $2 trillion in investment—were waiting in queues to get connection approvals at the end of 2021.[26] In each of the nation's regional grids, hundreds of projects are awaiting approval to connect, with the highest number of projects—more than 1,500 in 2021—located in the PJM Interconnection organization that coordinates electricity across thirteen states stretching from Illinois to North Carolina. It's a big problem. Together, the clean energy projects awaiting connection approval nationwide could produce more energy than the entire existing capacity of the U.S. power system. In other words, developers are ready and standing by with enough clean energy projects that could generate more energy than we can use—enough to replace all the fossil-fuel-generated electricity generated in America and then some—if only they could get their projects connected to the grid.

"It doesn't matter how cheap the clean energy is," Spencer Nelson, former managing director of research at ClearPath Foundation, an energy-focused nonprofit, told the *New York Times*.[27] "If developers can't get through the interconnection process quickly enough and get enough steel in the ground, we won't hit our climate change goals."

Getting new clean energy projects connected to the grid is just part of the problem. Getting power from existing clean energy projects to where it's most needed on today's antiquated power grid is another problem—one playing out in real time in California and other parts of the West.

California has long led the nation in renewable energy development. In 2018, it passed a law requiring all electricity sold in the state to come from renewable or other zero-carbon sources beginning in 2045, a path and plan that other states later followed. On many days, especially in the spring and summer months, the most populous state in the nation already gets 100 percent of its power from clean energy.[28] On days when the sun is brightest and during nights when the winds are strongest, California produces way more renewable energy than its grid can handle or its residents can use. As a result, the operator of the California grid, called the California Independent System Operator (CAISO), has to issue "curtailments" ordering wind and solar projects to stop putting more of their clean energy onto the overburdened grid. Throughout 2022, about 2.4 terawatt hours of electricity produced by wind and solar companies in California was curtailed, according to CAISO. The agency had to turn off the electricity spigots from wind and solar during peak production in every month of that year, with the highest numbers of curtailments occurring in March through May.

More battery and storage projects will help, by storing some of that excess clean energy for use later, when demand is higher and clean energy supplies are lower. But battery storage only goes so far. What's needed is a better grid. With a better, regionalized grid, clean energy projects in California could more easily and efficiently move the excess energy they generate on sunny days or windy nights to other states that might need it more on a particularly cold or cloudy day. Similarly, when the sun's not shining and the wind's not blowing in California, a regionalized grid could help the state buy and import clean power produced in Nevada or Arizona or other states more easily and quickly. That would benefit both developers and users of energy, not to mention civilization, because it would help avoid the need to fire up dirtier and more expensive gas- or coal-fired power plants to meet demand. According to a Department of Energy report, a regionalized Western grid could reduce overall electricity costs by 8 percent and decrease California's carbon emissions by about 7 percent.[29] In 2023, a coalition of state and national clean energy, business, and environmental groups joined together to urge passage of state legislation to create a regional transmission organization that could improve and better manage the West's electricity grid. According to the *Lights on California* coalition, such a grid could save consumers and businesses $563 million in annual energy costs, foster enough new clean energy to power ninety thousand homes, and create 139,000 new jobs.[30]

On a federal level, the bipartisan infrastructure law passed in late 2021 includes $65 billion for grid improvement, resilience, and other programs.[31] It's more than has ever been dedicated to improve the grid—but it's also just a drop in the bucket for what's needed. To successfully build and deploy the wind and solar power necessary to meet U.S. climate goals, the United States will need to expand its power transmission grid by 60 percent by 2030 and may need to triple it by 2050, according to research from Princeton.[32] That costs a lot of money. Just upgrading the two hundred thousand miles of high-voltage transmission lines that crisscross America to carry more renewable energy would cost about $700 billion, analytical firm Wood Mackenzie estimates—more than ten times the investment set aside by the infrastructure act.[33]

Money is just part of the problem. Everybody wants cheaper, more reliable power, and most people would rather get it from clean sources like solar or wind. But nobody likes power lines running across their yards or wind turbines or solar farms obstructing their views. Between 2008–2021, more than fifty utility-scale solar, wind, geothermal, and transmission projects in twenty-eight states were blocked after local groups protested, one study shows.[34] If the United States is going to meet its climate goals, policymakers, business, and the public must figure out ways to work together to expand transmission and clean energy projects in equitable and economic ways that the public can accept.

"The current power grid took 150 years to build," said Princeton's Jenkins. "Now, to get to net-zero emissions by 2050, we have to build that amount of transmission again in the next 15 years and then build that much more again in the 15 years after that. It's a huge amount of change."[35]

How hard will it be to expand and improve the grid to where it needs to be? For an example, look to the Southwest. In 2006, as solar and wind projects began sprouting up across the region, Phoenix-based SouthWestern Power Group announced plans to build a five-hundred-mile-long power line stretching from New Mexico to Arizona.[36] The idea behind the line, called SunZia by its developer, is to supply new sources of electricity for fast-growing Phoenix, while also providing more modern lines that could help spur even more renewable energy development throughout the region. A study by project backer Pattern Energy Group, the biggest wind energy producer in New Mexico, showed that the line could generate more than $20 billion in economic benefits, including the creation of two thousand new construction jobs and enough clean energy to keep the lights on for more than three million residents.[37]

Yet even amid the desert dunes and sparsely populated flatlands between the two states, the idea of a big new powerline sparked protests in ranching communities and neighborhoods along its proposed path. More than seventeen years after it was proposed, the federal government in May 2023 finally approved the SunZia line. Another major clean energy transmission line, the 732-mile TransWest Express project, connecting the giant Chokecherry and Sierra Madre wind farms in Wyoming to parts of Colorado, Utah, Nevada, and California, was approved by federal regulators in April 2023—fifteen years after it was proposed.

Department of Energy Secretary Jennifer Granholm said the United States must figure out how to improve the nation's power grid—and do it quickly. "It should not take over 10 years . . . to get a transmission line permitted at a moment when we must invest in the grid," she said during a *Washington Post* forum.[38] "We've got to essentially double the capacity of our grid to make sure we get to goals of 100 percent clean energy by 2035," Granholm added. "It is clear that speeding up permitting . . . has to happen if we really are to take action to prevent the biggest harms to our planet."

In May 2023, White House senior advisor John Podesta, who was tapped by the president to implement the administration's climate policies and spending, announced a plan to speed up transmission line development. Podesta understood firsthand how long and arduous the government can be when it comes to permitting new electricity transmission lines. Back in 2014, when he served as a special counsel to then–president Barack Obama, one of the issues that came across his desk involved the permitting of a major transmission line. Eight years later, after he returned to the White House with President Biden, Podesta learned in his first week on the job that the same transmission line was still awaiting approval. "That's unacceptable," he said. "We have to fix this problem now."[39]

It takes so long to get new transmission lines approved mainly because there are so many different bureaucratic bodies involved. At the federal level alone, a transmission line approval can require approval from as many as twenty different agencies, including the Department of Energy, the Department of the Interior, and the Federal Energy Regulatory Commission for starters, but also the Department of Commerce, Homeland Security, Housing and Urban Development, Department of Defense, and more. And that comes on top of the dizzying regulatory red tape at the state and local permitting levels.

The plan announced by Podesta requires the myriad agencies that are involved in permitting to work more closely and collaboratively on permitting. It also gives more power to the Department of Energy to exercise its authority under the Federal Power Act to oversee and streamline the permitting of transmission lines.[40]

It's not the first attempt at speeding up the permitting of transmission lines and other major infrastructure. In 2015, Congress passed a law known as FAST-41 that created a federal Permitting Council that can move projects it deems most important to the front of the line for permitting and special attention. As part of the IRA, Congress allocated $350 million to the Permitting Council to make improvements, including hiring more staff and better technology.[41] Ultimately, though, Podesta acknowledged, it's permitting reform legislation from Congress that will make the real difference—something both Republicans and Democrats on Capitol Hill can agree on. "This administration is doing all we can with the tools we have, but frankly, we could use more tools to go even further and faster," he said.[42]

There's a good reason why the man in charge of distributing IRA funding is obsessed with permitting. If transmission lines and renewable energy projects can't get permitted, the IRA funding for those projects will have a hard time getting out the door, especially with a new Congress or new administration in the White House. "Permitting is no longer an issue where the status quo is sufficient," said Alex Herrgott, president of The Permitting Institute, a nonprofit organization that advocates for permitting reform.[43] "There's significant concern that much of the IRA money will be left in a fallow nature because projects will not be able to move forward. That's a significant motivator."

Back at Scout Clean Energy, Michael Rucker agreed that grid and transmission connection problems are among the biggest problems facing companies like his. And it's not always just the government's fault. Often, utilities will add unnecessary costs to connection requests from clean energy developers like Scout, essentially blackmailing them in exchange for connection approvals, according to Rucker. He recounted an instance in Illinois where his company was under contract to build a three-hundred-megawatt solar project. But to connect to the grid, the local utility wanted Scout to build an entirely new fiber optic network and make other unrelated upgrades to the utility's infrastructure, all for $92 million. Sometimes, it's the government that gets in the way. In Arkansas, Scout had been working on building a new wind farm since 2016, renewing permits with the Federal Aviation Administration every two years even before it was able to begin construction. More than six years later, just as the project was finally ready to get started, the military decided to lower the minimum altitude of a flight path near it, prompting the FAA to warn it may have to cancel the project after all, according to Rucker. The military eventually negotiated revisions to the training route that would let the project move forward but with added delay and cost to an already expensive project.

Still despite all the uncertainties, the American transition to clean energy is well underway. The people, businesses, and communities that are positioned to take advantage of the new federal climate and clean energy programs and investments are benefitting.

That includes Rucker and Scout Clean Energy. Late in the summer of 2022, while Senators Joe Manchin and Chuck Schumer were secretly hammering out the details of the IRA, Rucker was secretly hammering out a different agreement—one to sell his company. For years, Scout's growth and success attracted the eye of many suitors. As America's new clean energy policies became clearer, the company grew even more attractive. In September 2022, a month after President Biden signed the IRA, one of the world's biggest clean energy investment funds,

Brookfield Renewable Partners, announced an agreement to buy Scout Clean Energy for $1 billion, a threshold known in the business world as "unicorn" status because of its rarity.

"I can't believe it," Rucker said shortly after the sale. "But I can honestly say I founded a unicorn company."

CHAPTER 5

Engines

"This Changes Everything Now"

FOR MORE THAN FIFTY YEARS, THE ANNUAL CONSUMER ELECTRONICS Show (CES) has served as the launchpad for some of the biggest technological changes in the world. The first videocassette recorder was introduced there in 1970, as was the first thin-screen television, the first tablet PC, and countless computers and video games. Over the decades, some of the brightest and most respected minds in technology have laid out their visions of the future at CES, often predicting the rise of technologies that would forever change the world, including mobile phones and touch-screen technology, internet commerce, and digital music.

The sweeping predictions and prognostications delivered by the keynote speaker at the 2022 CES, therefore, weren't particularly unusual or surprising. What was somewhat surprising was the keynoter herself: Not some internet icon or Silicon Valley wunderkind, but the daughter of a Detroit auto factory worker who grew up to run one of the most slow-to-innovate companies in American history. The subject of her speech had nothing to do with computers, televisions, or cell phones or other gadgets typically considered consumer electronic devices, but about the technological transformation of something much more ingrained in the history and fabric of our economy and society: The American automobile.

In her keynote remarks, General Motors (GM) CEO Mary Barra laid out plans for the biggest transformation in GM's history. Within thirteen years, she said, the company that had manufactured gas-powered cars and trucks for 114 years would make only vehicles powered by electricity. To do so, she announced, GM would invest $35 billion into electric and autonomous vehicle production. It would immediately launch a program to convert more than half of its factories to solely build EVs. And it would open four new giant battery plants across America. She also explained how GM was looking to expand beyond just cars, detailing recent investments in electric engines for locomotives and boats and funding innovation to build hydrogen-powered engines for aircraft.[1] Wall Street liked what Barra had to say, pushing GM's stock to an all-time high the next day.[2]

"Make no mistake," Barra said, "this is a movement."

Three decades earlier, GM introduced the world's first mass-produced EV, a squatty sedan called the EV1.[3] It was a hit with owners but was canceled in 1999 after only 1,100 were sold. This time, though, it's different, and GM is all in on EVs. By 2035, the company says it will produce thirty models of EVs across every price point, from the utilitarian Chevrolet Equinox sport utility vehicle (SUV) to the glitzy Cadillac Lyriq to the massive GMC Hummer. It is also investing nearly $750 million to build out a nationwide EV charging network to ensure GM vehicles can get juice on the road. As part of its corporate goal to be carbon neutral by 2040, GM plans to power all its U.S. factories with 100 percent clean energy.

What's good for GM is good for the country, the adage goes. But as Barra put it in a *Wall Street Journal* piece after her CES speech, the global shift to EVs "is good for business, the people of GM, customers and America."[4]

GM isn't alone. Every automaker in the world is ramping up production of EVs, with many taking the same road as GM—and before it, Tesla—to go 100 percent electric within the next decade or so. From high-end brands like Bentley, Jaguar, Porsche, and Mercedes-Benz, to middle-class mainstays such as Hyundai, Honda, BMW, and Volkswagen, to newcomers like Rivian and VinFast, the number of automakers saying they'll go fully electric is growing each year. At the beginning of 2023, there were fewer than fifty EV models available in the United States. By the end of 2024, that number is expected to be closer to 130.[5]

To build all those cars, automakers are building factories. In the first year after the IRA was signed into law, automakers, battery companies and suppliers to the EV industry announced more than $60 billion in investments in nearly one hundred new major manufacturing plants and other projects around the country.[6] Automakers that aren't fully plugged into the electric movement face being left in the dust. As *Bloomberg News* put it in a headline after worldwide EV sales topped $1 trillion for the first time, "Alarm bells are ringing at manufacturers that have been reluctant to ditch combustion."[7] See table 5.1.

The shift to EVs and the unprecedented growth of new factories represents the greatest transition in the U.S. automotive sector since its beginnings at the end of the nineteenth century. For years, the United States lagged behind other countries when it came to investments in EVs. Now, it's leading the world.

At the forefront is the American company credited with creating the US auto industry, Ford Motor Company. In addition to the battery plant it is planning in Michigan, Ford is investing $5.8 billion to build twin battery factories in Kentucky and another $90 million in an EV technician training center in Texas. And in the biggest investment in the company's history, Ford is spending $11.5 billion to quite literally build a new city in Tennessee to manufacture EVs and the batteries that go in them.[8]

Called BlueOval City, after Ford's signature nameplate, the 3,600-acre project next to the town of Stanton, Tennessee, will include battery production, vehicle assembly, and supplier operations spread over nearly six square miles. Ford plans to hire 5,800 workers there to make the Ford F-150 Lightning Electric truck and, with Korean partner SK On, the batteries that power them. In June 2023, the Department of Energy's Loan Programs Office announced a $9.2 billion loan to Ford and battery partner SK On to build the factories in Kentucky and Tennessee and provide another boost to battery and EV manufacturing in America.[9]

The project is changing the Stanton area like music and the Mississippi River changed Memphis. With a population of about five hundred, Stanton is more country community than city. Homes dating to the Civil War, along with a hodgepodge of newer brick ranch models, surround a forgotten downtown nestled beneath a big white water tower you can

Table 5.1. Electric Vehicle Factory Announcements in Year 1 of the Inflation Reduction Act

Company	Jobs	Investment	Location	State
Advanced Nano	93	$50,000,000	Elizabethtown	Kentucky
Factorial Energy	166	$45,000,000	Methuen	Massachusetts
Toyota	350	$2,500,000,000	Liberty	North Carolina
ABB E-Mobility	n/a	$4,000,000	Columbia	South Carolina
General Motors	n/a	$491,000,000	Marion	Indiana
Aspen Aerogels	75	n/a	Marlborough	Massachusetts
General Motors	n/a	$760,000,000	Toledo	Ohio
Daejin	83	$10,200,000	Cumberland	Tennessee
Our Next Energy	2,112	$1,600,000,000	Van Buren	Michigan
Gotion	2,300	$2,360,000,000	Big Rapids	Michigan
Honda	109	$233,000,000	Anna	Ohio
Honda	109	$233,000,000	East Liberty	Ohio
Honda	109	$233,000,000	Marysville	Ohio
Honda, LG	2,200	$3,500,000,000	Jeffersonville	Ohio
BMW	n/a	$1,000,000,000	Spartanburg	South Carolina
BMW	300	$700,000,000	Woodruff	South Carolina
Magna	920	$426,000,000	Saint Clair	Michigan
Bosch	350	$260,000,000	Charleston	South Carolina
Magna	155	$96,000,000	Shelby	Michigan
Hyundai	400	$205,000,000	Montgomery	Alabama
Canoo	n/a	n/a	Pryor	Oklahoma
Joon Georgia, Inc	630	$317,000,000	Statesboro	Georgia
Canoo	500	n/a	Oklahoma City	Oklahoma

SK Signet	183	n/a	Plano	Texas
General Motors	n/a	$45,000,000	Bedford	Indiana
LG Chem	860	$3,200,000,000	Clarksville	Tennessee
Hyundai	1,500	$926,000,000	Richmond Hill	Georgia
Ultium Cells	400	$275,000,000	Spring Hill	Tennessee
Envision	1,170	$810,000,000	Florence	South Carolina
Evercharge	n/a	n/a	Hayward	California
Sion Power	150	$341,000,000	Tucson	Arizona
Hyundai & SK On	3,500	$4,000,000,000	Bartow County	Georgia
Kontrolmatik	575	$279,000,000	Walterboro	South Carolina
Soulbrain MI	75	$75,000,000	Kokomo	Indiana
Lear Corp	n/a	n/a	Traverse City	Michigan
Lear Corp	500	$112,500,000	Independence	Michigan
Lear Corp	n/a	n/a	Macomb County	Michigan
Redwood Materials	1,500	$3,500,000,000	Ridgeville	South Carolina
Siemens	100	n/a	Carrollton	Texas
Cirba Solutions	150	$200,000,000	Lancaster	Ohio
Autokinition	150	$15,000,000	Bellevue	Ohio
Ecoplastics Corp.	456	$205,000,000	Register	Georgia
Revel	n/a	n/a	Maspeth	New York
Tesla	n/a	$717,000,000	Austin	Texas
Quench Chargers	n/a	n/a	Shelton	Connecticut
GM	n/a	$56,000,000	Rochester	New York
GM	n/a	$8,000,000	Defiance	Ohio
Nissan	n/a	$250,000,000	Decherd	Tennessee

(continued)

Company	Jobs	Investment	Location	State
Tesla	3,000	$3,500,000,000	Sparks	Nevada
Liochem	141	$104,000,000	Franklin	Kentucky
Cabot Corp.	75	$75,000,000	Pampa	Texas
Seoyon E-HWA	740	$76,000,000	Bloomingdale	Georgia
Kempower	601	$41,200,000	Durham	North Carolina
Redwood Materials	1,600	$2,000,000,000	McCarran	Nevada
Ford & CATL	2,500	$3,500,000,000	Marshall	Michigan
Tritium	250	n/a	Lebanon	Tennessee
Sewon America	740	$300,000,000	Rincon	Georgia
Ecobat	60	n/a	Casa Grande	Arizona
Li-Cycle	1,270	n/a	Rochester	New York
Stellantis	265	$155,000,000	Kokomo	Indiana
Scout Motors	4,000	$2,000,000,000	Blythewood	South Carolina
PHA	402	$67,000,000	Savanah	Georgia
EVelution Energy	360	$200,000,000	Yuma County	Arizona
Shyft Group	n/a	$16,000,000	Charlotte	Michigan
Entek	642	$1,500,000,000	Terre Haute	Indiana
Albemarle Corp.	300	$1,300,000,000	Chester	South Carolina
Cirba Solutions	300	$300,000,000	Columbia	South Carolina
LG Energy Solution	n/a	$1,800,000,000	Queen Creek	Arizona
Magna	500	$100,000,000	Auburn Hills	Michigan
BorgWarner	186	$20,600,000	Detroit	Michigan
UCore North America	100	$75,000,000	Alexandria	Louisiana
Seohan Auto	180	$72,000,000	Liberty County	Georgia
BorgWarner	122	$42,000,000	Seneca	South Carolina

Company	Jobs	Investment	City	State
Bosch	n/a	$1,500,000,000	Roseville	California
Rivian	218	$10,000,000	Shepherdsville	Kentucky
Atom Power	205	$4,200,000	Huntersville	North Carolina
Ingeteam	100	$20,000,000	Milwaukee	Wisconsin
Hanon Systems	160	$40,000,000	Statesboro	Georgia
Alpitronic Americas LLC	300	$18,300,000	Charlotte	North Carolina
Toyota	n/a	$2,100,000,000	Liberty	North Carolina
Manner Polymers	60	$54,000,000	Mt. Vernon	Illinois
Woory Industrial Co	130	$18,000,000	Dublin	Georgia
Toyota	n/a	$50,000,000	York Township	Michigan
NVH Korea	160	$72,000,000	Locust Grove	Georgia
Enchem America Inc	190	$152,500,000	Brownsville	Tennessee
Cenntro Electric Group	n/a	n/a	Ontario	California
Hitachi Astemo Americas	167	$153,000,000	Berea	Kentucky
Kia	n/a	$200,000,000	West Point	Georgia
Magna	750	$790 million (split)	Stanton	Tennessee
Magna	300	$790 million (split)	Stanton	Tennessee
Magna	250	$790 million (split)	Lawrenceburg	Tennessee
Bollinger	n/a	$44 million (split)	Oak Park	Michigan
Bollinger	n/a	$44 million (split)	Livonia	Michigan
Junchuang NA	120	$21,000,000	Fort Worth	Texas
XCharge	n/a	n/a	Kyle	Texas
Hanon Systems	600	$170,000,000	Loudon	Tennessee
Wolfspeed	1,800	$5,000,000,000	Siler City	North Carolina

SOURCE: E2. "CLEAN ECONOMY WORKS: IRA ONE-YEAR REVIEW." HTTPS://E2.ORG/REPORTS/CLEAN-ECONOMY-WORKS -2023/.

spot from Highway 79 on the way into town. Before Ford, the biggest economic story in Stanton was its founding, when the Memphis & Ohio Railroad picked a route through the middle of J. B. Stanton's family farm back in 1856 and put the place on the map. Production won't begin at BlueOval City before early 2025, but the economic earthquake it is producing began shaking up the region immediately. Houses that listed for $250,000 before Ford announced the project in September 2021 were selling for $550,000 or more a year later.[10] Vacant farmland that nobody wanted to buy a few years earlier was suddenly going for $470,000 an acre or more.

As the biggest investment in the history of Tennessee, the project promises to transform not just Stanton but the entire state. But it also will be just as transformational for Ford—and indeed, the entire auto industry.

"For most of the last 100 years, (the auto industry) hasn't changed a lot," said Bill Ford, executive chair of the company his great-grandfather Henry founded in 1903. "There have been a series of evolutions, but very few revolutions. This changes everything now."[11]

No carmaker has been more transformed by the era of electrification than Volkswagen. The German company founded in 1937 was long known as the leading producer of vehicles that ran on the dirtiest of fuels, diesel. Even when it came to its cleanest models, Volkswagen couldn't make them clean enough to meet U.S. air-quality standards. So it cheated. In September 2015, after being tipped off by researchers that Volkswagen's "clean diesel" vehicles weren't as clean as they were billed, the U.S. EPA found that Volkswagen had intentionally installed software "defeat devices" that could surreptitiously reprogram its diesel engines to appear much cleaner than they were. When the vehicles were hooked up to laboratory testing equipment, they passed federal and state of California emissions standards with flying colors. But when on the road in the real world, Volkswagen's diesel-powered Jettas and Golfs produced up to forty times more nitrogen oxide and other emissions, officials with EPA and the California Air Resources Board discovered. The "dieselgate" scandal cost the company $25 billion in fines, penalties, and costs to buy back or repair 580,000 vehicles.[12] It was much more costly than just that for the company, however. Six Volkswagen executives were indicted for conspiracy to cheat U.S. emissions tests. Its CEO resigned. And any credibility the foreign carmaker had earned with environmentally minded drivers who bought into its "clean diesel" marketing was roadkill.

In March 2023, as it continued to weave its way down the road to recovery from the dieselgate scandal, Volkswagen announced a stunning plan to go electric that rivaled GM's and Ford's. The company said it would invest more than $192 billion over five years as part of its plans to put thirty new EVs on the market, with a particular eye on markets in China and the United States. In America, that includes refitting and expanding its 3,800-employee factory in Chattanooga, Tennessee, where it builds its popular ID.4 electric car, and also a new four-thousand-employee, $2 billion factory in Blythewood, South Carolina, north of Columbia, where the German company plans to do nothing less than resurrect and electrify an American automotive icon.

Long before SUVs became the vehicles of choice for many Americans, an Indiana tractor company built one of the first. International Harvester produced the rugged and boxy four-wheel drive Scout brand of SUVs and trucks from 1960 until 1980, rolling out more than 500,000 of them from its factory in Fort Wayne, Indiana, until the cash-strapped company ended the line to focus on more profitable commercial vehicles. Today, original Scouts are collector's items. At fan clubs across the country, owners tout the rough-and-tumble ruggedness of their retro 4x4s. They recall nostalgically how Scouts regularly beat Jeeps in the mother of all off-road races, the Baja 1000. How their trusty trucks dutifully pulled the family boat up to the lake in weekends past.

In 2021, Volkswagen acquired the Scout name and brand after its German-based Traton Group commercial truck subsidiary merged with Navistar, the U.S. successor to International Harvester. Two years later, with the market for EVs looking more promising than ever, with its competition moving quicker than ever to win it, and with federal and state governments finally providing the market signal and incentives the EV market long needed, Volkswagen shifted Scout back into gear. After looking at more than seventy other sites across numerous states, it landed on the South Carolina site for its new factory, which is expected to produce more than 200,000 Scout SUVs and trucks annually beginning in 2026.[13]

"We view it simplistically a little bit like the Gold Rush," Scout Motors CEO Scott Keogh told reporters at a press conference in South Carolina. "There's never been a better time to build a factory in America."[14]

Federal tax credits for new battery and car factories are making it the best time to build a new EV factory in America. And the federal tax credits for purchasing them—$7,500 for new EVs and $4,000 for used EVs—are making it the best time to buy one. In 2022, new EV registrations grew by nearly 60 percent, even as the overall auto market fell by about 11 percent.[15] By the first quarter of 2023, the all-electric Tesla displaced the Toyota Camry as the best-selling car in America, coming in second only to the Ford F-150 pickup truck among all vehicles sold.[16] True, the overall market share of EVs is still small, under 10 percent at the beginning of 2023, but it's growing fast. S&P Global Mobility forecasts that EV sales in the U.S. could reach more than 40 percent by 2030, while Bloomberg NEF estimates come in slightly higher at 50 percent.[17] That's right at the goal the Biden administration set for EV sales in America when it first crafted its climate and clean energy plans.

But even if the tax incentives alone aren't enough to drive EV adoption to 50 percent by 2030, other policies, combined with market demand and innovation, will help put that goal within reach. For starters, the federal carrot of tax incentives also comes with a regulatory stick. In April 2023, the U.S. EPA announced the strongest auto pollution standards in the world. By requiring automakers to reduce greenhouse gas emissions from their overall fleets, the EPA predicts that about 67 percent of new light-duty vehicles and 46 percent of medium-duty vehicles will be electric by 2032.

That would be a huge jump from the less than 6 percent market share that EVs had in 2022. Understandably, critics—many from the auto and petroleum industry—say there's no way that can happen, that it's a goal that's simply too big, too soon. But consider that—even without the new credits, even without the most stringent car pollution regulations in the world, even without every automaker shifting quickly to EVs—the rate of growth for EV market share essentially doubled each year between 2020–2022. If only that pace were to continue on its own, it would mean EVs would reach a 50 percent market share by 2026—four years ahead of the Biden administration's goals and in line with what scientists say we need to do in the transportation sector to prevent the worst impacts of climate change.

Federal policies are just part of what is driving the tremendous growth and opportunity in the EV business. Long before Washington got involved in limiting greenhouse gas pollution from automobiles, the biggest car state in the country was already doing it. In 2002, California passed the first-ever greenhouse gas vehicle emissions standards in the world, paving the way for the state to require any automaker that wants to sell cars in the biggest state in the nation to meet tailpipe emissions standards that are stronger than the federal government requires in the rest of the country. At the time, automakers and the petroleum industry fought the rule tooth and nail in Sacramento and in the courthouse. Such a regulation, they howled, would kill the auto industry, ruin the petroleum industry, and eviscerate California's—and the country's—economy. Instead what happened was innovation. Automakers figured out how to meet the new California standards, and then some. Hybrid vehicles, little more than a thing of fancy when the California law went into effect, became commonplace. And Tesla, which got its start in California, flourished and forever changed the industry. Twenty years after the California law was enacted, plug-in hybrid vehicles made up almost 25 percent of all new vehicle sales in California. All-electric vehicles accounted for about 20 percent of all sales.[18] Meanwhile, seventeen other states, representing the vast majority of car sales in the country, also adopted the California standards. The federal EPA also used the California standards to guide its national car emissions standards.

New state regulations will help push EV sales even higher. In August 2022, the California Air Resources Board approved a landmark new rule, the Advanced Clean Cars II standard, that requires 100 percent of new vehicles sold in the state to be powered by electricity or some other zero-emissions engine by the year 2035. In other words, if any carmaker wants to sell a vehicle in the state that is the country's biggest market for vehicles and is on its own the fifth-biggest economy in the world, that vehicle can't produce any emissions. Other states stretching from New York and Massachusetts to Washington and Oregon have followed California's lead in adopting all or portions of the Advanced Clean Cars II rule and will allow only electric or other zero-emissions vehicles to be sold within their borders in the next decade or so.

Next, California and other states are turning to trucks. In 2022, California began developing its Advanced Clean Fleets regulations that could require every medium- or heavy-duty truck sold in the state to be zero-emission by 2036.[19] As with the California 100 percent EV standard for cars, other states also are expected to follow the big trucks rule.

Even states that eschew adopting California-like car standards, and whose conservative elected officials push back on the idea of federal regulations for car pollution, are helping drive the EV revolution because they want the jobs and private investments that come with it. South Carolina, for instance, approved a $1.3 billion incentive package to win Volkswagen's Scout factory. In neighboring North Carolina, the state government put together a $1.2 billion incentive package that includes road improvements, job training programs, and other benefits to attract Vietnamese EV maker VinFast, which is building a $4 billion, 7,500-employee factory west of Raleigh. In Georgia, state officials approved up to $1.8 billion in tax breaks to land Hyundai Motor Group's $5.5 billion, 8,100-employee EV factory near Savannah. States see the incentives as good investments, not just for the long-term, good-paying jobs and direct investments they bring, but also for the follow-on suppliers they attract. After Hyundai picked Georgia for its first EV factory in the United States, at least a half-dozen other suppliers announced their factories throughout the state, investing an additional $1 billion and creating an additional eight thousand jobs.[20] "Not only do these generational projects solidify our spot at the vanguard of the EV transition, but they also ensure that thousands of Georgians across the state will benefit from the jobs of the future," Georgia economic development commissioner Pat Wilson said in a statement.[21]

Producing EVs and convincing consumers and businesses to buy them are just part of the revolution taking place as the auto industry shifts from internal combustion engines to electric engines. For EVs to work, they have to be charged. And while the vast majority of EV owners charge their vehicles at home or their place of work, there has to be a national infrastructure of charging stations that can deliver the fuel for the next generation of vehicles as dependably and as reliably as gas stations have for more than a century.

Under the bipartisan infrastructure act, Congress approved $7.5 billion in federal spending for EV charging and infrastructure. The Biden administration has set a goal to deploy that money by adding 500,000 public EV chargers across the country by 2030, including charging stations every fifty miles along major interstate highways.[22] That would be a huge increase—nearly fourfold from the 130,000 or so public charging stations there were in 2023—but it's not nearly enough.[23] According to an analysis by consulting firm PwC, the number of charging stations needs to grow to an estimated 35 million by 2030—about seventy times the Biden administration's goals—to meet the charging needs of the estimated twenty-seven million EVs expected to be on the road by then.[24]

Deploying that many chargers in that amount of time is driving a boom in the electric vehicle supply equipment (EVSE) industry that nobody could've predicted just a few years earlier. PwC estimates that the EVSE market will grow at 15 percent annually, from about $7 billion in 2023 to about $100 billion by 2040.[25] The consulting firm predicts that the fastest growth will occur in offices and other commercial buildings across America as businesses lead the shift to EVs. Apartments and other multi-unit buildings are expected to follow.

Putting more charging stations at office buildings and apartments is one thing. Replacing the nation's network of more than 145,000 gas stations with a national network of 35 million or so EV charging stations for on-the-go charging will be harder. How can America possibly roll out enough charging stations quickly enough to make sure EVs don't die on the highways in between fill-ups? History provides some clues. In 1905, Henry Ford's company and others were manufacturing about 25,000 automobiles per year, and by 1907 there were about 140,000 cars and trucks registered in America.[26] Yet there wasn't a single gas station. Back then, car owners would fill up using gas they purchased by the bucketful from a general store or hardware dealer, or in some cases at the occasional forward-thinking local blacksmith or livery stable. The first true drive-up filling station didn't open until 1913 when Gulf Oil company opened its Good Gulf Gasoline station on Baum Boulevard in Pittsburgh—about seventeen years after the first gas-powered cars hit the road in America and five years after Henry Ford introduced one of the first mass-market cars, the Model T. The first gas station sold about thirty gallons of fuel on its first day for 27 cents per gallon—about $9.25 per gallon when adjusted for inflation.[27] After that, the number of gas stations began to grow as fast as the number of gas automobiles.

Not too dissimilar from the early days of gas-powered vehicles, EV drivers tend to fill up on their own, at home. About 80 percent of EV charging is done at home, according to the Department of Energy, while about 60 percent of EV drivers say they rarely or never use public charging.[28] But just as with early gas-powered vehicles, that will change as EVs become more common, and drivers get more comfortable with longer trips. At least that's what investors are betting. In 2022, investors pumped more than $5 billion worth of capital into car charging companies globally, with much of it directed at U.S. companies poised to benefit from the government's big car charging plans.[29] The number one charging network in the country, ChargePoint, raised $600 million in funding, including $127 million in new funding in 2020.[30] New policies are sparking the growth of new players in the industry, too, and providing some signals as to where new charging stations will likely pop up.

Following the passage of the federal climate and clean energy policies, Georgia-based EV charging company EnviroSpark raised $15 million from founders and executives of companies including Chick-fil-A, apartment builder Post Properties, and others.[31] In Brooklyn, New York, a company called itselectric wants to build a network of small, curbside chargers on city streets in New York and elsewhere that can provide passive income to building owners. The start-up raised $2.2 million for a pilot program.[32] And then there's the world's biggest retailer, Walmart. The company that changed how America shops now wants to change how America fuels its automobiles. It plans to add fast chargers at thousands of its stores and warehouse clubs across the country, allowing shoppers to fill up their electric cars and trucks outside at the same time they're filling up their shopping baskets inside. With more than 10,500 locations nationwide, and a store within ten miles of approximately 90 percent of all Americans, Walmart essentially has a footprint bigger than any gas station chain, spread across every state, including many in rural areas, where car charging is otherwise hard to find.[33] "We are uniquely positioned to deliver a convenient charging option that will help make EV ownership possible whether people live in rural, suburban or urban areas," Vishal Kapadia, senior vice president for energy transformation at Walmart wrote in a blog announcing the company's EV charging plans. "Easy access to on-the-go charging is a game changer for drivers who have been hesitant to purchase an EV for concerns they won't be able to find a charger in a clean, bright and safe location when needed."

In addition to third-party operators, automakers themselves are betting big on vehicle charging. Buoyed by Tesla's success with its nationwide charging network, high-end electric truck maker Rivian is rolling out its own EV charging network with plans for more than 3,500 chargers nationwide.[34] Volkswagen is doubling down on its subsidiary Electrify America, teaming up with energy and electric infrastructure giant Siemens to inject $450 million into the car charging network that has pledged to build 1,800 charging stations and more than 10,000 ultrafast chargers in the United States and Canada by 2026.[35] Ford, GM, and other carmakers also are investing in partnerships with existing car charging networks to offer buyers of their vehicles free or discounted charging to make it more attractive to buy their vehicles.[36]

Once again, the growth at big companies is filtering down to small businesses. In 2017, Los Angeles entrepreneur Ariel Fan started one of the first certified women- and minority-owned EV charging companies in the state of California. Since then, her GreenWealth Energy Partners has designed and installed more than one thousand charging systems across the state. When car charging grants and investments started flowing from the bipartisan infrastructure bill to states and municipalities, GreenWealth found itself with as much work as it could handle. "Honestly, we have as much business as we can execute on," she said.[37] "We don't have enough capacity to do any more." In less than eighteen months, Fan's company quadrupled in size, to twenty employees. After landing new contracts with the county of Los Angeles and other municipalities in early 2023, she was planning to double the company's workforce again. "It's a very, very exciting time," she said. "But it also comes with some growing pains."

More availability of public chargers may help convince more Americans to buy and drive EVs. But the huge number of old chargers that simply don't work certainly doesn't help the cause. In 2022, University of California Berkeley researchers tested every one of the more than 650 public DC chargers in nine counties around the greater San Francisco Bay area. The researchers found that nearly 30 percent of the devices were broken. About 5 percent wouldn't work because their cables were too short to reach the charging outlets on their vehicles.[38]

Broken chargers are a huge problem. Kameale Terry learned this as head of customer experience for EV Connect, a charging company based in El Segundo, California. After hearing customers constantly complain about broken chargers, Terry and partner Evette Ellis in 2020 started ChargerHelp, which bills charging station operators a monthly fee to repair, maintain, and manage their stations. "I knew that mass EV adoption would never happen if we had a ton of broken charging stations," Terry said.[39] In March 2023, a group of investors led by Blue Bear Capital and Exelon Corp agreed, awarding ChargerHelp $17.5 million in Series A funding. The capital will be used by the women- and minority-owned company, which claims to be the first independent charger maintenance and operations company of its kind, to expand beyond its Southern California base.

Knowing that broken car chargers represent one of the biggest roadblocks for EV expansion, the Biden administration in September 2023 announced the availability of $100 million in federal funding for companies and individuals to repair broken car chargers. According to the administration, the funding made possible by the bipartisan Infrastructure Act should be enough to fix every broken charger in the country. "Charging your electric vehicle should be as easy and convenient as filling up a gas tank—and this investment will make our EV charging network more reliable, full stop," said Federal Highway Administrator Shailen Bhatt.[40]

Building out an EV charging network that's big and robust enough to support the nation's transition to electric cars is a huge enough feat in itself. Building a charging network robust enough to keep the nation's fleet of medium- and heavy-duty trucks charged up and rolling is going to be an even bigger feat.

Short-haul trucks are less of a problem. Delivery companies can install enough EV charging infrastructure at their warehouses and terminals to fill up electric trucks overnight and have them ready to hit the road to deliver packages, food, or other goods the very next morning.

In California's Central Valley, a potato chip company is showing the way. At first glance, the 500,000-square-foot Frito-Lay plant in Modesto, California, looks like any other manufacturing operation. Inside, more than 1,100 workers churn out packages of Fritos, Lay's, Doritos, Cheetos, and other munchies that are shipped throughout the West. Look closer, however, and you'll see the future of commercial transportation. In the warehouse, twelve battery-powered forklifts zoom around, moving pallets full of chips from one end of the warehouse to the other. In the parking lot, eight electric yard tractors operate twenty hours a day, buzzing around like busy worker bees as they move more than 150 trailers in and out of loading docks and around the lot, pausing only for operator breaks and two hours of charging each day. When it's time to hit the highway, chips are loaded into fifteen fully operational electric big rigs—the first Tesla trucks to be deployed anywhere—that can go up to four hundred miles on just one hour of charging. For closer-in deliveries, the company uses six Peterbilt electric box trucks that can easily cover the region before returning to the Modesto plant for recharging overnight. All the EVs, along with the entire factory, are powered by 100 percent renewable energy, some of which comes from a one-megawatt solar carport that keeps vehicles cool while they're parked under the blazing Central California sunshine.[41]

The modern-day makeover of the plant cost around $30 million, which was paid for by Frito-Lay parent PepsiCo Inc. and through matching grants from the California Air Resources Board and other state and local agencies. The investment will not only reduce the plant's operating costs but also reduce greenhouse gas emissions at the factory by more than 90 percent, company officials say. In a place like California's Central Valley, which has some of the worst air quality in the nation, that matters.

On-site charging works for companies like Frito-Lay. But charging for long-haul, over-the-road trucks is another matter. The amount of electricity needed to charge an electric big rig is exponentially more than the amount needed to charge up a car or local delivery truck. According to a study by National Grid, the amount of juice needed to power chargers at a typical highway charging station during its busiest hours could use as much power as a professional sports stadium. A truck stop where dozens of big-rig drivers might stop overnight and charge up while sleeping could use enough energy as a small town.[42] It's going to take a lot more investment, a lot more infrastructure, and a lot better technology to transition the nation's heavy-duty transportation sector to electricity.

Even so, that transition is underway.

In 2022, San Francisco–based TeraWatt Infrastructure announced plans to build the first network of high-powered charging centers for medium- and heavy-duty trucks along the Interstate 10 corridor stretching from the Port of Long Beach, California, to El Paso, Texas. The company raised more than $1 billion in capital to help deploy the network, backed by investors such as Vision Ridge Partners, which also is a major investor in car charging network EVgo, in the Norwegian electric ferry company Fjord1.

Electrifying big rigs is a formidable challenge, TeraWatt CEO and cofounder Neha Palmer acknowledges. But, she added, it's happening. And when it does, it's going to be big, and it's going to be relatively fast.

"There's a huge amount of infrastructure that has to be built," Palmer told television network CNBC.[43] "We think about it as the kind of infrastructure that gets built once a century. You had the railroads two centuries ago, you had the national highway network a century ago, and the scale (for national EV charging networks) is very similar to that."

CHAPTER 6

Electrification

"Heat Pumps Are Sexy"

WITH MILD WINTERS AND SUMMER DAYS AVERAGING NEARLY NINE-
ty-five degrees, the town of Tyler, Texas, typically isn't a frigid place. But
just about once a week, inside the Trane Technologies building tucked
between a Walmart Supercenter and a mobile home park off Troup
Highway in Tyler, it snows.

Tyler is home to Trane's high-tech SEET center—short for Systems
Extreme Environmental Test center—where the company is working on
technology to make high-efficiency heat pumps that can heat homes,
offices, and schools in the coldest of conditions. Heat pumps are currently
the most efficient way to heat and cool a building, using much less energy
and emitting a fraction of the emissions of gas or electric HVAC systems.
But heat pumps don't always work well in the coldest temperatures. To
try and fix that, Trane, Carrier, Lennox, and just about every other major
HVAC manufacturer in 2022 joined a Department of Energy program
designed to help manufacturers solve the cold-weather problem. After
months of testing at its Tyler factory, Trane and other HVAC manufacturers in November 2022 traveled to the Department of Energy's
Oak Ridge National Laboratory in Tennessee to show off their innovation. Trane's prototype heat pump performed at negative twenty-three
degrees—three degrees cooler than the DOE's program requirement of
negative twenty degrees.[1]

Heat pumps, which despite the name can both heat and cool buildings, have been around for nearly two centuries. The first heat pump was built by Austrian inventor Peter von Rittinger in 1856 not for heating or cooling buildings but for drying salt.[2] Development of the compressor, refrigerant, and other advances, along with their efficiency and relatively low costs, made heat pumps popular in foreign countries long before most Americans ever knew they existed.

Heat pumps work by extracting heat from an outside source—whether it's the surrounding air, geothermal energy underground, or waste heat from industrial operations—and transferring or "pumping" it inside a building where it's needed. To cool buildings, heat pumps essentially work in reverse. They extract warm air from a room and pump it outside, replacing it with air that's cooled using a refrigerant.[3] Heat pumps can also be used for smaller applications. Put one on top of a home hot water tank for instance, and it works four times more efficiently than a typical gas or electric water tank, saving hundreds of dollars each year.[4]

Heat pumps don't turn electricity (or gas or any other fuel) to heat, like traditional HVAC systems such as boilers. Instead they use electricity to gather heat, condition it with refrigerant, and move it around.[5] That takes a lot less electricity—so much less that heat pumps are typically three to five times more efficient than traditional HVAC systems. If Trane and other companies can mass produce all-electric heat pumps that can heat and cool buildings in every condition, it could be a game changer, for the environment and the economy. Buildings use about 40 percent of all the energy consumed in the United States and produce about 30 percent of total greenhouse gas emissions. About half of that—15 percent of the country's overall emissions—are related to HVAC systems, and primarily those emissions come from burning gas, oil, or propane for heating. Heating and cooling buildings are also some of the biggest costs for building owners, and in turn their tenants.[6]

As a result, the electrification of buildings, with heat pumps at the center of it all, is now at the core of the business of energy efficiency. Replacing old and inefficient fossil-fuel-powered HVAC equipment with all-electric, heat pump HVAC and hot water systems can save the average household about $500 a year on average, according to research and advocacy group Rewiring America. At least 85 percent of all households would reduce their energy costs by switching to energy-efficient heat pumps and water heaters, saving a cumulative $37 billion a year, the organization estimates.[7]

The potential for commercial buildings is even greater. Approximately one-third of the nation's nearly six million commercial buildings rely on gas, primarily for heating, while about 1 percent still rely on even dirtier fuel oil.[8] While electrification has come a long way in commercial buildings, growing from about 40 percent in 1979 to 60 percent in 2018, the market potential for heat pump HVAC, hot water systems, and other electric equipment remains huge.

That potential has the otherwise boring business of heat pumps sizzling. In 2022, Americans bought more electric heat pumps than gas furnaces for the first time, with annual sales exceeding four million units.[9] Globally, growth was even stronger, jumping nearly 40 percent in Europe alone as more homeowners and businesses made the switch to electric heat pumps amid soaring gas prices and supply shortages resulting from Russia's invasion of Ukraine.[10] Not long ago, talking about heat pumps was as exciting as talking about toasters or coffee pots. Today, heat pumps are strangely (with an emphasis on *strangely*) sexy. In the United Kingdom, a heat pump fanboy named Mike Fell created a website, pumpchic.com, and Instagram feed dedicated to appliances, complete with a photo gallery "featuring the hottest heat pumps and landscaping" and links that let you virtually see what a heat pump would look like in your backyard and hear what it might sound like when running.[11] In a separate Twitter feed, Fell posts side-by-side photos of heat pumps and movie star George Clooney (once People magazine's "sexiest man alive") to illustrate their supposed similarities. There's a sleek black-and-white heat pump situated next to a svelte, tuxedo-clad Clooney, for instance, as well as a retro-looking heat pump alongside a 1980s photo of Clooney with a mullet haircut and polka-dot silk shirt.[12] In Alabama, a local clean energy advocacy group took it even further, selling shirts that read: "Heat Pumps Are Sexy."[13]

The even less sexy business of public policy is driving the growth of heat pumps and other energy-efficiency products further and faster. Through the IRA, consumers and businesses can receive a 30 percent tax credit (up to $2,000) for the installation of heat pumps, and another $6,500 if needed to upgrade their circuit box or wiring. Low-income households that earn 80 percent or less than the median household income in their communities can receive a rebate of up to $8,000 for a heat pump, enough to cover the entire cost of a system. Heat pumps are so key to reducing carbon emissions and improving the country's energy security that, in addition to the purchaser tax breaks, the Biden administration in 2023 invoked the Defense Production Act to authorize $250 million to help manufacturers build new factories to produce more made-in-America heat pumps.[14]

The government's focus on heat pumps is paying off. During a White House roundtable with HVAC company executives in 2023, the CEO of LG Electronics North America revealed plans to build the company's first heat pump factory in the United States. Other companies are pumping up their heat pump production too. Immediately following the passage of the IRA, Carrier rolled out a new program specifically to help businesses and homeowners tap into heat pump tax credits and rebates and also announced it was expanding its heat pump factory and research center in Collierville, Tennesse.[15] And then in April 2023, Carrier doubled down, agreeing to buy German clean energy giant Viessmann Climate Solutions, an 11,000-employee company that specializes in heat pumps, solar, batteries, and services.[16] Carrier CEO David Gitlin called the massive, $13 billion deal a "once-in-a-generation" opportunity that would position his company as a leader in the hottest growth area in the global HVAC business. Bloomberg News opined in a piece headlined "Who Wants to Become a Heat-Pump Billionaire" that if the 1967 movie classic *The Graduate* were made today, "heat pumps are the new plastics."[17]

It's not just federal policies driving the move to heat pumps and other electric appliances and spurring the quest to electrify homes and make them more energy efficient. Cities and states have led the way for years, beginning with the liberal academic community of Berkeley, California.

In July 2019, the San Francisco Bay area city became the first in the country to ban gas connections in new buildings. In doing so, the Berkeley City Council pioneered a new approach for cities to reduce greenhouse gases to combat climate change and address other cataclysmic threats. In writing the ordinance, city council member Kate Harrison noted that since Berkeley is a coastal city, it is extremely vulnerable to sea level rise caused by climate change. It's also located along a "wildland-urban" interface, making it vulnerable to wildfires resulting from drier conditions and higher temperatures that come with climate change. Finally, Berkeley also sits in an earthquake zone, the Hayward fault. So if wildfires and sea level rise don't potentially wipe out the city, gas lines severed by an earthquake could spark building fires that could burn Berkeley to the ground.[18]

Replacing gas with cleaner, cheaper electricity generated from renewable energy could also save consumers money and reduce health problems like asthma, city officials said. Electrifying buildings also can provide a charge to the economy, driving sales of heat pumps, electric water heaters, stoves, and other appliances and creating jobs for electricians and other contractors as well. "We really believe we have the underpinnings of good legislation with economic, health and safety and climate impacts," councilmember Harrison said at the time. "We can do this, and we'll end up a lot healthier and cleaner for it."[19]

Other cities and states agreed. Berkeley's landmark policy gave new life to a nascent national movement by cities and states to decarbonize and electrify buildings. Following Berkeley, more than seventy other California cities advanced or passed similar ordinances. One year after Berkeley passed its ordinance, heat pump sales in California outpaced the sale of traditional, typically gas-powered furnaces for the first time. The use of electricity to heat homes also rose sharply, while gas heating fell.[20]

The success and solid support of the action by cities also attracted the attention of state policymakers. In August 2021, California regulators approved statewide building code changes that require builders of all new homes to include upgraded electric supply panels and circuitry needed to support all-electric appliances, including HVAC systems, water heaters, and stoves.[21] In 2022, Governor Gavin Newsom zeroed in on heat pumps specifically, directing state regulators to come up with regulations and standards designed to reach a goal of deploying at least six million heat pumps statewide by 2030, as part of a broader goal to have seven million "climate-friendly" homes by 2035.[22] In a state of 40 million residents, Newsom's moves were baby steps. But considering California was still a top state for natural gas production, Newsom and other state officials knew that being more aggressive would risk picking a bigger fight with the deep-pocketed fossil fuel industry and other business organizations.

The city of Berkeley learned that the hard way. In April 2023, the Ninth U.S. Circuit Court of Appeals sided with the California Restaurant Association, whose members overwhelmingly use gas stoves and ovens in their kitchens, in a lawsuit challenging Berkeley's ordinance.[23] In its ruling, the court said the city overextended its reach because federal law gives the authority to set energy use and efficiency standards to the federal government, not to cities. (Berkeley officials contend that their ordinance doesn't set efficiency standards; it simply prohibits gas in buildings.)

While the Berkeley ruling casts a cloud over the movement to electrify buildings and the appliances in them, it hasn't stopped it. To the contrary, by 2023 more than one hundred local governments in eleven states had approved zero-emissions building ordinances designed to phase out gas and other fossil fuels and electrify buildings, according to the Building Decarbonization Coalition.[24] The nation's biggest city, New York, passed legislation that would require most new buildings built after 2027 to use electricity or other non-fossil fuel sources for heating and cooking. The nation's second-biggest city, Los Angeles, followed, passing an ordinance to ban gas in new buildings and shift to all-electric appliances as part of its goal to become a net-zero emission city by 2030.[25] Like in Berkeley, members of the Los Angeles City Council also noted their city's propensity for earthquakes and wildfires as reasons to get the gas out of its buildings, in addition to the overall need to cut greenhouse gas emissions.

The aggressive moves by cities also prodded other officials into action. The state legislature in New York in May 2023 approved the nation's first statewide ban on gas in new buildings, delivering on a promise Governor

Kathy Hochul made in her State of the State address four months earlier. Beginning in 2026, any new building shorter than seven stories in New York will have to come with all-electric heating and stoves; after 2029, the rule will apply to taller buildings, though many businesses, including most factories and restaurants, are exempt.[26]

On the other side of the continent, Washington state in November 2023 passed new building codes designed to electrify buildings, expand the use of heat pumps, and reduce energy consumption in homes and other buildings by 70 percent by 2031.[27] Despite the Ninth Circuit's decision in the Berkeley case, "this is a movement that can't be stopped," Berkeley councilmember Harrison said.[28]

Something else is driving the movement to electrify buildings: savings.

According to a Department of Energy study, the combined impacts of the IRA and the bipartisan infrastructure law are expected to reduce energy costs in America by nearly 10 percent by 2030, saving consumers as much as $38 billion.[29] Businesses are expected to see a 13–15 percent cost savings. Switching more homes and buildings to electricity and using more efficient HVAC and other appliances that come with federal rebates and tax credits is part of the solution. Getting more of that electricity from new solar, wind, and other renewable projects made possible by federal policies—renewable projects that can produce electricity more cheaply than oil and gas—is the other part.

Energy and environmental think tank RMI studied the economics of building electrification in seven major cities across the country. In every case, it found that shifting to electric appliances and getting off gas would result in significant savings for homeowners. In New York City, an all-electric home would reduce annual utility bills by 10 percent and save $6,800 over fifteen years, according to RMI—not to mention a reduction of forty-six tons of carbon dioxide emissions.[30] In chilly Minneapolis, all-electric homes can save $1,900 over fifteen years, while in Austin, Texas, owners of all-electric homes can save $4,400 compared with homes that run on gas.[31]

Ripping out old gas lines, installing new electrical panels, and wiring up all-electric appliances also can drive economic growth and create a lot of jobs. Research by E2 shows that if New York state were to shift to electricity for the majority of its buildings, the number of electricians, construction laborers, and other energy-efficiency workers would increase nearly fourfold, to more than four hundred thousand workers.[32] In the city of Chicago, a similar E2 study showed that building decarbonization would also create thousands of new jobs and shore up careers for the twelve thousand workers currently employed in energy-efficiency businesses. They include workers like Erik Eticitty, an electrician apprentice who works for the Chicago company Verde Energy Efficiency Experts. "The transition to all-electric buildings is an opportunity for growth and job creation," Eticitty told E2.[33]

Eticitty followed in the footsteps of his grandfather into the electrical business. In his grandfather's days, old inefficient incandescent lighting systems lit up buildings twenty-four-seven until the bulbs burned out. Big, energy-wasting boilers and chillers heated and cooled around the clock, even when offices were empty. Today, Eticitty and Verde Energy Efficiency Experts specialize in LED lighting systems, heat pumps, high-efficiency HVAC systems, and building automation systems that intelligently control it all depending on demand and usage. "From my vantage point, there is huge potential to electrify churches, schools, and hospitals that are still running on gas and water-cooled compressors," Etcitty told E2. Recently, Verde also branched out beyond buildings to capitalize on another booming business: Installing EV charging stations.

The move to electrification is creating new opportunities for electricians everywhere. Steve Eubanks got into the electrical business working for his dad's company in North Carolina and then as an electrician in the Navy. Over a career of more than thirty years, he's done just about everything there is to do involving wires and electricity, from hooking up ceiling fans and light switches to running circuits and adding breaker boxes. Now, he and his coworkers also get lots of calls for solar panel and heat pump installations and more recently car charging stations. "These days it seems like every other call is from somebody wanting to install an EV charger," at their home, he said.[34]

Few companies have embraced the business potential of building electrification and energy efficiency like Trane. Founded as a plumbing and heating business by immigrant James Trane in 1885, the company in

2019 changed its name to Trane Technologies and simultaneously said it was changing its focus and mission to be not just an HVAC and refrigeration company, but a "climate company" dedicated to refocusing all of its brands "and connecting them to take action on climate challenges.[35]

CEO Dave Regnery has spent his entire career at Trane. He started in little-known corners of the company, working in and eventually running divisions that sold pumps, valves, tools, and later, security and safety solutions for buildings such as schools and hospitals. In 2007, he took over the company's Thermo King division, which sells cooling and refrigeration equipment for trucks, railcars, cargo ships, and storage units used to ship food and other goods. He went on to run daily operations of its entire industrial and climate businesses, which include Thermo King, Trane, and Club Car, the golf cart maker.[36] Working across all of Trane's divisions, Regnery began to see both the potential of his company to have a real impact on climate change—and the potential business opportunities that would come with it. After taking over as CEO in 2021, he began to emphasize both the societal and business opportunities that come with combating climate change.

"The megatrends around sustainability and decarbonization are only intensifying," Regnery told investors at an industrial technology conference in New York.[37] "Unfortunately, the pace of global warming continues to accelerate. We need to act now if we're going to bend the curve on climate change."

With 15 percent of the world's greenhouse gas emissions coming from HVAC systems in buildings and another 10 percent coming from food waste—much of it from goods that spoil in unrefrigerated trucks and containers—"we knew we could have a big impact on carbon emissions," Regnery said.[38] To both address climate change and capitalize on the business of doing so, Trane set a goal to reduce greenhouse gas emissions by one gigaton by 2030, an amount equivalent to about 2 percent of the entire world's annual emissions. At the core of Trane's climate-focused business strategy are its all-electric HVAC systems that replace the need for separate gas-fired heating and cooling systems that are in older buildings. Trane claims its single-unit, all-electric systems are 350 percent more efficient than gas-fueled HVAC systems and—if used with on-site solar, wind, and batteries—can dramatically reduce operational costs.

Also key to the company's gigaton goal are its combined heat-and-power systems that use waste heat to power buildings and its automated control systems that monitor electricity usage and turn off and on HVAC, lighting, and other electric devices as they're needed. In its other big business line, Thermo King, Trane in 2022 introduced a new line of mobile refrigeration systems it claims can reduce vehicle emissions by 30 percent. It also rolled out new all-electric refrigeration systems that run on batteries and could someday become standard, especially as more medium- and heavy-duty electric trucks hit the streets.

Still, Regnery understands the importance of policy to drive the adoption of electric appliances and energy efficiency. "We're always innovating . . . (but) we don't have to wait for new innovations to start bending the curve on climate change. We can bend the curve now by adopting policies that encourage businesses and consumers to transition to sustainable technologies," he says. "We need to act now, and we need to act boldly."[39]

Along with heat pump HVAC systems, heat pump water heaters are at the heart of building electrification and efficiency. Using the same technology as heat pump HVAC systems, heat pump water heaters essentially work like refrigerators in reverse. Instead of generating heat to warm up water like a kettle on a flame, they use electricity to spin a fan that pulls heat from the surrounding air and transfers it to a tank, where it warms up the water. Just as refrigerators give off heat as they cool what's inside them, heat pump water heaters give off cool air as they heat what's inside them.[40] What makes them so attractive is that they can be as much as seven times more efficient than gas-powered water heaters, and three and a half times as efficient as traditional electric water heaters.[41] Water heaters typically consume nearly 20 percent of a home's electricity usage, so homeowners can expect to save between $300 and $500 on their energy costs each year, according to some estimates.[42] Commercial and multifamily building owners can benefit even more, reducing their energy costs by as much as 75 percent by switching to heat pump water heaters, according to Rheem, one of the biggest manufacturers of water heaters.[43]

Like heat pump HVAC systems, the business of heat pump water heaters is hot. Between 2016 and 2020, U.S. sales doubled. Even so, they still represent just about 2 percent of the overall water heater market. There is a lot of room for growth, and federal, state, and local policies are once again helping spur that growth. As part of the IRA, buyers of heat pump water heaters can get tax credits of up to $2,000 and low-income households can get rebates of 100 percent of the costs, up to $1,750.[44] Commercial building operators also can receive major tax breaks for retrofits that incorporate heat pump water heaters.

Those rebates, coupled with city and state policies that seek to ban gas and electrify buildings, as well as game-changing mandates like Washington state's requirement for all new homes to include heat pump HVAC and hot water systems, and New York's building electrification law, are pushing manufacturers to expand, creating jobs and driving investments as they do.

Nyle Systems, based in the town of Brewer, Maine, got its start in the 1970s making kilns used to dry green lumber forested in Maine and beyond. Later, it expanded its expertise in drying stuff to the food business, manufacturing commercial food dehydrators used to make beef jerky and the fruit used in trail mix. As businesses and consumers in the United States became increasingly more concerned with climate change and emissions reductions, Nyle Systems CEO Ton Mathissen saw a market in producing commercial heat pump water heaters, which are relatively common in his native Europe. In March 2023, with a $6 million cash infusion from cleantech investment firm Aligned Climate Capital, Nyle Systems announced it would open a new factory in nearby Bangor, Maine, that will produce commercial heat pump water heaters that the company claims are 60 percent more efficient than traditional commercial water heaters. The factory is expected to create two hundred new jobs when it opens in what used to be a warehouse for online retailer Wayfair.

"The need for these kinds of products is only going to grow," Mathissen told television station WABI in Bangor.[45] "And so, we really anticipate over the next five to 10 years that we're going to be growing this business quite dramatically. Each of the last couple of years we tripled it, of course from a very small base. But, in the coming years we expect to double this business every year."

Heat pumps may be sexy for some people, and water heaters can be a hot topic. But a third major appliance at the center of building electrification and efficiency is causing the biggest stir when it comes to the politics of it all.

It started in January 2023, when federal Consumer Product Safety Commissioner Richard Trumka Jr. suggested in a press interview with *Bloomberg News* that his agency could consider new regulations or possibly even a ban on gas stoves over concerns about the unhealthy indoor air pollution they emit. The Biden administration already had been encouraging consumers and businesses to shift from gas to electric stoves, including with a $840 tax credit for new electric stoves under the IRA. Trumka's comments, however, sparked a theatrical tizzy among the fossil fuel industry and its conservative supporters. Texas Republican Representative Ronny Jackson tweeted, "If the maniacs in the White House come for my stove, they can pry it from my cold, dead hands."[46] Florida Governor Ron DeSantis, echoing a conservative theme, tweeted, "Don't tread on Florida, and don't mess with gas stoves!" The American Gas Association, meanwhile, pushed back using its bank account, funding studies to dispute the connections between gas stoves and health issues like asthma, paying for surveys showing gas stoves are overwhelmingly popular with restaurateurs, and hiring consultants to testify at public hearings extolling the safety of gas stoves.[47]

Unintentionally, the clash over cooking appliances also sparked something else: An explosion in interest in the newest type of electric stove, the induction stove, which uses copper wires and electromagnetic energy to heat food more efficiently, more safely, and more quickly than any other stove on the market. "The Biggest Winner of the Gas Stove Fight Is Induction Ranges," *Bloomberg Businessweek* declared in a cover story for the magazine titled "Dawn of the Induction Age." The cover featured a rendering of a head-scratching caveman heating a T-bone steak over a cookpot powered by a magnet.[48] In North America, the market for induction cooktops was worth about $5.6 billion in 2019 and was expected to grow by more than 8 percent a year between 2021 and 2028, according to Grand View Research.[49]

Because of their efficiency—induction stoves are as much as 10 percent more efficient than conventional electric stoves and three times more efficient than gas stoves—they can reduce energy costs for consumers and businesses. According to the EPA's Energy Star program, if all cooktops sold in the United States in 2021 were induction stoves, the energy cost savings would've exceeded $125 million, and the amount of electricity saved would have been equal to one thousand gigawatt hours.[50]

Along with environmental benefits and the savings, though, it's performance—and sometimes aesthetics—that's driving growth in induction stoves. That's forcing old-school appliance companies to rethink their product lines and also opening opportunities for innovative new companies intent on becoming the Tesla or the Apple Computer of the otherwise pedestrian oven and stove business.

Among them is Impulse Labs Inc., a San Francisco area company that got its start when founder Sam D'Amico was looking for a way to build a battery-powered indoor pizza oven. "What started as a cool idea to make pizza became a mission to reframe the home appliance industry," D'Amico explained in a company blog.[51] One of the biggest hurdles for many potential buyers of induction stoves is making sure their kitchen has enough electricity to run them. Most induction stoves require a 220-volt power outlet, which often means homeowners and restaurants have to upgrade electrical panels and wiring if they want to switch. Impulse Labs claims it has the solution for that costly problem. Its models come with an integrated battery, which offsets the need for higher voltage. Having a battery backup creates other benefits too. Users can still do their cooking in a blackout, for starters. The stove battery can also be configured to keep the refrigerator or other kitchen appliances running while the lights are out, essentially turning your oven into a cake-baking battery backup for your entire kitchen. In November 2022, a group of venture capital firms led by New York's Lux Capital agreed to invest $20 million in Impulse and D'Amico's vision to reframe the home appliance industry.

Impulse isn't the only start-up seeking to shake up the business. Another San Francisco Bay area company, Channing Street Copper Co., also introduced an electric induction stove with a battery backup that also comes with a cute name: "Charlie."[52] In Florida, a start-up called Invisacook wants to do away with the idea of a separate stove and oven altogether. It builds induction cooktops directly into countertop materials, eliminating the need for a separate kitchen appliance and creating a cool factor for chefs who can dazzle their guests by boiling water or frying up a couple of eggs in a pan placed directly on their countertop.[53]

Beyond flash and fancy, new climate and clean energy policies are also providing a jolt to blue-collar energy-efficiency businesses and jobs that don't have anything to do with electrification. In addition to tax credits and investments for heat pumps, electric stoves, and other energy-efficient appliances, the federal IRA and the bipartisan infrastructure act together will unleash billions of dollars in credits and rebates for less high-tech improvements like insulation, windows, and doors.

In a country where 80 percent of existing buildings are more than twenty years old, that creates a lot of potential for the nation's 382,000 energy-efficiency companies and the 2.2 million workers they employ, according to statistics from E2 and E4theFuture, an energy-efficiency advocacy group.[54] The energy-efficiency investments and credits in the IRA and Infrastructure Act alone are forecast to create 49,000 new energy-efficiency jobs while reducing energy expenses for homeowners and building owners by $85 billion by 2030.[55]

Insulation rebates and other energy-efficiency policies also will help support businesses and entrepreneurs like Jessica Azarelo, the self-proclaimed Attic Queen of Tampa, Florida. In 2021, after leaving behind a career in the banking and mortgage business, Azarelo started her own insulation company. Today, she spends her days crawling around in scorching hot Florida attics, blowing insulation, sealing leaks, and making homes more efficient, a job she says she loves.

"There is no better feeling than a customer reaching out after a job is complete to say how much better they feel, how much more comfortable they are in their home or how much money they've saved," Azarelo told E4theFuture.[56] She said the only regret she has is that she didn't start her company sooner.

"This is a $10 billion industry," Azarelo said. "There will always be a need for home performance and healthy home companies. There is much more work to be done."

CHAPTER 7

Emerging Innovation

"Looking to the Future, and It's Very Bright"

IN DECEMBER 2022, AT THE SPRAWLING LAWRENCE LIVERMORE National Laboratory east of San Francisco Bay, scientists did something that had never been done before.

They produced energy just like the sun does.

By concentrating enough powerful lasers at a pellet of fuel, researchers at the Department of Energy laboratory produced a fusion reaction that for the first time yielded more energy than it required to produce. It was a baby step—albeit a big one—toward creating a new form of zero-carbon energy that could provide civilization with limitless power for electricity, transportation, and other needs.

The discovery was probably the lab's biggest since it opened in the 1950s to design and later monitor the health of America's nuclear weapons. It sent reverberations throughout the scientific community and around the world. "Simply put," said Department of Energy Secretary Jennifer Granholm, "this is one of the most impressive scientific feats of the 21st century."[1]

Department of Energy's ability to achieve fusion ignition for the first time—eight months later Livermore researchers would do it again, with even higher yields—is incredibly significant.[2] It also validated the work of not just researchers at the Department of Energy but those at private companies who also have been working on creating fusion power for decades and in myriad ways. In 2022, more than thirty private companies across the country were working on fusion energy, according to the Fusion Industry Association.[3] Together, they attracted nearly $3 billion in private funding in 2022 alone, a whopping 140 percent increase from the year before, according to the association.

At the site of a former U.S. Army base in Devens, Massachusetts, Commonwealth Fusion Systems is working with the Massachusetts Institute of Technology to build a fusion reactor that will use high-powered magnets instead of lasers to ignite fusion energy.[4] In Everett, Washington, Helion Energy is trying to perfect a way to smash together plasma formed from helium and deuterium to generate energy inside a six-foot-high, barbell-shaped reactor.[5] Not far away, Seattle's Zap Energy won a $1 million grant from local authorities to repurpose a coal-fired power plant in central Washington that closed in 2006 into a fusion-powered plant. According to Zap, just one ounce of its fusion fuel carries as much stored energy as 25 tons of coal.[6]

There's a catch to fusion, though.

Despite the Department of Energy's groundbreaking discovery at Lawrence Livermore and the similarly promising work at private companies, the possibility of commercial fusion energy could be still decades away. Most fusion companies aren't expected to have a product ready for commercialization until after 2030 (Helion has said it expects to have a commercial product ready by 2028, but some experts doubt that ambitious timeline).[7] In addition to the billions that have already been spent, the costs of developing reactors and producing fusion energy are astronomical compared with the cost of renewable energy today. Someday our homes or flying cars very well may be powered by "Mr. Fusion" devices like the one that powered Dr. Emmett Brown's (Christopher Lloyd's) DeLorean in the *Back to the Future* movies. It wasn't that long ago, after all, that now-commonplace technologies like videoconferencing and watches that can monitor your heart rate and communicate like walkie-talkies were considered far off into the future. But it will take a while.

Like fusion (which fuses atoms to make energy), fission (which splits atoms to make energy through a nuclear reaction), is an incredibly promising technology for a zero-emissions future. Globally, companies from giant equipment manufacturers to boot-strapped start-ups have introduced more than fifty small modular reactors (SMRs) that are designed to use fission to produce nuclear energy, according to the International Atomic Energy Agency.[8]

The IRA opens a host of tax credits up to the nuclear industry, including Advanced Energy Project (48C) credits, Clean Energy Investment Tax (48E) credits, and others. Like tax credits for other forms of clean energy, credits for nuclear energy can be transferred and monetized—meaning companies can sell the credits to investors in exchange for cash upfront to fund research, hire employees, and build plants.

The tax credits and other government investments are helping drive down the cost of small nuclear reactors, and spurring interest in developing them. In 2023, the Tennessee Valley Authority, GE Hitachi Nuclear Energy, and other partners agreed to invest $400 million to help develop SMRs that could someday produce energy at plants in Tennessee, Canada, and Poland. Elsewhere, NuScale Power Corp., the Department of Energy, and a group of utilities had been working on what they said would be the first SMR project to market. NuScale's Carbon Free Power Project planned near the Department of Energy's Idaho National Laboratory in Idaho Falls intends to deploy six SMRs, each housed in thick containers about twice the size of a typical overseas shipping container or big rig trailer and weighing seven hundred tons apiece.[9] Together, the nuclear reactors could provide more than 460 megawatts of nuclear power to fast-growing communities in nearby Utah and other parts of the Intermountain West.[10]

But like fusion, fission also has a long and expensive path ahead. It will likely be a long time before small nuclear reactors produce power as cheaply as solar or wind. In March 2023, NuScale and Utah Associated Municipal Power Systems, a consortium of fifty utilities across seven states that is working with NuScale on the project, announced that the price tag for the project had soared, to $9.2 billion from the original projections of $5.3 billion. Several of the city-owned utilities involved in the consortium decided to bail out of the project, indicating they would instead look to cheaper alternatives such as solar and wind.[11] The 75 percent increase in cost estimates drew concerns and comparisons to the last nuclear project built in America, the Plant Vogtle nuclear plant expansion in Georgia, where cost overruns, safety issues, and years-long delays drove the price tag from $14 billion to nearly $35 billion—costs that will be borne by customers of plant owner Southern Co. The Plant Vogtle project was approved in 2012 and was supposed to be operating by 2016. It didn't start operating until the summer of 2023, seven years late, with the bill to Georgia ratepayers still climbing.[12]

While we wait on fusion and fission, three major game-changing clean energy technologies are closer to commercialization. Together, thanks again to federal and state policy drivers, they are attracting both private investors and innovators.

HYDROGEN

We already know how to make hydrogen, and we already make plenty of it. U.S. companies produce about ten million metric tons of hydrogen annually, enough to cover about 1 percent of the country's entire energy usage—if only it were used for that. Instead, the majority of hydrogen is used to refine petroleum and create ammonia and other chemicals used for everything from making fertilizer to treating metals. Even more problematic is the way we currently make it. Today, hydrogen is predominantly produced commercially by stripping it off natural gas, which contains hydrogen (in China, it is predominantly produced from coal). The technical process is called "steam methane reformation" and what it produces is referred to as "gray" hydrogen as a shorthand. The problem is that using gas to create hydrogen releases about 100 million metric tons of carbon dioxide every year, almost 2 percent of the country's entire annual carbon emissions.[13]

Beyond its use in the chemicals and petroleum industries, hydrogen can be what some call a veritable "Swiss Army Knife" for energy because of its versatility.[14] For now, at least, electricity generated from renewable energy is cheaper and more practical to power homes, offices, and passenger vehicles. But hydrogen can be a better fuel for a broader range of bigger applications that require huge amounts of energy, such as steel production, big manufacturing plants, heavy-duty trucks, ships, and airplanes.

Key, though, are the colorful ways in which hydrogen is made. "Gray" hydrogen takes us in the wrong direction environmentally, since producing it using gas or coal creates much more emissions than using energy from hydrogen can save. But we can and should clean up the production of hydrogen. One of the most promising pathways involves using electricity and devices known as electrolyzers to split the elements of water—hydrogen and oxygen—apart. "Green" hydrogen is produced when the electricity used in the process is renewably sourced, producing zero-emission energy with zero-emission energy sources. Green hydrogen is more beneficial than gray hydrogen for sure. Now that solar and wind are the cheapest power sources available, they also can be cheaper to produce than the rest of the rainbow of hydrogen flavors. That includes not just "gray," but also "blue" hydrogen, which uses natural gas in a similar process to gray hydrogen production but captures and sequesters the carbon emissions it produces, and "pink" hydrogen that uses nuclear power in the electrolysis process.

There remain significant uncertainties around the scope of hydrogen's role in the clean economy, but by some estimates, the market potential could be huge. Market research firm Grand View Research estimates the U.S. market for green hydrogen market will expand by nearly 40 percent each year between 2022 and 2030, as heavy industries like steel manufacturing shift to cleaner energy sources and manufacturers of heavy-duty trucks and other vehicles figure out how to fill up with hydrogen instead of diesel or gasoline.[15] By 2050, global demand for hydrogen could grow by as much as sixfold, according to consulting firm McKinsey & Co.[16]

The IRA for the first time created tax credits specifically for hydrogen produced with at least 60 percent fewer emissions compared with today's "gray" hydrogen. The Section 45V Production Tax Credit gives hydrogen producers up to $3 per kilogram of clean hydrogen they produce, in addition to other tax credits (48C) for construction of advanced energy projects.[17] To claim the very lucrative top credit of $3 per kilogram, projects must have near-zero carbon emissions. How to ensure that projects have near-zero emissions with veracity is a subject of heated debate. Environmental advocates and others argue that electrolyzers can only achieve near-zero emissions if they are powered 100 percent by *new* clean energy that is not currently on the grid (so as not to divert existing clean energy that is already serving demand, and increase demand from coal and gas power plants to meet the gap); located within a practical distance (to ensure that the clean energy is being delivered to the grid where an electrolyzer is located) and operating only during the hours that clean energy is available (i.e., when the sun is shining or the wind is blowing). Without abiding by these "three pillars," producing hydrogen at mass scale will produce more greenhouse gases than it reduces, studies show.[18] Oil and gas companies and some hydrogen and renewable energy companies say such rules are too strict. Instead, they would prefer looser rules that enable them to be powered by existing clean energy on the grid or power their electrolyzers at any time during the day—regardless of whether wind and solar are available. Essentially, that could extend and expand the use of fossil fuels, which is turbocharging climate change to begin with.

Some climate and environmental justice organizations say hydrogen is a bad idea no matter how it's made. In August 2023, a group of national, state, and local organizations from across the country signed a letter urging the Department of Energy to reject all applications for hydrogen hubs and abandon the idea. The organizations, which included the Center for Biological Diversity, 350.org, and others, said a large-scale buildout of hydrogen would exacerbate the climate crisis, harm communities, and, because much of hydrogen today is produced using gas, would increase and extend the use of fossil fuels.[19]

Oil and gas companies see hydrogen, carbon capture, and other energy-related businesses as a big part of their future as demand for fossil fuels continues to decline. The world's biggest fossil fuel companies—including BP, Shell, and TotalEnergies—have announced plans to spend billions of dollars on new hydrogen projects, potentially parlaying their expertise in drilling, refining, and building big energy operations into a new and promising arena.[20] The problem is that—with rare exceptions—the oil and gas businesses want to produce "blue" hydrogen projects that would burn gas or other fossil fuels to power electrolyzers, and then inject the carbon emissions they capture from such operations into wells to help pump out more oil and gas, that in turn will produce more carbon emissions when burned, and, of course, also extend and expand our reliance on fossil fuels.

In addition to the tax credits made possible by the IRA, money also is flowing to hydrogen from the bipartisan infrastructure law. In June 2022, the Department of Energy announced plans to release $8 billion in funding made possible by the infrastructure law to develop clean hydrogen "hubs" across the country that will serve as the cornerstones of a foundation for hydrogen energy. The announcement was the starting gun for states, cities, and businesses to assemble plans and players to try and land Department of Energy funding and attract companies that will produce, store, and distribute hydrogen. The Department of Energy received nearly eighty applications for funding, with states and cities in every part of the country banding together, sometimes with universities, labor unions, and private industry, to develop potential regional hubs that could attract thousands of jobs and put their communities on the forefront of the next big thing in clean energy.

A year before the Department of Energy unveiled its hydrogen hubs, the agency's Loan Program Office announced its first loan guarantee in nearly a decade. The $504 million loan guarantee will support the construction of one of the largest green hydrogen and energy storage facilities in the world. The Energy Department's loan guarantee for Utah's Advanced Clean Energy Storage Project (ACES), a consortium that includes Mitsubishi Power Americas and Magnum Development, is also expected to be one of the first hydrogen power plants in the country.[21] Initially, plans call for the hydrogen to be blended with gas (30 percent hydrogen; 70 percent gas) beginning in 2025, as the power plant shifts off coal. Ultimately, the plant is expected to run on 100 percent hydrogen that is produced from excess renewable energy produced by nearby solar and wind projects that often generate more clean energy than its customers can use. The region's renewable energy potential is so good that project managers say that they can produce more green hydrogen than they can use. Excess hydrogen will be stored in nearby underground salt caverns for use when renewable energy and fresh-made green hydrogen aren't available.[22] In addition to hydrogen, the ACES project is expected to pump $2 billion in investments into the region between 2022–2026, supporting more than five hundred construction jobs and a total of 1,100 jobs locally and statewide.[23]

The jobs, investments, and unique potential of the Utah project are making hydrogen more attractive not just to clean energy proponents and Democrats, but also to Republican supporters of fossil fuels who might otherwise criticize the Department of Energy's loan program and investments as big-government interference in the free market. It's helping bridge the partisan divide over clean energy. "This is not only a win for Millard County and Utah, but it is also an important step toward developing new energy technologies as we utilize an 'all of the above' approach to meet our energy demands," said Utah Republican Senator Mitt Romney, who has been critical of the Department of Energy loan program.[24] Utah Republican Representative John Curtis, who founded the GOP's Conservative Climate Caucus, said it was "exciting to see the ACES project secure funding from the Department of Energy and move one step closer to completion. Hydrogen can, and should, play a large role in powering our society."

No company has more at stake when it comes to hydrogen than Pennsylvania-based Air Products, the huge and appropriately named company that got its start in the 1940s selling oxygen-generating machines to steel mills and later the U.S. military to keep fighter jet pilots breathing and alive at high altitudes. Today, Air Products is one of the world's biggest suppliers of hydrogen, for use in everything from petroleum refining and chemical manufacturing to fuel for NASA rockets. Now, the company is betting big on hydrogen as tomorrow's go-to energy source for steel mills and other heavy industrial operations, and also for heavy vehicles such as trucks, trains, ships, and planes. In addition to investing in new hydrogen plants, Air Products is building new commercial hydrogen filling stations, starting in Alberta, Canada, where it plans to open a two-lane station where truckers can top off the tanks of their hydrogen-powered big rigs on one side and while drivers of electric fuel cell vehicles charge up on the other.[25]

Currently, almost all of Air Products' hydrogen is "gray" hydrogen made from electricity generated by burning gas or coal. Company Chairman and CEO Seifi Ghasemi makes no apologies for the dirty business, telling investors on a webinar with Reuters that its use of fossil fuels to make hydrogen "will continue for a long time."[26] That said, the industry is also in the midst of a cleaner transition, one that Ghasemi and Air Products want to lead, he said. Domestically, that transition starts in Louisiana, where the company is building a massive $4.5 billion "blue" hydrogen plant. When the Louisiana plant opens in 2026, it will be powered by gas, but Air Products has said it plans to capture and sequester 95 percent of the carbon dioxide emissions it produces. In Saudi Arabia, meanwhile, Air Products is building what it claims will be the largest "green" hydrogen plant in the world, with electrolyzers that run on 100 percent renewable energy producing up to six hundred tons of hydrogen per day and 1.2 million tons of ammonia per year.

Back in the states, Air Products and power company partner AES Corporation are investing $4 billion into a green hydrogen plant in Wilbarger County, Texas, that—like the big hydrogen project in Utah—is located at a former coal-fired power plant. For thirty-four years, the old Oklaunion coal plant south of the Oklahoma border produced power by burning coal, until New York–based Frontier Energy bought it in 2020 with the initial intention of converting it from coal to gas. As renewable energy grew cheaper and natural gas got more expensive, however, Frontier decided to shut down the power plant and instead build solar and wind farms there. Frontier is creating a cottage industry out of turning dirty industrial projects into clean ones. Through its Frontier Solar Holdings subsidiary, it has also purchased old steel mills, power plants, and industrial properties across the country on the cheap and turned them into renewable energy projects.[27] At the Texas site, wind turbines and solar panels will generate 1.4 gigawatts of clean energy that in turn will be used to produce two hundred metric tons of hydrogen each day, which Air Products claims will make it the largest green hydrogen plant in the country.[28] Building the Texas plant will also create more than 1,300 construction jobs and another 115 permanent on-site jobs after it opens in 2027, according to Air Products and AES. It also will generate about $500 million in local tax revenues, the companies predict. Shortly after announcing the Texas green hydrogen plant, Air Products announced its $500 million Massena, New York, green hydrogen plant, which will employ nearly one hundred workers.

Air Products CEO Ghasemi said the IRA and other federal policies were key to why the company is shifting from gray hydrogen, which today accounts for about 20 percent of its global revenues, to cleaner forms of hydrogen with the ultimate goal of getting to 100 percent green hydrogen.

"I think that gray hydrogen is not going to grow significantly," he said on the call with investors and Reuters.[29] "I think by 2035, we will be selling mainly blue and green hydrogen, and by 2050 mainly green hydrogen."

To get past gray hydrogen, however, Air Products and other companies like it are relying on another emerging technology: Carbon capture.

CARBON CAPTURE AND STORAGE

The Heidelberg Materials cement plant in southern Indiana has been in operation since 1902, when the company's founders discovered rich reserves of limestone they could use to meet the growing need for construction materials as new cities and towns sprung up throughout the Midwest. Ever since then, the plant has been an integral part of the town of Mitchell, Indiana (population 4,000), and one of its biggest and most important employers. "Generations of families have worked here," said Dennis Dolan, regional vice president for Heidelberg, formerly known as Lehigh Hanson Inc.[30] "It's not unusual for employees to work (here) 40, 50 or more years, making the cement industry and our company their life's work." In October 2019, Dolan joined local elected officials and workers at a groundbreaking ceremony for a new $600 million plant in Mitchell in the biggest corporate investment the town has ever seen. When complete, it will be the company's largest and most modern cement plant. And if the new technology the company is pioneering there with support from the Department of Energy works like it's supposed to, it could become one of the cleanest cement plants in the country.

The cement industry is one of the biggest industrial emitters of carbon dioxide pollution in the world. It's responsible for about 8 percent of the world's carbon dioxide emissions.[31] Cement is also ubiquitous and shows no signs of going away as the main ingredient in concrete, the primary building material for homes, office towers, roads, and bridges. Reducing greenhouse gas emissions from concrete production is huge. After water, concrete is the second-most-consumed material in the world, and by far the most widely used building material. Since about 90 percent of the emissions from the concrete come from cement, federal and state governments have zeroed in on the industry to reduce carbon emissions and combat climate change.

In 2022, the Department of Energy awarded Heidelberg a $4.7 million grant to install new carbon capture equipment at its Mitchell cement factory. The company will contribute another $1.1 million toward the project. Using giant filters and proprietary, ammonia-based solvents, the equipment designed by Mitsubishi Heavy Industries America is expected to capture about 95 percent of the carbon emissions produced at the cement plant and sequester it in the sandstone and dolomite formations deep underground.[32] If successful, the project could become a model for cement factories nationwide, potentially helping transform yet another century-old US industry. Some locals say it could be the biggest thing to come out of the little town of Mitchell since native son and astronaut Gus Grissom became the second American to fly in space in 1961.[33]

The Mitchell, Indiana, project grant was one of ten major grants awarded for carbon capture and storage projects by the federal government through the bipartisan infrastructure act. In all, the Department of Energy doled out $31 million for carbon capture and sequestration projects located at iron, cement, and power plants in Texas, Kentucky, and Illinois, as well as carbon capture research projects in other states.[34]

In addition to the federal grants and investments, the IRA extended and increased the tax credit for carbon capture and sequestration projects. As a result, projects can get a tax break of $85 for every ton of carbon they capture and store from industrial operations (up from $50 per ton previously), and $60 per ton for carbon used in a product, like cement (up from $35/ton previously). Direct air capture projects, which are still unproven and harder to build and operate, can receive tax credits of $180 per ton for carbon that's sequestered underground and $130 per ton that's used to create other products or for enhanced oil recovery.[35] Importantly, projects can receive direct pay credits for the first five years. That means they can essentially get a refund on their tax bill upfront rather than wait for their credits, which provides capital to start projects more quickly and get them going.

The federal government also has set aside $3.5 billion to figure out the tricky and expensive problem of direct air capture. The Department of Energy plans to divide the money between four "regional direct air capture hubs" that can each suck up at least one million metric tons of carbon annually and either sequester it underground or create new products from it. In August 2023, the Department of Energy announced the first two regional sites, agreeing to invest $1.2 billion into two direct air capture projects, right in the heart of the nation's oil and gas industry.[36]

One project, being developed by a subsidiary of Occidental Petroleum in Texas, the biggest state for terrestrial oil drilling, promises to vacuum up to one million tons of carbon dioxide from the air each year and sequester it underground. Though the process—and the involvement of fossil fuel companies that have previously avoided any responsibility for addressing climate change—have raised skepticism, Occidental and other oil and gas companies say they see technologies like direct air capture and hydrogen as their future. "We believe that our direct capture technology is going to be the technology that helps to preserve our industry over time," Occidental CEO Vicki Hollub told the audience at an annual oil and gas conference in Houston, which for the first time included more sessions on hydrogen and other new technologies than on oil.[37] "This gives our industry a license to continue to operate for the 60, 70, 80 years that I think it's going to be very much needed."

In addition to the Texas project, a second regional direct air capture hub project was funded in Louisiana, the biggest state for offshore drilling. There, a group led by carbon capture companies Climeworks AG and Heirloom Carbon Technologies will similarly suck carbon dioxide directly from the atmosphere and store it in giant underground wells that are approved and permitted by the EPA.

Capturing and storing carbon dioxide underground is just the start, however. Many companies see a much brighter—and much more profitable—future. Heirloom's technology is particularly interesting. The company essentially uses limestone, one of the most abundant materials in the world, as a giant carbon dioxide sponge. At a trial at its Brisbane, California, headquarters in February 2023, Heirloom demonstrated how it works. First, Heirloom used heat to remove naturally occurring carbon dioxide from limestone and sequestered it not underground but in giant bottles. Then, it set the "cleaned" limestone out on racks of massive baking sheet–like trays each the size of a Starbucks store, where it naturally sucked up carbon dioxide from the atmosphere like a thirsty sponge. But instead of taking years to absorb CO_2 naturally, Heirloom's technology sped up the process, reducing the time it took for the sheets of limestone to fill up with carbon dioxide to just three days. Just like a sponge squeezed out and reused over and over, the limestone can be reused repeatedly.

But what to do with all the carbon dioxide the company wrings out from the limestone? In the February 2023 test, Heirloom took its bottled carbon dioxide to a nearby concrete plant. There, not unlike a giant SodaStream machine used to make sparkling water, the CO_2 was injected into reclaimed water to produce ready-mix concrete, sequestering the greenhouse gas in the building material, potentially forever. According to Heirloom, it was the first time carbon dioxide obtained by direct air capture was permanently stored in concrete. The company plans to scale up its technology at its first commercial facility, in California's Central Valley, and later at an even bigger scale including at the Louisiana project, said Vikrum Aiyer, policy chief for Heirloom." The history we made in the Bay Area illustrates that we can capture carbon dioxide from the air, permanently store it into a medium like concrete, and have that material be upcycled, so to speak, by pouring it back into local housing and transportation infrastructure projects in the built environment," he said.[38]

Not far from Heirloom's San Francisco Bay area headquarters, another company is taking another approach to sequestering carbon dioxide in concrete. Start-up Blue Planet Systems is working with utility Calpine Corporation to convert carbon dioxide emissions from a gas-fired power plant in Pittsburg, California, combine it with calcium from waste concrete, and turn it into synthetic limestone aggregate that can be used to make concrete. In 2022, Blue Planet broke ground on a prototype concrete aggregate plant in Pittsburg that it claims could eventually capture 175,000 tons of carbon dioxide each year and use it to produce enough limestone aggregate to supply 250,000 yards of concrete, or enough to fill about 25,000 concrete trucks. When that concrete is used for buildings, roads, or bridges, it has the additional benefit of sequestering and storing that carbon dioxide forever. Even when the building or other structure is eventually demolished, the carbon dioxide stored inside the concrete is permanently sequestered, just like other ingredients like water and aggregate. Only extreme heat or acid could decompose the synthetic limestone, according to Blue Planet.[39]

Another example of what direct air capture projects might look like may soon be found on the wide-open plains of Wyoming. A Los Angeles–based company called CarbonCapture Inc. plans to build what it says will be the country's largest direct air capture project in an undisclosed location in the state, using tractor-trailer-sized modules it plans to stack together to suck carbon dioxide out of the air, clean it up and sequester it underground. The company claims that by 2030, its Project Bison operation will be able to capture up to five million tons of carbon dioxide from the air, first using gas but eventually using renewable energy to power the big fans and devices.[40] CarbonCapture plans to make money in two ways.[41] First, for every ton of carbon dioxide it captures and buries underground, it will sell a carbon removal "credit"—at a price tag of $500 or more per ton as of 2023—to companies that are trying to reach corporate net-zero emissions goals. In March 2023, Project Bison landed its first big customer, Microsoft Corporation, which agreed to buy carbon removal credits from the project to help meet the software company's heady internal goal of removing as much carbon dioxide from the atmosphere that it has produced since it was founded in 1975.[42] CarbonCapture doesn't plan to sequester underground all the carbon it sucks out of the air, however. It also plans to bottle and sell it for use in making products ranging from sustainable jet fuel to concrete.

Those sorts of products are still in their infancy and are not commercially viable yet, casting a big cloud over Project Bison and a herd of other direct air capture projects like it. Still, CarbonCapture CEO Adrian Corless said the pieces are coming together, thanks to the federal climate policies. "With the passage of the Inflation Reduction Act, the prolifer-ation of companies seeking high-quality carbon removal credits and a disruptive low-cost technology, we now have the ingredients needed to scale (direct air capture) to mega-ton levels by the end of this decade," he said in announcing Project Bison in 2022.

State policies also are helping drive carbon capture and storage projects. In 2021, California passed legislation that requires all cement producers operating in the state to reduce their net emissions to zero by 2045. It's a big deal: California is the nation's number two cement producer behind Texas, and cement plants operating in California and elsewhere rely heavily on coal and gas and other toxic fuels, including burning old tires.[43] To meet the state's goals, cement plants in the state will have to convert to cleaner fuels such as hydrogen or electricity, increase energy efficiency, and invest in carbon-capture technology, cre-ating a new market for businesses across those fields.

LONG-DURATION STORAGE

In February 2021, one of the worst winter storms in Texas history slammed into the state, freezing natural gas wells and pipelines, shutting down coal and nuclear power plants, and icing wind turbines to the point they couldn't turn. More than 250 Texans died and 4.5 million homes and businesses were left without power, causing about $200 billion in economic damage by some estimates.[44]

Almost exactly two years later, companies from Finland and Cal-ifornia announced what could be part of the solution to preventing similar outages in the future. Helsinki-based Wartsila Corporation and Burlingame, California-based Elioan LP announced they had completed financing for a two-hundred-megawatt battery storage project in the south Texas town of Mission that could keep the lights on for hundreds of thousands of homes for hours or even days the next time power plants failed. The companies claim their project is the world's biggest battery project of its type. Just as significantly, they noted, it is the first energy storage project ever financed using tax credits made possible through the IRA.[45] In announcing plans for its Madero and Ignacio battery proj-ect, Eolian CEO Aaron Zubaty emphasized the importance of energy storage in preventing blackouts like Texas experienced during its Big Freeze. "The new face of grid resilience is fast and flexible energy storage to fill in the gaps when other resources are too slow or too fragile," he said.[46] In the aftermath of the Texas freeze, the demand for energy storage heated up. In Texas alone, battery storage is expected to increase nearly fifteenfold by the end of the decade, from about two gigawatts in 2022 to about twenty-nine gigawatts, S&P Global predicts.[47]

Projects like Eolian's are hot with investors too. In 2022, corporate, venture, and private equity funding into energy storage companies soared by 55 percent to a record $26 billion. Start-up storage companies also are attracting suitors. At least twenty-eight energy storage companies were acquired in 2022, also a record number, according to data from Mercom Capital Group.[48]

Lithium-ion batteries are key for energy storage today. But other nascent technologies can last longer, operate more cheaply, and have fewer impacts on the environment they're helping to save. Along with private investments, federal policies and investments and new pressure from state and regional regulators eager to avoid another Texas-style freeze are giving a huge boost to long-duration storage. In November 2022, the Department of Energy announced nearly $350 million to fund eleven emerging long-duration energy storage projects through funding made possible by the bipartisan infrastructure act. The funding was on top of $30 million for research projects to advance long-duration storage and $9 million for a fund and program called Energy Storage for Social Equity, or ES4SA, to help make energy storage more accessible and affordable in economically disadvantaged communities.[49]

As in other areas of the clean energy revolution, the IRA's tax credits also are driving growth in storage. The law for the first time included energy storage in the investment tax credit program that for years was exclusive to solar, wind, and other energy projects. In the case of Eolian's Texas storage project, for instance, the company was able to transfer its tax credits to investors looking for ways to reduce their corporate tax burdens over the long term in exchange for the cash Eolian needed to start the project.

Another company is working on building a different type of long-duration storage that relies on the simple ingredients of water and gravity. Since its founding in 2018, Salt Lake City–based clean energy development company rPlus Energies has developed solar and wind projects throughout the Western United States. Now, it's doubling down on pumped-hydro storage, beginning with what could become one of the biggest energy storage projects in the country, in the middle of the Nevada desert.

The technology behind pumped-hydro storage is simple. It has been around for decades. In essence, water from a lower reservoir is pumped uphill to an upper reservoir when electricity is cheap. When electricity is more expensive or in short supply, the water from the upper reservoir is released, cascading through giant turbines that produce electricity that can be transferred to the grid. Since operators control when the water is released, they can deliver power whenever it's most needed, day or night.

At its White Pine project in Nevada, rPlus Energies plans to construct two reservoirs outside the town of Ely, one about two thousand feet high up a cliff and the other at the base of the hill. When nearby solar panels and wind turbines are producing more electricity than is needed, the company will use the excess energy to pump water up the cliff. Later, at night, when the wind isn't blowing, or when energy demand is high, it will release the water from the upper reservoir, driving turbines that produce electricity as it flows back down to the lower reservoir. Able to generate as much as one thousand megawatts, the project could be one of the biggest energy storage projects in the country, storing and producing enough electricity to fully meet one-eighth of Nevada's energy needs at peak usage times, according to the company. It is expected to generate other benefits too, including $12 million in state and local tax revenues and more than five hundred construction jobs throughout the project, rPlus Energies claims.[50] Buoyed by the inclusion of storage for clean energy tax credits for the first time under the IRA, the project is just one of nearly a dozen pumped-hydro projects rPlus Energies is planning. Others are in the works for Oregon, New Mexico, Washington, California, and Utah.[51]

In September 2023, the Department of Energy announced $325 million in grants made possible by the bipartisan infrastructure law to nine companies on the cutting edge of energy storage.[52] Two of the grant winners are companies that are recycling and repurposing used electric vehicle batteries for renewable energy storage in low-income communities. Others are building batteries based on new chemical combinations that could prove to be better than conventional lithium-ion. A company called Energy Dome claims it can store energy using a technology that compresses carbon dioxide in dome-like tanks. The company plans to build its first project in Wisconsin. In Alaska, a grant will help the remote community of Healy to develop a new storage system that uses heat pumps and concrete blocks housed in a former coal-fired power plant to store energy that can keep the lights on locally for as long as ten hours, filling in the gaps left when solar and wind energy isn't available.[53]

Another grant winner is pioneering a new kind of technology that we all know about: Rusting metal.

In the town of Cambridge, Minnesota, Form Energy and partner Great River Energy plan to install a 1.5-megawatt "iron-air" battery array at the site of a gas-fired power plant that can supply energy to the region without burning fossil fuels.[54] Form Energy's batteries, each about the size of a side-by-side washer and dryer, run on a technology that essentially uses electrical charges and air to cause "reversible rusting" on iron metal. While discharging, the batteries absorb oxygen from the air, causing the metal to rust. While charging, an electrical current converts rust back to iron, and the batteries release oxygen. The result is energy without carbon emissions, as long as the electrical currents used in the process come from renewable energy. Form Energy claims its iron-air batteries store power at less than one-tenth the cost of lithium-ion batteries and can deliver it for one hundred hours or more, filling electricity gaps left by renewables.

The company's technology has attracted nearly $1 billion from a long list of investors, led by Bill Gates's Breakthrough Energy Ventures. In December 2022, not long after Gates met with West Virginia Senator Joe Manchin over the IRA, Form Energy announced it would build a $760 million battery plant in Weirton, West Virginia, to make its iron-air batteries. The factory, made possible by federal tax credits and a $290 million incentive package from the state, is expected to create new jobs for as many as 750 West Virginians. The company has said the jobs will pay an average of $63,000 a year—nearly 20 percent higher than the average annual salary in the state.[55]

In a statement, Manchin said the West Virginia battery factory was "exactly what I had in mind as I negotiated the Inflation Reduction Act." Republican Governor Jim Justice proclaimed it was one of the biggest and most important investments for the state, particularly for the town of Weirton. "At one point, Weirton was one of America's most important steel towns—a national leader in steel production," Justice said.[56] "Now, this historic city is looking toward the future, and it's very bright."

VIRTUAL POWER PLANTS

From the heart of the oil and gas industry, Houston-based Sunnova Energy is on the dawn of a new way to generate and distribute clean, renewable energy. The company essentially wants to install solar and battery backup systems on more than 75,000 homes across the country at little cost to homeowners, use its software to link them all together, and in doing so create a new kind of power plant.

The idea of a "virtual power plant" like Sunnova is building isn't entirely new. In 2022, solar company Sunrun linked together five thousand solar installations to create a virtual power plant serving New England. Similar systems are planned in Texas and California.[57] Sunnova has been in business since 2012 and is one of the leading rooftop solar companies in the country, with more than 250,000 customers. For years, it has been building "micro-grids" that link residential solar and battery projects together, allowing users to put excess power they generate or store but don't need on the grid for use by users on other parts of the grid where it might be cloudy or dark.

But the size and scope of the program Sunnova is calling Project Hestia (named after the Greek goddess of hearth and home) could ultimately change the way we think about power plants and energy distribution. In April 2023, Project Hestia got a huge boost when the Department of Energy awarded Sunnova a $3 billion loan guarantee to move it forward. The company plans to use the money in turn to offer low-interest loans to homeowners, particularly in low-income and disadvantaged communities. One of the places the company is starting is in Puerto Rico, where hurricanes and other climate-related disasters have made power outages a regular occurrence. Within twenty-five years, the company expects to install 568 megawatts of solar over forty states, creating more than 3,400 jobs along the way, according to the Department of Energy.[58]

One of the biggest fans of virtual power plants is the Department of Energy official who agreed to loan Sunnova and Project Hestia $3 billion: Jigar Shah, director of the department's Loan Programs Office. Shah knows something about solar, batteries, financing, and business. In 2003, he founded SunEdison, which pioneered the idea of financing solar installations and created the "solar as a service" model that helped the solar business grow exponentially by making it easier for users to finance rooftop solar systems. Shah later started the clean energy investment company Generate Capital before joining the Department of Energy in 2021.

Virtual power plants are something Shah likes to bring up at conferences, in media interviews, and with anybody who will listen. A former podcast host, he even created a series of "bite-sized blogs" about virtual power plants he calls "VPPieces" that he posts on the Department of Energy's website. For Shah and others at the Department of Energy, virtual power plants address several Biden administration priorities. In addition to making more renewable energy available generally, with government assistance and guidance they can also help make solar and batteries more affordable and more available specifically in low- and moderate-income communities and communities of color that have been passed over in the past—something Shah likes to call the "democratization" of clean energy. Rooftop solar and batteries can also be installed relatively quickly, as compared to big utility-scale projects, which means more of them can be deployed more quickly. Deploying more renewables and connecting them to create virtual power plants avoids the need for building more coal or gas-fired power plants and all the carbon pollution they generate.

"There's really sort of a lack of understanding of how (clean energy) technology can scale up and get commercialized," Shah said. "That's what we're trying to do."[59]

CHAPTER 8

Equity

"Now Is the Time"

THE DIVIDING LINE THAT SEPARATES THE HAVES AND THE HAVE-NOTS
at the epicenter of America's last big economic transformation runs along
a fifty-foot-wide creek bed in San Mateo County, California.

On the one side of the often-dry San Francisquito Creek and Highway 101 is the town of Palo Alto, one of the most expensive zip codes
in America and home to the elite—and almost entirely white male—
founders of the tech industry boom, including Meta's Mark Zuckerberg,
Alphabet's Larry Page, and the family of Apple cofounder Steve Jobs.

On the other side of San Francisquito Creek is the town of East Palo
Alto. There, 70 percent of the population is Hispanic or Black. Nearly
12 percent of the population lives below the poverty level. While the rest
of Silicon Valley in the 1990s was solidifying its spot as the center of the
internet universe, East Palo Alto became the center of the Bay Area drug
trade, earning the dubious distinction in 1992 as the country's most dangerous neighborhood and the murder capital of America.[1] Easy access
to capital and good education helped drive the technology boom that
created modern-day Palo Alto and the tech millionaires and billionaires
who now live there. Easy access to crack cocaine and guns and fewer job
opportunities for anybody without a college degree left residents on the
other side of the creek behind.

This didn't happen by accident. Segregation and redlining have been
part of the region's history for more than a century. Policy mattered as

much then as it does today. In 1920, the Palo Alto Chamber of Commerce passed a resolution calling for local lawmakers to create a "segregated district" for Asian and Black residents coming to the area. In the 1960s, U.S. 101 was planned and built to go right through the middle of minority residents' neighborhoods and homes, creating what the NAACP would later call a "concrete curtain" between white neighborhoods and Black, Asian, and Hispanic neighborhoods. More recently, the offshoring of manufacturing, including in the semiconductor and solar industries, has worsened the divide between locals who have college degrees and those without degrees searching for work in an economy with a dearth of jobs they're qualified to get.

The lack of equity between Palo Alto and East Palo Alto is emblematic of Silicon Valley and the tech industry as a whole, and the results are obvious to anybody who visits the area. After New York and Hong Kong, Silicon Valley is home to one of the greatest concentrations of billionaires in the world. It's also home to some of the greatest income inequality. In 2022, the median wage for high-skilled tech industry workers in the region was about $137,000, nearly three times the median wage for less-skilled, nontech workers in the region. Like skills, race matters. Average wages for white, non-Hispanic workers were more than 60 percent higher than for Hispanic, Latino, and Black workers.[2]

Of course even the highest earners struggle to live in Silicon Valley. In 2022, the region's median home price hit a record-breaking $1.53 million. Childcare costs have risen 85 percent in the last decade.[3] More than 40 percent of children in the Silicon Valley counties of San Mateo and Santa Clara live in households that are not self-sufficient. As many as one in five households are at risk for food insecurity but can't get public assistance because they don't meet income requirements, thanks to the region's relatively high wages compared with the rest of the state and country.[4] Living in Silicon Valley can be hard for almost anybody but the richest residents. But it's much, much harder for the low-wage workers who build and clean the homes and offices of tech titans, feed them at local restaurants, and take care of their children.

It's this sort of social, racial, and economic inequity and division created during previous economic revolutions in America that architects of the new economic revolution want to avoid.

It won't be easy.

Just like the technology revolution, the clean energy revolution so far has been something primarily for rich, white people—people who can afford to put solar panels on their rooftops and park a Tesla in their garage. The median income for households that installed solar panels in 2021 was $110,000—about $31,000 more than the national median household income.[5] The typical Tesla Model 3 owner is a white man who owns his own home and has a household income of nearly $134,000 a year, according to automotive research firm Hedges & Company.[6]

On the other end of the spectrum, poor areas, indigenous communities, and communities of color often bear the brunt of the negative consequences of clean energy, such as mining. In Thacker Pass, Nevada, for instance, Canadian mining company Lithium Americas Corporation is developing an 18,000-acre mine in an area that includes the ancestral home of the Paiute, Shoshone, and Bannock people. The U.S. Department of the Interior gave final approval to the $2.2 billion project in May 2023 despite protests by the tribes, which said it would irreversibly harm the region and bring even more dishonor to a place where more than thirty Paiute people were massacred by U.S. soldiers in 1865.[7]

It was the murder of another person of color that motivated President Biden to include equity and environmental justice in his clean economy policies. During a year of racial unrest following the May 2020 killing of Black Minneapolis resident George Floyd by police, then-candidate Biden pledged if elected to address race and inequity, including when it came to the economy and environment. One week after taking office, Biden signed a series of executive orders aimed at addressing environmental justice and racial and economic inequity in ways that no other president had done before. He ordered the establishment of a White House Environmental Justice Advisory Council within the EPA. He laid out a whole-of-government blueprint requiring all federal agencies to develop plans to infuse equity and inclusion into everything they did. He ordered the White House Council on Environmental Quality to develop a climate and economic justice screening tool to identify and highlight disadvantaged communities and those impacted by environmental disasters from the past. He set a goal for 40 percent of federal investments in clean energy and other areas to go specifically to disadvantaged communities and to businesses, nonprofits, and other organizations working on expanding clean energy and opportunities in the clean economy to more people and communities of color.

The new administration called its program Justice40.

"We need to make equity and justice part of what we do every day—today, tomorrow, and every day," Biden said.[8]

Longtime champions for equity are holding out hope that Justice40 will truly be transformational in preventing the sorts of disparities that define Silicon Valley and the tech industry. "Between CHIPS, IRA and the infrastructure bills, entire new sectors are being developed, creating hundreds of thousands of new green jobs and revitalizing entire communities," said Tom Soto, a Latino investor from Los Angeles whose Latimer Partners focuses on investments at the intersection of clean energy, climate and equity. "And now, under Justice40, those communities that had been on the margins now have a seat at the table."[9]

It's a seat that has been off-limits to people and communities of color for a long time. For Latinos in particular, it stems back to the U.S. annexation of California back when it was still part of Mexico, according to Soto, an eighth-generation Californian whose mother and father both served in the state legislature. According to family lore, the Sotos once controlled thousands of acres in the San Gabriel Valley east of modern-day Los Angeles. During the California Gold Rush, the family turned it all over to the government in exchange for $50, a house in Pomona, a buckboard wagon, and U.S. citizenship, according to Soto. The land was later divided between white settlers who would go on to become some of the richest and most powerful families in the Los Angeles area.

Today, Soto sees inequity from another perspective, bubbling up in the clean economy. Less than 2 percent of the estimated $82 trillion in money controlled by asset management firms is managed by diverse-owned firms, according to a 2021 study by the Knight Foundation.[10] That lack of diversity among investors, along with the lack of access to capital for clean energy entrepreneurs—especially among people of color—prompted Soto to help start the Los Angeles Cleantech Incubator (LACI) in his hometown. Since its founding in 2011, LACI has helped more than 375 start-up companies raise more than $1 billion in investments to pioneer new cutting-edge clean energy innovations. Nearly 70 percent of LACI-backed businesses are owned by people of color or women, according to Soto, who serves on the board of the organization. In 2023, LACI led a national coalition of cleantech incubators to adopt a new set of principles designed specifically to support Justice40 goals by prioritizing investments to underrepresented cleantech entrepreneurs.

"Yes, the next chapter of this discrimination is in the climate tech sector," Soto said. "It's a fight."

In addition to Justice40 and equity-minded investors like Soto and organizations like LACI, the Biden administration also is banking heavily on organized labor in the fight for equity in the new clean economy. Through collective bargaining agreements and better pay, unions are proven to reduce racial wage gaps and improve equity for all workers. One study by the University of Chicago, for instance, showed that wage gaps between Black and white women workers would be reduced by as much as 30 percent if the country had higher unionization rates.[11]

Proponents have been fighting for decades to improve equity in the clean economy. Creating more "green jobs" was a big plank in Barack Obama's platform in the 2008 presidential campaign. It later became a huge part of his American Recovery and Reinvestment Act as well as the failed American Clean Energy and Security Act of 2009 (better known as Waxman-Markey, after its congressional authors). More recently, liberal Democrats' "Green New Deal" was the most far-reaching attempt to level the playing field for underrepresented and underserved communities.

What the Biden administration did—first with executive orders and later through legislation—was weave equity and environmental justice into the fabric of the clean economy that was first spun with those earlier policies. There's a long way to go, and it remains to be seen how successful these policies will be. But now, at least, equity and environmental justice considerations are embedded in the operations of the federal agencies responsible for implementing these policies, and they're now being implemented through programs touching every part of America.

The Department of Transportation, for instance, is responsible for doling out $7.5 billion from the infrastructure law for community block grants, investments, and loans to build out a national network of car chargers. But EV chargers aren't needed so much in affluent areas where wealthy Tesla drivers can charge up at their houses. They're needed in inner cities where more residents rent than own and in rural areas where EV charging isn't otherwise available. Under the law, at least 40 percent of all Transportation Department grants for vehicle charging stations are directed specifically to disadvantaged, low-income, rural, and tribal communities. Another $1.1 billion is earmarked for grants to state and local governments to buy zero-emission and low-emission buses.

Similarly, the IRA authorized $11.7 billion for the Department of Energy's Loan Programs Office to provide loans and grants for cutting-edge clean energy businesses; for retooling or repurposing existing energy projects like power plants and pipelines, and for helping battery and clean vehicle factories get started. It also authorized the agency to lend as much as $400 billion overall, as long as the money is appropriated by Congress. To qualify for funding through the Loan Programs Office, or for grants through the bipartisan Infrastructure Act, applicants must submit "Community Benefits Plans" detailing how they will work with local communities and stakeholders to advance job quality and access and help bring economic and environmental benefits of new jobs and investments to communities that have often been left behind in previous economic transitions. "That plan is 20 percent of the application," explained former Department of Energy senior advisor Kate Gordon.[12] "For the first time, we are not only asking for it, we're scoring it and it's written into the contracts when we provide the awards."

The Department of Energy is trying to get more federal resources into the hands of more people of color in other ways too. In June 2023, it awarded $1.5 million in funding to six organizations working to help get more people of color into the clean energy industry. Some of the programs funded through the agency's Inclusive Energy Innovation Prize include groups that help Black entrepreneurs in Oregon get their climate-focused businesses up and running; provide clean energy work-force training programs for New Yorkers in disadvantaged communities and, in New Orleans, an effort called "Get Lit, Stay Lit" that hires young people to install solar panels and create microgrids at local restaurants, especially in disadvantaged parts of the city. Inspired by what happened in the aftermath of Hurricane Ida, when residents in disadvantaged areas turned to a handful of locally owned, solar-powered restaurants for food, shelter, cooling, and charging their cell phones, "Get Lit, Stay Lit" wants to equip hundreds of New Orleans restaurants to serve as solar-powered shelters before the next big storm.[13]

Businesses can't apply for loans and grants unless they know about them. With that in mind, the Department of Energy in March 2023 awarded $6.3 million to a unique start-up organization called Black Owners of Solar Services (BOSS) to develop programs in three Southeastern states to better educate minority-owned clean energy businesses about the availability of Department of Energy grants, loans, and other programs.

"Now is the time," said BOSS cofounder Ajulo Othow.[14] "The moment is really now to try and create as wide an opening as possible for people in the industry to come in."

Othow is an example of how hard it is for people of color to break into the clean energy industry. She grew up and still lives on a small farm her family has owned for generations in the rural community of Oxford, North Carolina, north of Raleigh. After graduating with a master's degree from George Washington University and then a law degree from Northeastern University, she went into the nonprofit world to work on rural economic development issues. In 2015, in the middle of North Carolina's solar boom, she switched to the private sector, working at companies that develop utility-scale solar in rural areas. It wasn't the right fit for her, however, and she didn't see a future for herself in the companies where she worked. "I love rural communities," Othow said. "But I felt that the investments (by solar companies) that were being made in many rural communities . . . could've been put to better use. I felt like it was still a very extractive practice. I wanted to figure out a better business model." In 2017, while simultaneously running a small law practice, she also started a solar company. Her EnerWealth Solutions was founded on the idea of developing small solar arrays to supply power to local farming communities and to electric co-ops in rural communities in North Carolina.

And then, three years later and 1,200 miles away, came the murder of George Floyd. Like much of the rest of America, especially Black America, Othow was shocked and shaken. And like Biden and others, she was motivated to do something to try and make a difference.

"When all the racial reckoning after George Floyd's murder happened, right as the (clean energy industry) was growing . . . a few of us got together because we wondered if we were the only ones working in this field," she said. "We felt like the least we could do is create some sort of network, some community, among ourselves." With cofounder Dana Clare Redden, another Black female solar entrepreneur in Atlanta, she started BOSS. Today, the nonprofit has more than fifty business members and a network of 2,500 other supporters nationwide.

Othow and Redden are definitely in the minority in clean energy.

Overwhelmingly, clean energy workers are white men. Women represent less than 30 percent of the clean energy workforce, even though they make up 50 percent of the nation's population. Blacks and African Americans make up just 8 percent of the clean energy workforce, compared with about 13 percent of the nation's total workforce.[15] When it comes to the C-suite or ownership of clean energy companies, the disparities are even greater. In 2019, nearly 90 percent of senior executives of U.S. solar companies were white and 80 percent were male, according to an industry study.[16] And when it comes to getting funding, launching, and owning companies, it's even worse. Of the $216 billion in venture capital allocated across all industries in 2022, only about 1 percent went to Black start-up founders.[17] Women entrepreneurs fared only slightly better, with companies founded solely by women garnering just 2 percent of total venture capital.[18]

Tonya Hicks is about as rare as it gets in business—particularly the clean energy business.

Growing up in Meridian, Mississippi, she excelled in math and aspired to follow in the footsteps of pioneering Black female mathematicians like those who helped NASA launch America's space program in the 1960s, the women who were featured in the movie *Hidden Figures*. She earned a math scholarship to Central State University in Ohio. But then, in her sophomore year, a professor crushed her spirit and changed her life. Black women, he told her, couldn't get jobs as mathematicians in government. Instead, she was told, she should become a schoolteacher. Soon after, Hicks quit college, went back home, and became something entirely different: An electrician. She was the first woman electrician in her hometown, the first Black woman electrician in the state of Mississippi, and in 1994 the first woman to complete the five-year training program to become an International Brotherhood of Electrical Workers "journeyman wireman" in her union local.

"When you're the only one, you don't have anybody to copy," she said.[19] "You're underestimated everywhere you go, even with other women, because nobody's used to seeing anybody who looks like me and does what I do."

In 1998, Hicks moved to Atlanta. At the age of twenty-eight and with a six-year-old son, she started her own electrical contracting business, working mainly on new commercial construction projects that were sprouting up all across fast-growing Atlanta. Then in 2022, excited by the possibility of federal clean energy policies, she shifted to doing residential solar installations and building efficiency work and even started an EV car charger manufacturing and installation company. Hicks called her new residential company SHE, for Smart Home Energy, and her EV charging company SHE-EV.

"I got excited about the IRA and the infrastructure law because they don't have enough electrical contractors to do half of the stuff they're talking about," she said. "There's no choice but to give me some work. And the good thing is, I'm prepared to do it."

In more than twenty-five years in business, there's one thing Hicks was never able to do: Convince investors to give her money to start any of her companies. "I've been turned down several times . . . to the point where there's really no expectation that I would get funding. So I bootstrapped everything the entire way," she said.

Finding funding is a common problem for all entrepreneurs, but particularly for entrepreneurs of color and women. It's one of the reasons there are very few large minority-owned clean energy companies, or clean energy companies located in or focused on communities of color. That creates another problem. It's harder to convince people of color to come to work in clean energy when their communities and their families don't have any experience with things like solar, EVs, or energy efficiency. This is especially notable in jobs in construction, which—between energy-efficiency jobs installing lighting, HVAC systems, insulation, and windows and doors and erecting wind and solar projects—accounts for nearly half of all clean energy jobs in America. Construction workers know they can always get a job building houses or roads or office buildings. They're understandably less sure of the future of jobs in newer sectors of the economy like solar, wind, or energy efficiency. That's another reason why unions are important to provide job security for workers amid a transitioning economy.

Regardless of color, people who come from low- and moderate-income communities are most likely to seek jobs in the most secure businesses they can find, not in small, unproven businesses in industries they know little about.

"Think about it," said Devin Hampton, CEO of Utility API, a data management and software company that helps solar and other clean energy providers manage their demand and usage. "We're trying to bring in more people who statistically come from families with less wealth, who are statistically likely to be the first generation to go to college, and we're saying to them, "Oh, hey, come work for this risky start-up."[20] People with backgrounds like that, he said, naturally seek out the most stable, dependable jobs they can find, in industries that are well-known to them and their families.

Hampton knows this from experience. As a Black man who grew up in Seattle, he could've taken a lot of different career paths. He began in a blue-collar job in what he thought was a stable position at one of the region's biggest employers. For five years, Hampton worked in ramp operations at Alaska Airlines, spending his days throwing baggage on and off of airplanes. After he got laid off in 2005, he took a job tending bar, where one of his regulars announced he was running for city council and asked Hampton to get involved in the campaign. That led to Hampton eventually working on a much bigger campaign—Barack Obama's run for president—which ultimately led to an eight-year career at the Department of Energy and the U.S. Trade and Development Agency. After Obama left office, Hampton joined Oakland, California–based Utility API, a company he learned about while he was at the Department of Energy.

Compelled to do something after the murder of George Floyd, Hampton and a colleague in 2021 launched EDICT (Empowering Diverse Climate Talent) to help more people of color get into the clean energy industry. EDICT, through its affiliation with the nonprofit Clean Energy Leadership Institute and the cleantech investment group Elemental Excelerator, works with nearly one hundred clean energy companies to create and offer paid internships for young people of color seeking careers in clean energy. Diversifying the clean energy workforce, Hampton said, doesn't just create new opportunities for young people of color. It also helps strengthen the industry and the companies in it.

"What we were trying to do was make sure that clean tech doesn't look like regular tech," Hampton said. "It's not just that we're helping (young, diverse) people out, it actually also helps businesses become stronger."

New policies could also help get more clean energy into communities of color, and more funding to people of color trying to start clean energy companies.

As part of the IRA, the EPA is responsible for the $27 billion Greenhouse Gas Reduction Fund, a first-of-its-kind federal program designed to make clean energy accessible in more places and support more clean energy entrepreneurs, with a major emphasis on disadvantaged communities and communities and people of color. The fund is modeled after state and regional "green banks" that leverage limited state money to attract private investors and provide loans to clean energy entrepreneurs who in turn can hire local workers and provide communities with cleaner, healthier energy.[21]

The EPA plans to distribute the funding from three basic buckets.[22]

- $14 billion will go to creating a green bank-style National Clean Investment Fund that will provide grants to several national nonprofit groups to partner with banks and other private capital providers to make loans to businesses and community groups for clean energy projects in low-income and disadvantaged communities.

- $6 billion will go to create a "Clean Communities Investment Accelerator" competition that will fund nonprofit groups in up to seven designated hubs across the country to help households and businesses in low-income and disadvantaged communities get financing for clean energy and energy-efficiency improvements.

- $7 billion will provide up to sixty "Solar for All" grants to states, tribal governments, municipalities, and nonprofits to expand solar in low-income and disadvantaged communities.

Senate Majority Leader Schumer called the Greenhouse Gas Reduction Fund "one of the most transformative" pieces of the legislation.[23] Based on the size and scope of the program, he could be right. At $27 billion, the fund is bigger than some of the biggest venture capital firms in the world, according to tracking firm DealRoom.[24] By comparison, one of Silicon Valley's most venerated VC firms, Sequoia Capital, has about $28 billion under management. Kleiner Perkins, which over fifty years financed generations of tech start-ups, from America Online and Amazon to Netscape and Google, has about $7 billion under management.

Just as importantly, the EPA Greenhouse Reduction Fund money will go to clean energy entrepreneurs, businesses, and programs in communities that would have been hard-pressed to get funding of any kind, much less venture capital funding. These include businesses located all across the country, not just in the nation's technology hubs or university towns or states that are dependent on geological resources, like deposits of coal or gas.

"This is going to completely, completely transform our communities," said EPA Administrator Michael Regan.[25] "People who have been disproportionately impacted, who traditionally have not had a seat at the table, will finally get a chance to compete for billions of dollars."

For Regan, equity and environmental justice is personal. It's something he has tried to infuse throughout the EPA since becoming the first African American man to run the agency beginning in March 2021. Regan was six years old when the environmental justice movement got its unofficial start about an hour and a half away from his hometown of Goldsboro, North Carolina. In 1978, an out-of-state trucking company hired to dispose of toxic oil filled with PCBs from a transformer factory decided to circumvent EPA regulations and cut costs by getting rid of it in another way: By dumping it along 240 miles of North Carolina highways in the middle of the night. Years later, the state finally decided to clean up the toxic waste, but it needed a place to store it. State officials ended up buying property in a place that they thought wouldn't attract attention, a plot of farmland in a predominately Black community in Warren County, near the Virginia border. Residents, led by the NAACP and other groups, had another idea. Beginning in September 1982, as trucks began rolling to the site in the town of Afton, they staged a massive protest that lasted six weeks.[26] Daily, country roads leading to the site were filled with mainly Black protesters who marched and laid down in front of convoys of dump trucks filled with PCB waste to try and stop them. More than five hundred protesters were arrested. They failed to stop the landfill, but they forever raised national awareness about how poor and minority communities are often targeted for environmentally hazardous dumping grounds and projects, sparking the idea of environmental justice that later would ripple across the country. Regan was too young to remember much about the protests, but "I remember my parents discussing the heroism of the women and men who locked arms and laid down brazenly in front of trucks carrying dirt laced with PCBs," he said at a celebration marking the fortieth anniversary of the protests.

It was at the Warren County anniversary celebration, one month after the passage of the IRA, where Regan announced the EPA's new Office of Environmental Justice and External Civil Rights, where a staff of two hundred is responsible for analyzing everything the agency does—from implementing the Greenhouse Gas Reduction Fund to issuing regulations—and ensuring it's done with equity and environmental justice in mind. As Regan likes to say, "EJ is part of the DNA at EPA."[27]

There's a difference between an economic revolution funded by public money and one funded by private and venture-capital money, like the personal technology revolution that made—and divided—Silicon Valley. The people doling out the money this time are not motivated by short-term profits or discovering the next killer social media app. They're motivated by a mission to combat climate change and directed by the president of the United States to do it with equity and environmental justice in mind. It's a dynamic for economic transformation that America hasn't seen at this scale since President Roosevelt's New Deal. As a result, some of the most unlikely places are suddenly becoming key players in America's clean economy revolution.

Take Vidalia, Louisiana.

Located on the easternmost edge of the state, Vidalia is a town whose history was shaped by racism, inequity, climate disasters—and soon, by the clean economy. It's a suburb of Natchez, Mississippi, its bigger city cousin located on the opposite bank of the Mississippi River a scant two miles or so away. The river that splits the two towns can be both a blessing and a curse. In February 1937, the region faced massive flooding after the river crested at a record 58.04 feet. A year later, the entire town of Vidalia was picked up and moved a mile inland to stay dry and make room for new levees. In 2011, the water reached another record high at Vidalia-Natchez, when the Mississippi crested at sixty-one feet amid some of the worst and most damaging flooding ever recorded. Today, the region has the dubious distinction of straddling the border of two of the three worst states for potential climate disasters in America. Mississippi and Louisiana are numbers two and three, respectively, among the worst states for climate-related impacts such as flooding, extreme heat, and weather disasters. Only Florida is higher in the rankings from the insurance industry research group Policygenius.[28]

During the antebellum era, this whole region was at the heart of the cotton country, built on the backs of enslaved persons and connected to the rest of the world by America's second-longest river. Vidalia's Tacony Plantation once owned more than six hundred enslaved people and was one of the biggest cotton producers of its time.[29] Natchez was home to the Deep South's second-busiest slave market between 1830–1863.[30] A century later, it would become a hotbed for the Ku Klux Klan.

Today, descendants of those enslaved persons are among the region's 49,000 residents. About half of the population of the greater Natchez-Vidalia metropolitan area is Black, and about 30 percent live below the poverty level, nearly three times the national average.[31] Hospitals and social service agencies are some of the region's biggest employers, along with McDonald's, Dollar General, and the Magnolia Bluffs Casino.

But that's changing.

Lured to America by the growing market for electric vehicles, Australia-based Syrah Resources announced in February 2022 that it was investing $176 million to expand a small plant it owned in Vidalia that processes graphite material for lithium-ion batteries used to power EVs and store renewable energy. Employment at the plant more than doubled, from about twenty workers to more than fifty. Five months later, employment doubled again, after the Department of Energy issued a $102 million loan to help Syrah expand even more. And then in October 2022, the Vidalia operation won an additional $220 million in federal matching funds from the Department of Energy after Syrah was selected along with nineteen other companies for grants made possible by the bipartisan Infrastructure Act to build and expand the nation's battery-making infrastructure.[32] With the additional $220 million in federal funding—matched by Syrah's contribution of $224 million—the company plans to build what could become America's first graphite active anode material production facility. Using sophisticated machinery, employees will take graphite mined by Syrah and shipped from Mozambique and grind, shape, and polish it so it can be applied to anodes, which when paired with cathodes in a lithium-ion battery cell can store the energy used to power vehicles or keep the lights on. The federal grant will allow the company to create another one hundred local jobs in the greater Natchez area that are expected to pay 20 to 70 percent better than the typical local wage. As part of its Department of Energy–required community benefit plan, the company said it will also partner with more than 150 other local vendors for everything from construction services to supplies. It also is required to meet specific commitments on workforce training, job quality, and benefits to low- and moderate-income communities.

Syrah was one of two energy storage companies working in Louisiana that received money from the first $2.8 billion tranche of infrastructure law funding designated to build a battery industry in America. The other was Koura Global, an offshoot of a Mexico-based company that develops chemicals and other materials used in the production of batteries and other goods. Koura received $100 million in federal matching money to expand an existing factory in St. Gabriel, Louisiana, that is expected to become the first major U.S.-based producer of an essential battery production compound called lithium hexafluorophosphate, which traditionally was supplied entirely by Asian companies.[33]

"These massive investments will have transformational impacts in Vidalia and St. Gabriel and create hundreds of jobs," said Louisiana Governor John Bel Edwards.[34] "This is another step forward in our important work to diversify and grow Louisiana's economy, create good-paying jobs, and become leaders in the global energy transition as we move toward our goal of net-zero carbon emissions by 2050."

Transformational, indeed.

In an area where the biggest employers are hospitals, fast food restaurants, discount stores, and casinos, the changes occurring in the Natchez-Vidalia region would have been unfathomable just a few years ago. Suddenly, the region and its residents are essential players in the biggest evolution in the automotive and renewable energy industries in recent history. That's ironic, considering that Louisiana and Mississippi rank as the two worst states in the country for EV sales and EV charging installations.[35]

Investments that previously would've gone to high-tech hubs are now flowing to the area, including from international companies based in countries known in the past for taking American jobs, not creating them. And in a place that's among the most impacted by climate change in the nation, where a third of the population lives below the poverty level and more than half are Black, clean energy jobs and opportunities that might've once seemed more befitting of Silicon Valley are now being created on the banks of the muddy Mississippi.

It's the sort of transition that's changing the face—and the future—of communities across America.

CHAPTER 9

States

"Right in the Middle of a Huge Revolution"

EVER SINCE THE MIDWEST REFINING COMPANY STRUCK OIL WITH ITS Hogback number one well near the Navajo Nation town of Shiprock in 1922, the fossil fuel industry has been a huge part of New Mexico's economy. The state is the number two producer of oil and gas in America—yes, ahead of Alaska and Louisiana—and behind only neighboring Texas.[1] Royalties from oil and gas leases on public lands contribute more than $2 billion annually to New Mexico's coffers.[2] And in Albuquerque, the state capital, the fossil fuel lobby is a powerful political force that has few rivals. Between 2017–2020, the oil and gas industry made an estimated $11.5 million in donations to industry-friendly politicians in the state.[3]

Yet none of that has kept the most powerful energy industry regulator in New Mexico from pushing her home state away from oil and gas and toward solar, wind, and other types of renewable energy.

As the state's Land Commissioner, Stephanie Garcia Richard is responsible for managing 13 million acres of public lands, including the leases for oil, gas—and now, renewable energy. There's little doubt about Garcia Richard's support of clean energy. Shortly after she was elected as the state's first female and first Latina land commissioner in 2018, the oil pumpjack that for years sat proudly in front of the Land Commission office on Old Santa Fe Trail was removed. At her office, she sometimes hands out the dime-sized blue and red lapel pins she and other commission employees wear that bear the official Land Office seal: A winding river leading down from majestic mountains, and, since she arrived, something new. "We added the wind turbines on them," she said proudly.[4]

It's not all for show. Within months after taking office, Garcia Richard established the state's first Office of Renewable Energy and announced a goal to triple renewable energy production on state lands. Four years later, she met that goal, inking a deal with Pattern Energy Company to build one of the largest wind farms in the Western Hemisphere, the 1,050-megawatt Western Spirit Wind project in central New Mexico. A few months after the Pattern Energy deal, she announced a smaller but perhaps just as noteworthy lease: An agreement with petroleum giant Chevron Corporation to lease 360 acres not for gas or oil, but for a huge 55,000-panel solar farm that will, ironically enough, provide clean energy to power Chevron's dirty oil and gas operations in the Permian Basin.[5] In her first term in office, the number of renewable energy leases approved by Garcia Richard increased more than 200 percent, hitting a record $12 million in 2022. That's just a drop in the bucket compared with the $2 billion from oil and gas leases, but a big and growing drop nonetheless.

For Garcia Richard, saving the planet for future generations is important. But more immediately, the former third grade teacher and mother of two is bullish on renewables mainly because they're helping to pay for kids' education today. In New Mexico, about 95 percent of money raised from public land leases goes to support the state's public education system. Oil and gas leases provide the bulk of that, but—better than many state policymakers—Garcia Richard sees clearly where energy in America is heading. "We all know oil is a finite resource and we can't rely on it forever," she said.[6] "I'm doing everything I can to build a solid foundation so our schools and institutions can thrive long into the future."

While federal climate policies are huge drivers of the clean energy revolution rippling across our economy, so are the actions of states and state officials like Garcia Richard. We all want to leave the world a better place for future generations. But just as important to many state officials is the potential for new lease and property tax revenues; new corporate investments and factories; new job opportunities for residents and sometimes, just good old-fashioned competition between states and their leaders.

The role of states in the clean economy revolution is critical. If America is to meet its goals and its promises to the world to reduce the nation's greenhouse gas emissions by 50 percent by 2030; generate 100 percent of its electricity from clean energy sources by 2035 and shift to 100 percent zero-emission vehicles by 2050, it will be in large part because of climate leadership in the states—leadership that began decades ago, often by unexpected champions.

You might not think of Iowa as a national leader in clean energy unless you happen to live there. But in 1983, Iowa became the first state in the country to enact a renewable portfolio standard requiring utilities to include clean energy in their mix. The standard was signed into law by Governor Terry Branstad, who was the longest-serving Republican governor in the country before President Donald Trump named him ambassador to China in 2017. Today, Iowa gets more than 60 percent of its energy from wind turbines.

It was another Republican governor who signed into law the most important climate policy in the history of America before the Biden administration's federal climate and clean energy laws. In 2006, Governor Arnold Schwarzenegger approved Assembly Bill 32, the California Global Warming Solutions Act, the first program in the country to take a comprehensive approach to addressing climate change.[7] The law paved the way for the nation's first carbon cap and trade program and requires California to reduce its greenhouse gas emissions by 30 percent below 1990 levels by 2020 and 40 percent by percent by 2030. There's little doubt the policies worked—and helped the state's economy along the way. California met its 2020 goals four years early. It attracted hundreds of billions of dollars in investments in solar, wind, and other clean energy projects; helped create more than 500,000 clean energy jobs; and became a global leader in clean energy. It's now on track to exceed its 2030 goals, especially with the addition of other laws after AB 32 that phase out gas and diesel-powered cars and trucks and require utilities to shift to 100 percent clean energy.[8]

The California law did more than just set the state on the path to lead the country in clean energy as if that wasn't enough. It also showed we don't have to rely solely on international treaties or the federal government to build a clean economy, according to Schwarzenegger.[9]

"We proved to the world that sub-national governments are very, very powerful," Schwarzenegger reflected at an event with E2 years later. But only, he added, "if they realize their power, and if they're willing" to use it.[10]

The pioneering policies in Iowa and California blazed a path for other states to follow. Twenty-eight other states and the District of Columbia went on to implement renewable energy standards, and twenty-three now have 100 percent clean energy goals.[11] Meanwhile, California's Global Warming Solutions Act served as a model to show other states, the federal government, and even other countries what they could do if they also used smart climate policy not just to help the environment, but to help the economy.

Unlike giant California or Texas or wide-open Iowa and New Mexico, the Commonwealth of Massachusetts doesn't have a lot of space for big wind and solar farms. Yet when it comes to clean energy—and the economic benefits that come with it—Massachusetts is huge.

While number forty-four among all states in total land acreage, Massachusetts is number seven in the country for the number of jobs in clean energy, with more than 113,000 workers. About 70 percent of those workers don't work in solar or wind or EVs, but in energy efficiency. Because of forward-leading state policies, Massachusetts is number two in the country for energy efficiency (behind only California) according to rankings from the American Council for an Energy-Efficient Economy.[12] The Commonwealth is a longtime leader in requiring utilities to provide energy-efficiency programs and rebates to customers and also has some of the strongest building and appliance standards in the country.[13] In addition to saving consumers and businesses money on their electricity bills, Massachusetts' energy-efficiency policies have helped create a clean economy that over the years added $28 billion to the gross state product and generated $5.3 billion in federal state and local taxes according to the Massachusetts Clean Energy Center, which was created in 2008 with the state's Green Jobs Act legislation signed by then-Governor Deval Patrick, a Democrat.[14]

It was another Massachusetts governor—a Republican—who signed into law an even bigger piece of clean energy and climate legislation that today is helping drive the clean economy revolution in New England. Governor Charlie Baker had already been one of the Republican party's most notable champions of clean energy and climate action when he signed one of the biggest climate and clean energy bills of any state into law in August 2022. The Massachusetts law requires the Commonwealth to develop new offshore wind resources and shift to 100 percent zero-emission new vehicles starting in 2035. It also gives some municipalities the authority to ban gas in buildings. The law is intended to help the state get closer to its goal of net-zero greenhouse gas emissions by 2050. But just as important to Baker was creating economic and job opportunities—fundamental tenets for most Republican politicians. Especially when it comes to offshore wind, "I continue to want us to be a pretty big player in that space because it's a sustainable way to create a lot of jobs, for a very long time," Baker told the *Boston Globe*.[15]

Jobs and economic opportunities aside, nothing pushed states into action more than the Trump administration's abdication of any responsibility for addressing climate change or helping America compete in the global market for clean energy. During his four years in office, President Trump rescinded or rolled back more than one hundred bedrock environmental laws and executive orders by previous administrations. And then on June 1, 2017, Trump announced he was pulling the country out of the Paris Climate Agreement, leaving America in the company of Iran, Libya, Syria, and Yemen as the only countries that didn't ratify the landmark agreement to hold temperatures well below two degrees Celsius.[16] President Biden rejoined the agreement immediately after taking office. But before that happened, the shock of America ceding its global responsibility and its previous promises and turning a blind eye to the international clean energy market reverberated around the globe and across America.

The same day Trump formally pulled out of the Paris Agreement, California Governor Jerry Brown, Washington Governor Jay Inslee, and

New York Governor Andrew Cuomo announced the formation of a coalition of states committed to upholding the promises the country made in the Paris Agreement and denouncing Trump's action. "I don't believe fighting reality is a good strategy—not for America, not for anybody," said California Governor Brown. "If the president is going to be AWOL in this profoundly important human endeavor, then California and other states will step up."[17] Together, the three states represented one-fifth of the entire U.S. GDP and were home to nearly one in five Americans. But California, New York, and Washington were just the start. Within weeks, twenty-three states, along with Puerto Rico and Guam, joined the U.S. Climate Alliance, representing 58 percent of the U.S. economy and 41 percent of the nation's greenhouse gas emissions.[18] While Democratic governors led most of the states, two Republicans—Massachusetts' Baker and Vermont Governor Phil Scott—also signed on.

From coast to coast, the Climate Alliance states have proven that reducing greenhouse gas emissions and tackling climate change by investing in clean energy pays off, according to Inslee.

"If you compare the economic and environmental performance of those 23 states . . . we together have reduced our emissions per GDP by 14 percent more than the non-climate alliance states," Inslee said at a climate leadership conference in 2023, where he was honored for forming the alliance and his overall climate leadership.[19] "And as a result, our GDP growth was 16 percent higher than those not in the climate alliance."

Like Republican Schwarzenegger, Democrat Inslee, who ran for president in 2020 on the most far-reaching climate platform of any candidate in history, sees state government action as key to the clean energy revolution. "We appreciate what President Biden has done to pull the rabbit out of the hat with the Inflation Reduction Act . . . and Congress has stepped up to the plate," he said. "But the fact is that states need to go farther and faster, and they can go farther and faster." Inslee pointed to his state's decision to enact building codes requiring all new homes and apartments in Washington state to come with electric-powered heat pumps as one example of how states can move quicker than the federal government. State laws prohibiting the sale of fossil-fuel-powered automobiles within their borders, he said, are another.

Especially under Inslee's leadership, Washington exemplifies how one state is leveraging its traditional economic strengths as well as its unique natural attributes to solidify its place in the clean economy revolution. Renowned for its cloudy days and drizzle, Washington state probably isn't going to be a powerhouse for solar energy anytime soon. But its relatively mild winters and summers make the state a perfect place to pioneer heat pump requirements. Similarly, Washington's status as a leader in the aviation industry—Boeing, Honeywell Aerospace, Alaska Airlines, and other major aviation companies all have headquarters or major operations in the state—making it a perfect place to lead another clean economy transition that's beginning to soar: The nascent business of clean aviation fuels.

On September 27, 2022, in the central Washington town of Moses Lake, a typical-looking white commuter plane took off from Grant County International Airport, rose to 3,500 feet, banked high, circled the airport, and landed flawlessly after about eight minutes in the air. The flight would have been inconsequential except for one fact: It was the first battery-operated airplane in the world to take flight.[20] Built by Arlington, Washington-based Eviation, the nine-passenger plane affectionately named Alice (after *Alice in Wonderland*) was powered by more than 21,500 batteries that collectively accounted for about half of the airplane's total weight. Eviation's Wright Brothers moment in Moses Lake was short, but its plans are big. The company claims when its planes hit the commercial market in 2027, they will have a range of up to 250 nautical miles. That would be enough juice to make it from New York to Boston or Washington, or from Los Angeles to Las Vegas. Even before its maiden flight, Eviation had a waiting list of customers. Commuter airlines Cape Air and Global Crossing Airlines placed orders for about 125 Alice airplanes, while cargo company DHL Express ordered twelve planes, according to Eviation.

If electric airplanes don't take off commercially, maybe hydrogen-powered planes will. Six months after Eviation launched Alice into the skies over central Washington, the first-ever hybrid hydrogen fuel cell-powered airplane took off from the same Moses Lake runway. California-based Universal Hydrogen's plane, nicknamed "Lightning McClean" was a little bigger and went a little farther than Alice, demonstrating the viability and versatility of hydrogen for more energy-intensive demands such as powering airplanes and rockets. Universal Hydrogen's modified Dash-8 turboprop airplane flew for about fifteen minutes, taking off with traditional fossil fuel before switching over to hydrogen to power the electric engines designed by Everett, Washington-based magniX, the same company that built the all-electric engine used by Eviation's battery-powered Alice. Two pilots and an engineer were the only people on board Universal Hydrogen's plane, but the company plans to someday carry as many as forty passengers as far as six hundred miles round-trip on its hydrogen-powered turboprops.[21]

It's not just electricity and hydrogen powering the airplanes of the future. Thanks to federal and state policies, cleaner versions of more traditional aviation fuel blended with biofuel, hydrogen, or other zero-carbon additives are now hitting the market too. Under the IRA, airlines and fuel producers can get a $1.25 tax credit for every gallon of sustainable aviation fuel (SAF) they use, whether they blend it into traditional feedstocks or use it directly.[22] The legislation also sets aside grants for companies to develop SAF technologies and refineries. U.S. senator Maria Cantwell of Washington, a longtime champion of SAF, said commercial carriers like Seattle-based Alaska Airlines are eager to use cleaner fuels—they just can't buy enough of it. "Alaska Airlines is all in," she said. "They have said to me over and over again, 'I will buy any amount of SAF you can make.'"[23] Indeed, Alaska Airlines is leading the SAF transition. In 2022, it announced an agreement to buy 185 million gallons of sustainable aviation fuel from Gevo Inc. as part of the airline's goal to completely phase out fossil fuels and become carbon net zero by 2040.[24]

Realizing the potential of SAF to Washington state—especially when coupled with federal tax credits—Governor Inslee on May 3, 2023, signed legislation into law that will provide state tax credits of up to $2 per gallon for producers or users of sustainable aviation fuels. Two weeks later, Dutch-based Sky NRG, a longtime partner of Boeing, announced plans for a $600 million plant in Washington that will produce as much as thirty million gallons of SAF annually beginning as early as 2028. The project is expected to create about six hundred construction jobs and about one hundred full-time jobs after the plant opens. SkyNRG CEO Philippe Lacamp told the *Seattle Times* that it was the new state legislation that convinced the company to build its first U.S. plant in Washington. It "positions Washington state as the most attractive, most supportive state for SAF," Lacamp said.[25]

When it comes to state incentives, few places stand out more than South Carolina. A package that the state's Republican governor created for one company in the 1990s—back when few people were talking about clean energy and electric vehicles seemed far off in the future—is now putting the Palmetto State at the forefront of the clean energy revolution and serving as a reminder of what America's investments could bring in the future.

In the early 1990s, South Carolina's economy was struggling. The textile industry that had been the foundation of much of its economy was leaving for China and other countries. Attempts to build a banking business that could compete with the financial hubs being built in Charlotte, North Carolina, and Atlanta, Georgia, floundered after South Carolina firms were bought up by competitors from neighboring states and the savings and loan crisis put others into bankruptcy. South Carolina Governor Carroll Campbell, a rising Republican star entering his second term, was looking for new ways to keep his state growing and reduce unemployment, which hovered near 8 percent.

He found the solution in Germany. In 1992, BMW Group was looking to build its first factory in America, initially settling on Nebraska over South Carolina for the auto plant. But Governor Campbell and his economic development chief Wayne Sterling, both of whom saw economic development among the states as bloodsport competition, weren't giving up. Wooing foreign manufacturers wasn't something foreign to them or to South Carolina. While the textile industry initially got the state on the radar of international companies, in 1975 South Carolina scored a major corporate coup when French tire maker Michelin picked Greenville for its U.S. headquarters, bringing an army of foreign suppliers along behind it. As with Michelin, Campbell knew that luring BMW to

South Carolina would mean more than landing a new factory. It would also mean landing a new industry with a long future ahead of it.

In the spring of 1992, Campbell flew to BMW's headquarters in Munich with hopes they could get Chairman Eberhard von Kuenheim to officially commit to South Carolina—only to leave downtrodden and rebuffed after Kuenheim told them he had selected Nebraska instead. Campbell pleaded with the BMW chief to hold off on announcing his decision for just a couple more weeks, while South Carolina put together a better incentive package. It would be worth his while, Campbell told him. And it was. The $131 million incentive package South Carolina ultimately offered BMW included $51 million worth of land that the state had purchased and assembled near Greenville—Spartanburg Airport; $15 million in income tax credits and $5 million in job training programs.[26]

That summer, BMW announced it had picked South Carolina over Nebraska for its $300 million factory, creating 1,700 jobs. Over the next twenty-five years, BMW invested more than $4 billion into expansions in South Carolina, creating more than 11,000 direct jobs and an estimated 43.000 indirect jobs at hundreds of BMW suppliers located throughout South Carolina and pumping nearly $27 billion annually into the state's economy.[27] Landing BMW was the biggest economic success story in South Carolina history—and now, the key to the state's continued success in the latest American economic revolution.

Two months after the IRA became law, BMW announced a $1 billion investment to retrofit and expand its South Carolina factory to make six fully electric BMW models. It also announced another $700 million to build a battery assembly factory.[28] Less than six months after that, another German automaker, Volkswagen, announced plans for its $2 billion, four-thousand-employee factory in Blythewood, South Carolina, where it will make electric Scout SUVs and trucks.

Just as suppliers followed Michelin and later BMW to South Carolina, new suppliers are now following the new EV operations to South Carolina, providing a clear illustration of the secondary impacts rippling across the new clean energy economy. In December 2022, Japanese battery company Envision ACSC announced plans to build a $810 million,

1,200-employee factory in Florence, South Carolina.[29] Another BMW supplier, Bosh, announced a $260 million investment to retrofit its diesel components factory in Charleston to make electric motors, creating another 350 new jobs there. Redwood Materials announced another $3.5 billion, 1,500-employee battery plant in Ridgeville. Battery recycling company Cirba Solutions announced a $300 million, three-hundred-employee plant in Columbia. Albemarle Corporation announced its $1.3 billion, three-hundred-employee lithium processing plant in Chester County.[30]

The list goes on and on.

In all, more than a dozen EV and battery-related companies announced $11 billion in investments and more than nine thousand jobs in South Carolina in just the first nine months after the IRA became law. The state has become such a hub for EVs and batteries, and the industry is expected to be such a big part of the state's economy, that Republican Governor Henry McMaster in 2022 signed an executive order directing state agencies to work together to coordinate with all the EV-related companies moving into South Carolina, improve the state's EV infrastructure—and recruit more EV companies. "The only way South Carolina has been able to maintain its status as an automotive industry leader for nearly three decades is by strategically adapting as the industry innovates," McMaster said in announcing the order.[31] "As the industry continues to move towards electric vehicles, South Carolina will move along with it."

To see how far South Carolina has already come, and to get a glimpse into where the auto industry is headed, drive a few miles outside of downtown Greenville to the Clemson University International Center for Automotive Research, also known as CU-ICAR. There, on a small campus that looks more like a sleek European industrial park than part of a southern college, researchers are designing new batteries, electrical systems, and just about everything else that might go into a vehicle. On any given day, students and corporate researchers might be guiding experimental vehicles between buildings, or gauging how drivers might react to new designs at a test center where a ring of cameras capture "drivers'" moves while they're seated in bucket seats with dashboard-like computer screens in front of them. BMW's Information Technology Research Center is located at the campus, appropriately right across from the Carroll A. Campbell Jr. Graduate Engineering Center and across from a garage that features a life-size Michelin Man statue where drivers can check their tire pressure and get some air if they need it. Soteria Battery Innovation Group, a consortium of battery company researchers, is located at CU-ICAR, and foreign auto component companies like carbon fiber maker Toho Tenax and ball bearing manufacturer Koyo JTEKT do research there.

Also located at CU-ICAR are the offices of the Upstate South Carolina Alliance, which oversees economic development efforts for the ten counties in the northwesternmost part of the state. There, Alliance president and CEO John Lummus explained how the region—and his job—is changing. "Before we used to talk just about costs—cheaper land, lower wages, that sort of thing," he said. "That's not the only thing anymore. People want to be here now."[32]

Today, more than 575 international companies have operations in Upstate South Carolina, many of them lured to the region after learning about it through BMW, which Lummus says is still his best sales tool when pitching the region to foreign companies.

Other states have adopted the economic development model South Carolina pioneered with BMW to try and get their slice of the clean economy pie. In 2021, Georgia officials cobbled together 2,900 acres west of Savannah with an eye on luring a major manufacturer of some sort to the state that could help rejuvenate the region's economy and create new jobs for an area where unemployment was above the state and national average.

"At the time we were taking a big risk," recalled Hugh "Trip" Tollison, president and CEO of the Savannah Economic Development Authority.[33] "When we bought the property in July 2021, we had no activity on it. We didn't have a prospect. But we did know the site was an incredible site. We knew we had something special to market."

Tollison knew it could take years to land a tenant, but his agency and the governor's office gambled that the wait would be worth it. They didn't have to wait as long as they expected. Just five months later, on Christmas

Eve 2021, Tollison got a phone call from a real estate consulting firm. They had a big fish on the line, a huge client looking for a huge site, and needing to move quickly. If Savannah and the state of Georgia wanted to get in the game, Tollison was told, his agency had to submit a proposal by January 6. Working nights and weekends over the holidays, they met the tight deadline, and soon after, a group of South Korean executives touched down in Georgia to visit Savannah. They were from Hyundai Motor Company.

Four months later, on May 20, 2022, Hyundai announced it had selected the Savannah site from a short list of four locations for its first U.S. electric vehicle factory. Impressed with the site's high location, natural drainage, and proximity to both a major interstate and world-class port and enticed by a $1.8 billion state incentive package that Tollison and the governor's office put together that included tax breaks, free land, and other benefits, the company said it would invest $5.5 billion to build the biggest manufacturing operation in Georgia's history. Hyundai's new complex is expected to include eleven buildings totaling seventeen million square feet that each year would produce as many as a half-million EVs as well as the batteries to power them. The project would create more than 8,100 jobs, Hyundai and state officials announced, and would also attract a wide range of Hyundai suppliers that would bring even more investments and thousands more jobs to the region.

They were right. As was the case with BMW in South Carolina, the return on Georgia's investment to land Hyundai is paying off. In just the first year since Hyundai announced it was coming to Savannah, suppliers broke ground on dozens of projects in the region, announcing more than $2 billion in investments and another five thousand jobs—nearly double what Georgia officials had estimated.[34] Even before it could complete its first factory, Hyundai and partner LG Energy Solutions in May 2023 announced a second battery plant in Georgia, a $4.3 billion project that will bring yet another 4,300 jobs to the state.[35]

Hyundai is one of several EV companies driving Georgia to the front of the clean economy revolution. Cutting-edge truck and SUV maker Rivian is planning a 7,500-employee plant east of Atlanta, thanks in part to another $1.5 billion in incentives offered by the state.[36] Kia, which since 2009 has built its Sorento and Optima models at a factory in West Point, Georgia, announced in 2023 that it will also begin to build its newest electric SUVs there.[37]

"What's crazy is that all of this is happening all at once," Tollison said. "Georgia is definitely right in the middle of a huge revolution."

Some states use land, tax credits, and other incentives to attract and support the companies and jobs that are driving the clean economy revolution. Others are using legislation and leveraging federal investments to attract new clean economy companies to their states.

In February 2023, Minnesota Democratic Governor Tim Walz signed into law legislation making his state the latest to shift to 100 percent clean electricity by requiring utilities that serve the state to use only carbon-free energy sources by 2040. Republican opponents were quick to attack the legislation, saying it would kill jobs and cause blackouts. But while big utilities may have been inclined to agree with them in the past, that's not what the state's biggest utility had to say in 2023. "This legislation will provide opportunities to innovate, create jobs, incorporate new technologies into the grid," Xcel Energy Minnesota president Chris Clark said in a statement.[38]

Three months after passing the 100 percent clean energy bill, the legislature passed an even more sweeping $2 billion climate and clean energy bill that includes rebates for Minnesotans who purchase electric vehicles or heat pumps and invests millions into grants to help schools and other public agencies to switch to solar power, which will save them money in the future.[39] The legislation also imposed some of the most far-reaching bans on PFAS chemicals in the country. In the Land of 10,000 Lakes, keeping PFAS and other chemicals out of water is hugely important. But so are creating jobs and driving economic investments, which is one of the biggest reasons why the state legislature was able to pass the 100 percent clean energy legislation, according to the sponsor of the bill, Minnesota House Majority Leader Jamie Long. "We don't have any fossil fuel production in Minnesota," Long told the nonprofit advocacy group Evergreen Action.[40] "We import $13 billion a year in fossil fuels to the state and those jobs are created somewhere else. I certainly can appreciate those states wanting to fight for those jobs, but it's my job to fight for Minnesota jobs and if we are installing wind and solar right here in the state . . . that will mean creating excellent jobs here in Minnesota." About 60,000 Minnesotans work in clean energy, according to E2, but that number is expected to grow substantially with the new state and federal clean energy policies.

If Minnesota is known for its lakes, New York is known for its buildings. In 2023, the New York Legislature passed the first statewide ban on fossil fuels in new buildings, which promises to drive a huge boost in business for electric heat pumps, stoves, water heaters, and other all-electric appliances. Under the All Electric Buildings Act, new buildings under seven stories won't be allowed to include gas hook-ups beginning in 2026.[41] By 2029, the all-electric standard will begin to apply to larger buildings. Since buildings are responsible for more than a quarter of the nation's greenhouse gas emissions, the legislation will make a significant dent in the state's greenhouse gas emissions. It will also save New Yorkers money. By shifting from oil and gas to cheaper electricity increasingly coming from cleaner renewable resources, New Yorkers could save $900 per year on their electricity bills, according to some estimates.[42] Switching to electricity also could create thousands of jobs for electricians, HVAC installers, and other workers. A 2022 report by E2 found that more than 120,000 New Yorkers worked in building electrification and decarbonation occupations, but with statewide building electrification policies, that number could nearly quadruple, to more than 400,000, by 2050.[43]

Leading the charge in New York, quite literally, is New York City. In 2021, then-mayor Bill de Blasio signed legislation phasing out fossil fuels and requiring all new buildings of any size to be fully electric by 2027 (commercial kitchens and a few other businesses are exempted).[44] A year later, the nation's biggest city launched a $4 billion program called "Leading the Charge," which will retrofit one hundred existing schools by removing oil, gas, or coal boilers and replacing them with all-electric HVAC systems and replacing inefficient lighting systems in eight hundred schools with high-efficiency LED lighting. The city also pledged that all schools built in the future will be all-electric, without fossil fuel boilers or power plants. New York City's schools program—the biggest of its kind in the nation—includes $14 million to train and hire workers.[45]

"Our city will never again build a new school that burns fossil fuel. Never again," said New York City Mayor Eric Adams.[46] In addition to reducing energy costs and making buildings and the air healthier for students and communities, "this whole concept of leading the charge will boost our economy and expand the green workforce," Adams said.

Of course no state has led the country on climate and clean energy legislation more than California. Long before Schwarzenegger signed the Global Warming Solutions Act into law, the state was setting the bar for the rest of the nation. In 1974, California became the first state to implement statewide energy-efficiency standards that have remarkably kept the state's overall energy consumption flat for a half-century even though its population has grown by more than 85 percent during that time.[47] Those laws have saved consumers and businesses billions of dollars and created a market for more than 53,000 businesses involved in energy efficiency, employing nearly 300,000 Californians.[48] It also served as a model for energy-efficiency policies in other states and ultimately at the federal level. In 1977, California developed the nation's first appliance energy standards for everything from air conditioners and dishwashers to refrigerators. That policy would become a blueprint for other states and the EPA's Energy Star program beginning in 1992.[49]

More recently, California has led the country on what has become the biggest source of greenhouse gases and the biggest growth area in the new clean economy: Transportation.

In 2002, California passed the first-ever greenhouse gas tailpipe emissions standard in the world, changing the auto industry forever. Under the California Clean Cars Rule—also known as the Pavley Bill after California Assemblymember Fran Pavley—automakers that wanted to sell new cars and trucks in California had to meet air-quality standards stricter than the rest of the country. In the years that followed, sixteen other states and the District of Columbia, representing more than a third of the nation's vehicle sales, also adopted the California rules. The law was ultimately used as a model for federal standards passed by the Obama administration. It's a fundamental reason why vehicles in America continue to get cleaner and more efficient, and it's also what jump-started the growth of hybrid vehicles and, later, EVs.

That groundbreaking policy also is the chassis on which California continues to build when it comes to clean vehicle laws. Twenty years after passing its landmark clean cars standard, California in 2022 adopted—and other states once again followed—the Advanced Clean Cars II standard that requires all new passenger vehicles sold in California to be zero-emission vehicles by 2035. The state later expanded its vehicle standards to require sellers of medium and heavy-duty trucks to sell an increasing percentage of zero-emission big rigs beginning in 2024, and for manufacturers to stop selling fossil fuel-powered trucks in the state by 2045.

The clean vehicle policies pioneered by California and adopted by states across the country helped lead every car manufacturer in the world to begin offering more EVs. Big rig makers ranging from Tesla to Peterbilt are rolling out electric heavy-duty trucks. In July 2023, the state and nearly every major truck maker reached an agreement to advance production of zero-emission vehicles. Next on California's clean transportation to-do list: Trains. In April 2023, the state passed the nation's first-ever emissions rules aimed at reducing pollution from diesel locomotives. Like with cars, train makers are now reacting. One month after the new rules were approved, train maker Pacific Harbor Line rolled out a new all-electric locomotive as part of a test between the ports of Long Beach and Los Angeles.[50] GM and Pittsburgh-based Wabtec Corporation also are testing both battery-powered and hydrogen-powered locomotives elsewhere in California.[51] And in August 2023, the Caltrain regional rail service in the Bay Area announced it was piloting the nation's first, bi-level, battery-powered electric commuter train.

Even though the federal EPA is also ratcheting up vehicle emissions standards nationally, California's leadership is illustrative of how states continue to be in the driver's seat when it comes to innovation and speed in policy implementation.

"We are sending the market signals so . . . manufacturers move forward as quickly as possible to bring these vehicles to market and get them deployed," said Liane Randolph, chair of the California Air Resources

Board. "This is such an incredible time for climate action both at the federal level and in the states."[52]

Unfortunately, this is also a time of incredibly partisan politics. And if there's anything that can stop the growth of the clean economy now, it's partisan politics. Beginning, illogically enough, in the state now benefiting the most from clean energy.

CHAPTER 10

Division (and Hope) on the Front Lines

"It's Not Either the Economy or the Environment"

THE FEDERAL GOVERNMENT DECLARED WAR ON TEXAS.

At least that's what the Republican Party of Texas claimed.

By supporting EVs and renewable energy "our Federal government has declared a war on fossil fuels, which is a war on the citizens and the economy of Texas," the state's GOP proclaimed in an official resolution on March 17, 2023.[1]

To counter Washington's "war" on Texas, the state's biggest and most powerful political party demanded that Governor Greg Abbott, Lieutenant Governor Dan Patrick, and legislators eliminate subsidies and rebates for clean energy and EVs, while simultaneously creating new tax breaks for purchasers of gas-powered stoves and other appliances. It insisted that lawmakers require wind, solar, and EV companies in Texas to turn over the federal incentives they received to pay for improvements to the power grid. It called on state lawmakers to somehow force the federal government to provide more subsidies to fossil fuel companies (on top of the myriad federal subsidies the fossil fuel industry already receives), require wind turbine manufacturers to implement systems to prevent collisions with birds, and force wind, solar and EV manufacturers to either recycle all their used components by 2030 or dispose of them someplace.

The fact that the leading political party in Texas would issue such a vitriolic call-to-arms—and equate the federal government's clean energy policies to a declaration of war was in some ways baffling. Texas is the biggest producer of clean energy in the country (number one in wind energy; a close number two in solar), home to country's biggest EV maker (Austin-based Tesla), and one of the hottest markets for battery storage. The fact that the governor, lieutenant governor, and state legislature would later follow the GOP resolution like a playbook for policy is a sign of just how vulnerable the shift to a cleaner economy is in America in an age when partisan politics and cultural ideologies can trump common sense and the common good.

But that's exactly what happened in Texas.

At the direction of their party, Republicans in the 2023 Texas legislature introduced more than a dozen bills aimed at stopping or slowing the growth of clean energy.[2] Stoking the flames at the statehouse were GOP Governor Abbott and Lieutenant Governor Patrick, who inaccurately and misleadingly claimed that renewable energy had to be curtailed because it somehow helped cause the grid to nearly collapse during Winter Storm Uri, even though numerous investigations clearly showed that the grid failure was mainly attributable to fossil fuel plants and pipelines that froze up from the unprecedented cold.[3]

One of the bills introduced by Texas Republicans in 2023, using language almost straight from the GOP resolution, would have required renewable energy companies to pay fees to access the Texas power grid, and also require them to buy reserve power, presumably from fossil fuel companies. Another bill would have forced wind and solar companies to pay new fees that would be used to subsidize fossil fuel plants. Yet another bill would have all but prohibited offshore wind energy development in the Gulf of Mexico by creating a new system of arduous permits and requiring wind developers to pay for and produce reports on how the state's oil industry might be impacted by their businesses.[4]

And then there was Texas Senate Bill 624. Among other things, that legislation would've allowed any landowner within twenty-five miles of a renewable energy project to file a formal complaint to stop it. It would've levied expensive new fees on solar and wind companies that would be held as deposits to dismantle renewable projects decades in the future. It would've created new setbacks outlining how close renewable projects could come to property lines and required myriad new permits for renewable projects. The new legislation would have done more than just stifle new renewable energy projects. It also would've penalized previous renewable projects as well, retroactively applying fees and requiring permits for wind and solar projects even if they had been operating for years. Tellingly, fossil fuel companies in Texas aren't subject to any state-mandated property setbacks and wouldn't have had to pay the same types of fees or deposits that renewable energy companies were suddenly facing.

Bill author Senator Lois Kolkhorst, a sixth-generation Texan who was first elected to the legislature in 2001, characterized her legislation as "an attempt to open a conversation," about the future of renewables in Texas, especially with billions of federal funding and tax credits for clean energy headed toward the state from the Biden administration's programs. She framed it as a bill to protect lands, water, and wildlife, and to make sure "our beloved Texas is not harmed in any way."[5]

The bill was so far-reaching and foreign to the way the GOP traditionally embraces business, landowner rights, and incentives for the energy industry that even some Republicans couldn't believe it. Among them was John Davis, whose family since the 1880s has owned the Pecan Spring Ranch in west Texas, where they've raised cattle, sheep, produce, and now, wind turbines. The latest crop at Pecan Spring includes seven wind turbines operated by a company that provides regular land lease payments to the family, helping pay the bills and ensure the future of the farm.[6] Now a self-proclaimed "energy rancher," Davis also happens to be a Republican who previously served as a state representative and worked side-by-side with Kolkhorst in the past. At a Senate hearing in 2023, Davis told Kolkhorst and his other fellow Republicans that her legislation flew in the face of the party's traditional values. "It doesn't make sense," he said, "unless of course it is to punish renewables."[7]

The raft of anti-renewable legislation proposed in Texas in 2023 would have punished more than just the renewable industry. It also would have punished landowners like Davis who make money off of wind leases; local school boards and governments that get tax revenues from projects; and small businesses that thrive when construction workers come to town and need hotel rooms, food, and supplies. According to the trade group American Clean Power, the Texas legislation would have put $50 billion in planned wind, solar, and battery investments at risk. During public hearings, companies including wind energy developer Örsted and renewable project developers Invenergy and Cypress Creek Renewables warned that the legislation could force them to reconsider their plans in the state. Others predicted that the signal being sent by the legislature could put a damper on corporate relocations generally, since most major companies now want cheaper and cleaner energy to power their operations. "Corporate customers are here because of lower power prices," from renewable energy, Jeff Clark, president of the Austin-based Advanced Power Alliance told state lawmakers.[8] This "puts every corporate contract at risk."

Fortunately, most of the proposals aimed at stopping clean energy growth in Texas, including Kolkhorst's legislation, failed. Dozens of environmental and business groups, including chambers of commerce, manufacturers, and even some oil, gas, and utility companies, helped convince lawmakers that their ill-conceived legislation would kill the Texas wind industry—and all the jobs and lease and tax revenues that came with it—just as the industry was hitting its stride. But as longtime Texas energy expert Doug Lewin pointed out, Texas Republicans' attacks on clean energy were unprecedented, unfounded, and unfortunately, not over. Anti-renewable energy politicians and their supporters, Lewin wrote on social media after the 2023 legislative session came to a close, "remain on a right-wing crusade against renewables, consumers, and, apparently, free-market capitalism itself."[9]

"Right-wingers against markets," Lewin added. "Strange days."

Strange days made even stranger when you consider how the renewable energy industry in Texas got started: By Republicans, including the one-time leader of the national Republican party.

On June 18, 1999, then–Governor George W. Bush signed into law Senate Bill 7. The sweeping energy legislation would've gotten much more attention if it wasn't overshadowed by some other news Bush made just four days earlier when he announced he was running for president. The legislation was best known for deregulating the state's electricity market. It struck down traditional utilities' monopoly over the state's electricity market and opened it up to companies like Enron, the notorious Houston-based energy trading company founded by Bush's longtime friend and campaign contributor Ken Lay. Enron barely benefited from the Texas law it helped create: Two years after it was passed, the company went bankrupt and Lay was found guilty of securities fraud in one of the biggest accounting scandals in history. Twenty years later, the market dynamics created by SB 7 were faulted for helping cause the near-collapse of the state's power grid during 2021's Winter Storm Uri.[10] And the main selling point for legislation, lower energy prices, proved to be wrong too, after consumer power bills ultimately went up, not down, amid soaring natural gas prices.[11]

But SB 7 also contained a less-noticed but much more successful provision. Under the law, power producers in Texas for the first time were required to include renewable energy in their generation plans. Specifically, the legislation required power producers to generate at least 2,880 megawatts of new renewable energy within a decade, enough to power about 1.6 million Texas homes. The state would easily exceed that goal in 2006, three years early.[12]

Texas would go on to become the number one producer of wind energy in the country, generating about a quarter of all wind energy in the United States. By 2023, it was also on its way to passing California as the nation's number one producer of solar energy.[13] The state's wind and solar farms generated more than 57,000 megawatts of energy in 2023—about twenty times the amount of renewable energy required under the legislation signed into law by Gov. George Bush.[14]

The legislation was also significant in another way. It was drafted by lawmakers from both sides of the political aisle—Republicans and Democrats working together on clean energy policy, something that in today's partisan world is rare. Republican state Senator David Sibley, a conservative, free-market proponent who had a career as a dentist before joining the state legislature, reportedly sketched out the initial legislation on an airplane cocktail napkin after a fact-finding visit to California. Alongside Sibley was state Representative Steve Wolens, a Dallas Democrat that *Texas Monthly* magazine once described as an "Intellectual Gladiator," for leveraging his knowledge and his penchant for detail to push through tough legislation during his twenty-four years in the state-house.[15] Together, Republican Sibley and Democrat Wolens and their staffs worked side by side for weeks in the basement of the state capitol in Austin to develop the language that would become SB 7.

Former Governor Bush joked about his role in the legislation years later. "I remember when I signed the bill, I said, 'there's a new day coming for wind,'" he recalled years later at a renewable energy conference.[16] "And they said, well, you're leaving the state, and a lot of hot air is going with it." Wisecracks aside, the former Texas oilman-turned-president heralded the Texas experience as evidence of what was possible. "Texas produces more wind energy than any other state in the union," Bush told attend-ees of the International Renewable Energy Conference in 2008. "If an oil state can produce wind energy, other states in America can produce wind energy."

Since Bush signed the 1999 Texas law, the boom in renewables has been profoundly profitable for the state and its residents. According to American Clean Power, renewable companies have invested nearly $100 billion in Texas, more than in any state in the country. Wind and solar companies pay about $350 million in annual lease agreements to Texas ranchers, farmers, and other landowners and another $340 mil-lion a year in state and local taxes that pay teachers, schools, police departments, and other local services.[17] In 2022 alone, more than nine gigawatts of wind, solar, and storage were developed in Texas, double the amount developed that year in the next closest state, California. All that investment has translated into jobs. Every day, more than 250,000 Tex-ans—a quarter million workers—pull on their boots and go to work in clean energy jobs. Only California has more clean energy jobs than Texas.[18] And while deregulation did little to reduce consumer prices, the fact that wind and solar are cheaper than gas, coal, or any other source of energy saved Texans approximately $32 billion since 2010, according to one study.[19]

What changed in the twenty-four years between when Texas Repub-lican Governor George Bush signed landmark legislation to expand renewable energy and Texas Republican Governor Greg Abbott and his legislative supporters tried to kill renewable energy has to do with money, politics, and cultural ideology.

When Texas passed its renewable energy mandate in 1999, solar and wind hardly existed in the state. Today, clean energy generates more than 26 percent of the state's electricity. That has the oil and gas industry worried. Ahead of the March 2022 state elections, the oil and gas industry contributed more than $19 million—about 90 percent of all its political giving in state elections nationwide—to Republicans in the Lone Star State, according to the watchdog group Open Secrets.[20] Of the top ten state officeholders nationally supported by the oil and gas industry in that election cycle, all were Republicans, and all but two were in Texas.

But divisions on the front lines of the clean economy revolution aren't limited to Texas. As *New York Times* columnist and Nobel Prize–winning economist Paul Krugman put it, the way Texas turned against clean energy was a sign that "renewable energy has become a victim of the anti-woke mind virus."[21]

It's a virus that is spreading to other states.

In Wyoming, Republican lawmakers in 2023 filed a resolution to prohibit sales of EVs, saying EVs "will have deleterious impacts on Wyoming's communities and will be detrimental to Wyoming's economy and the ability for the country to efficiently engage in commerce."[22] Prohibiting EVs in the nation's eighth-biggest state for oil, "will ensure the stability of Wyoming's oil and gas industry and will help preserve the country's critical minerals for vital purposes," according to the legislation. The bill died in committee a month after it was filed. Wyoming state Senator Jim Anderson, who sponsored the legislation, later told the *Washington Post* that he didn't really want to phase out EVs; he just wanted to make a point that if states like California could ban gas-powered vehicles, states like his could ban electric-powered vehicles.[23]

In Ohio, it's not electric cars, but solar and wind projects that can be banned. In 2021, the GOP-led legislature passed a law allowing local governments to proactively ban utility-scale solar and wind developments within their borders, even though no such laws exist for fossil fuel projects. At least ten Ohio counties later passed resolutions blocking wind and solar projects, keeping residents dependent on more expensive coal and gas imported from other states, and keeping clean energy companies guessing as to where and if they can build.[24] The Ohio anti-renewable law was just the latest blow against clean energy in the Buckeye State. In 2019, GOP legislators passed what *Vox* called "the worst energy bill of the 21st century."[25] The law dramatically scaled back the state's renewable energy and energy efficiency standards and bailed out financially struggling nuclear and coal plants in the state. Solar, wind, and other clean energy companies that had been growing in Ohio suddenly fled for more business-friendly states. The nuclear bailouts were later repealed after former Ohio House speaker Larry Householder and energy lobbyist and former Ohio Republican Party Chair Matt Borges were found guilty of federal racketeering charges for taking more than $60 million in bribes to push the law through.[26] Borges was sentenced to twenty years in prison and Borges was sentenced to five years. But the clean energy rollbacks remain in place.[27]

In Florida, Governor Ron DeSantis and other Republican lawmakers passed legislation preventing cities and other municipalities from phasing out natural gas in buildings, setting back goals by some of the state's biggest municipalities to shift to 100 percent clean energy.[28] A separate law signed by DeSantis bans local governments from requiring fuel retailers to add EV charging stations.[29] And if all that weren't enough, in August 2023, Republican presidential candidate DeSantis rejected $377 million in federal energy efficiency rebates and grants for Floridians, just to make a political statement against the Biden administration and its IRA. It didn't seem to matter that rejecting the funding meant losing hundred of millions of dollars in energy savings for Floridians, not to mention losing a business bonanza for the estimated sixteen thousand energy efficiency businesses in the state.[30]

DeSantis wasn't the only Republican presidential contender railing against federal clean energy policies during the 2024 election. Former President Trump vowed to kill the IRA and other Biden climate policies, even though they're creating more jobs and private industry investments in America than any federal policies in recent history, including any passed during his time in office. Former South Carolina Governor and GOP contender Nikki Haley—whose home state has benefited more than just about any other from the IRA, landing $11 billion in private investments and more than 10,000 new jobs because of the IRA in its first year alone—called the policy "a communist manifesto filled with tax hikes and green subsidies that benefit China," and said she'd repeal it.[31] South Carolina Senator Tim Scott, another early GOP presidential contender, also pledged to rescind the law that had resulted in the biggest economic investments in the history of his state.[32]

And then there's the U.S. Congress.

Nine months after every single Republican in Congress voted against the IRA, the GOP-led House faced another critical vote on the future of the law. This time there weren't just promises of a potential clean economy boom. It was happening, and faster than anybody ever predicted. In just a year after the IRA was signed into law, private companies announced plans to invest at least $86 billion into more than two hundred major clean energy factories and projects across the country creating 70,000 new jobs.[33]

The vast majority were in Republican congressional districts. More than 85 percent of all clean energy investments and 70 percent of the jobs announced by companies in the year following the signing of the IRA were in congressional districts represented by Republicans, according to E2. See table 10.1.

Twenty of the top twenty-five (and all of the top fifteen) congressional districts for clean energy investments in the first year of the IRA were in Republican districts. North Carolina's Ninth Congressional District, represented by Republican Representative Richard Hudson, led

Table 10.1. Clean Energy Projects by Congressional District, 2022–2023*

Party	Announcements	Jobs	Private-Sector Investments
Republican	121	53,656	$73.8 Billion
Democratic	68	15,550	$9.6 Billion
Unknown	21	3,111	$982 Million

*FIRST YEAR OF INFLATION REDUCTION ACT, AUGUST 2022 TO AUGUST 2023. *SOURCE: E2.* "CLEAN ECONOMY WORKS: IRA ONE-YEAR REVIEW," HTTPS://E2.ORG/REPORTS/CLEAN-ECONOMY -WORKS-2023/.

the way, attracting nearly $9.6 billion in investments, including Toyota's EV and battery factory. Georgia's Eleventh Congressional District, represented by Republican Representative Barry Loudermilk ($6.6 billion), and Nevada's Second Congressional District, represented by Republican Representative Mark Amodei (also $6.6 billion) followed. See table 10.2.

Even though investments and jobs were flowing in record amounts to Republican states and districts, bringing new opportunities to communities left behind by previous economic transformations, then–House Speaker Kevin McCarthy in the spring of 2023 pushed forward legislation that would have repealed almost all the new clean energy tax credits and investments in the IRA. Called the Limit, Save, Grow Act, the Republican-led legislation had no chance of passing the Senate or escaping a presidential veto.[34] But McCarthy was under pressure from the most conservative members of his party to make something happen in his new role as House Speaker. At the very least, he figured, the legislation could get congressional Democrats and President Biden to the bargaining table, where he might be able to extract at least a few concessions. On April 26, 2023, the House voted to pass the proposal 217–215. Four hard-right Republicans—Representatives Ken Buck, Matt Gaetz, Andy Biggs, and Tim Burchett—sided with Democrats in voting against the bill, not because they supported clean energy but because they said the legislation didn't do enough to reduce federal spending.[35]

After passing the bill, Speaker McCarthy used it for an even more economically dangerous ploy: Forcing a showdown with the Biden administration over the nation's debt ceiling. Traditionally, making sure the United States paid its bills and met the financial obligations approved by Congress had been a bipartisan prerogative. Since 1960, Congress raised or temporarily extended the nation's debt limit seventy-eight times—forty-nine times under Republican presidents and twenty-nine times under Democratic presidents.[36]

But things were different in the spring of 2023. Over the next four weeks, McCarthy used the legislation as a bargaining tool as he and House Republicans forced the Biden administration into the precarious position of potentially blowing through the country's debt ceiling and defaulting on its debts, or making big spending cuts to its signature

**Table 10.2. Top Congressional Districts for Private-Sector Clean Energy
Investments 2022–2023***

District	Representative	Party	Jobs	Private-Sector Investments
NC-9	Richard Hudson	R	2,150	$9,600,000,000
GA-11	Barry Loudermilk	R	5,660	$6,647,000,000
NV-2	Mark Amodei	R	5,050	$6,600,000,000
AZ-5	Andy Biggs	R	N/A	$4,100,000,000
TX-13	Ronny Jackson	R	1,690	$4,075,000,000
MI-5	Tim Walberg	R	2,500	$3,500,000,000
OH-15	Mike Carey	R	2,200	$3,500,000,000
SC-1	Nancy Mace	R	1,500	$3,500,000,000
TN-7	Mark E. Green	R	1,011	$3,280,200,000
GA-3	Drew Ferguson	R	923	$2,770,000,000
OK-2	Josh Brecheen	R	900	$2,450,000,000
MI-2	John Moolenaar	R	2,300	$2,360,000,000
SC-2	Joe Wilson	R	4,600	$2,094,000,000
SC-5	Ralph Norman	R	1,005	$1,808,900,000
SC-4	William Timmons	R	450	$1,705,000,000
MI-6	Debbie Dingell	D	2,112	$1,650,000,000
AZ-7	Raul Grijalva	D	1,750	$1,601,000,000
CA-3	Kevin Kiley	R	N/A	$1,500,000,000
IN-8	Larry Bucshon	R	642	$1,500,000,000
GA-1	Earl Carter	R	3,562	$1,441,000,000
AL-5	Dale Strong	R	900	$1,274,000,000
OH-9	Marcy Kaptur	D	150	$1,153,000,000
LA-3	Clay Higgins	R	700	$1,100,000,000
NM-1	Melanie Stansbury	D	1,800	$1,000,000,000
SC-6	James E. Clyburn	D	1,425	$872,000,000

*FIRST YEAR OF INFLATION REDUCTION ACT, AUGUST 2022 TO AUGUST 2023. *SOURCE: E2.*
"CLEAN ECONOMY WORKS: IRA ONE-YEAR REVIEW," HTTPS://E2.ORG/REPORTS/CLEAN-ECONOMY
-WORKS-2023/.

policies, beginning with clean energy tax credits and investments in the
IRA. On May 28, just days before the deadline to default on the country's debts or raise the debt ceiling, with negotiations hanging over the global economy like a guillotine, McCarthy and Biden announced they had reached a deal.[37] Their agreement included relatively minor caps on

nondefense spending, new work requirements for some older recipients of food stamps, and reduced funding for the Internal Revenue Service.

None of the clean energy investments and tax credits authorized by the IRA were repealed, or even reduced.

If there was a silver lining in the dangerous partisan parrying during the debt ceiling negotiations, it was that politicians in Washington—just like those in Austin, Texas—seemed to get the message, at least temporarily: Killing clean energy incentives that are creating jobs, driving investments, and attracting new companies to America isn't a good idea. By taking the IRA investments off the table in the debt ceiling negotiations, McCarthy and congressional Republicans signaled that they understood the economic benefits flowing to their states from the policies and that they didn't want to face the backlash from constituents if those investments, jobs, and new factories go away.

The partisan divide over climate change is still incredibly wide. Even after the debt ceiling debacle, congressional Republicans continued to mount attacks on the IRA and other clean energy and climate policies. Barely two weeks after the debt ceiling debacle, House Ways and Means Chairman Representative Jason Smith, a Missouri Republican, introduced the "Build It in America Act" that would repeal the IRA's clean energy and clean vehicle tax credits fueling the biggest boom in U.S. manufacturing in decades.[38]

In the lead-up to the 2024 election, the attacks on clean energy policies grew, as did politically motivated misinformation campaigns about clean energy and EVs to appeal to the Republican base of voters. Nobody distorted the truth more than the forty-fifth president of the United States. As president, Donald Trump outlandishly claimed that expanding renewable energy was a bad idea because solar "was not strong enough" and that Americans would be forced to turn off their television sets to save electricity if the wind wasn't blowing at night.[39] Back on the campaign trail as a candidate for president again in 2023, Trump claimed in a speech in Michigan that EVs would "decimate" the state and its automotive sector, ignoring the fact that thanks to the EV incentives passed with the IRA, the Michigan auto industry was in the middle of an unprecedented expansion, with carmakers announcing $8.2 billion in investments and more than dozen new EV factories or expansions and thousands of new jobs for Michigan autoworkers.[40] At another stump speech in South Carolina, Trump mocked EVs as "ridiculous" and warned that if more Americans bought EVs "everyone's going to be sitting on the highway . . . looking for a little plug-in." He didn't mention the fact that South Carolina was on track to become one of the biggest states for EV manufacturing in the country, with BMW, Volkswagen, and numerous battery and EV charging companies building or expanding factories in the state following the passage of the IRA.[41]

If Republicans need a playbook on how to stop the biggest American economic revolution in generations, they now have one. In the summer of 2023, as the world was baking in the hottest month in recorded history and smoke from wildfires choked cities across the country, the conservative and influential Heritage Foundation released Project 2025, a guidebook for a possible Republican presidential transition.[42] The nearly one-thousand-page plan calls for a new president to completely dismantle the Biden administration's climate policies, including the IRA and the bipartisan infrastructure act. It calls for dramatically increasing fossil fuel drilling and mining and eliminating regulations on greenhouse gas pollution while killing or eviscerating almost every clean energy program in the federal government—including the programs that are creating jobs and driving unprecedented investments and economic growth in Republican states.[43]

Even so, there are encouraging signs that the economics of climate change may be starting to bridge some of the divides on the front lines of the clean economy revolution. Take Trump's South Carolina campaign speech, for instance. Standing awkwardly next to the former president at the January 2023 event was the state's Republican governor, Henry McMaster. While McMaster didn't respond to Trump's pokes at EVs, the former lawyer and onetime assistant to legendary Southern conservative Senator Strom Thurmond has lauded and courted the EV industry—and with great success. In 2022, more than half of all private-sector investments in South Carolina came from EV companies, and McMaster hopes it's just the start. In October 2022, he signed an executive order establishing a far-reaching economic development program aimed at expanding the EV business and workforce in South Carolina.[44] The order directed the state Department of Commerce to designate a new "EV Coordinator" to oversee the recruitment of new companies; directed state agencies to work together on policies that make South Carolina more attractive to EV companies; and ordered the Department of Employment and Workforce to develop new EV-related worker training programs. McMaster has said he wants to make South Carolina "the place where the EV industry can transform the future."[45] That will be hard if his fellow Republicans in Washington roll back the policies making that future a reality.

Nobody understands the conundrum Republican politicians have with clean energy and climate change like former U.S. Representative Bob Inglis. For six terms, Republican Inglis represented South Carolina's conservative Fourth Congressional District, which includes Greenville and other Upstate cities. In 2010, he lost the Republican primary in a landslide for one primary reason: He said he believed climate change was real. Today, Inglis runs a nonprofit called republicEn, a group that champions conservative approaches to address climate change. He also watches closely how Republican politicians are reacting to the clean economy boom and talking about climate change—or not.

"To call it climate change is to capitulate to the left in front of your right-wing constituents—and that's politically dangerous," Inglis said, speaking from personal experience.[46] "So you can continue to say harsh things about . . . the Green New Deal and about Joe Biden, but meanwhile, if you're a capable governor, you realize we've got an (economic development) opportunity that's just irresistible."

While acknowledging the governor of his state and Republican leaders of other states need to tread carefully, Inglis said the failure of anti–clean energy legislation in Texas could be a lesson for Republicans everywhere—and also a sign of hope. "I sort of wish some of it would have passed, because as (former South Carolina senator) Fritz Hollings used to say, there's no education in the second kick of a mule," he said. "If they had passed those bills, it would have been like, what? You've just killed these businesses that are really thriving?

"Cooler heads prevailed, and maybe there's hope in that," Inglis said.

Whether Republican lawmakers like it or not, along with jobs and investments, the foreign companies now flocking to states like South Carolina and Georgia are bringing with them something else: Attention to climate change, a desire for more clean energy and sustainable business practices—all things that are typical in many countries but less so in red states throughout the southeast. The influence is beginning to rub off on the locals. Drive past BMW on I-85 in Spartanburg and the first thing you see are rows of four hundred solar panels that help power the parts of the campus.[47] Electric vehicles from BMW and other manufacturers aren't hard to spot. There are twice as many EV charging stations located throughout the Greenville-Spartanburg region as there are in the capital city of Columbia, which has twice the population.[48] In an October 2021 poll for the group Conservatives for Clean Energy, two-thirds of South Carolinians, including 64 percent of Republicans, said they thought it should be a priority for the state to increase solar and wind. About 70 percent of respondents, including 54 percent of Republicans, said expanding clean energy would encourage economic development throughout the state.[49]

"People here are starting to get it," said Lummus, CEO of the Upstate South Carolina Alliance. "But we've got a long way to go."

Likewise in Georgia, Lummus's counterpart Trip Tollison at the Savannah Economic Development Authority sees foreign companies' focus on environment and sustainability starting to impact the way people think about climate change and clean energy. At Hyundai's Savannah factory, solar panels will cover employee parking lots. Plans include $343 million in water infrastructure, including a state-of-the-art membrane bioreactor water treatment plant that will treat effluent wastewater that can then be used for irrigation and other uses at the plant. Employees and visitors will be able to access on-site hiking trails and parks that are bigger than some of the public parks in Savannah.[50]

"It really is going to be an ecological park, and I think it's going to get a lot of attention once it is complete," Tollison said.[51] That attention, he said, could help show some people that clean energy, EVs, and paying attention to the environment aren't just for tree-huggers in California or New York, but for people of all political stripes, in Georgia and every other state.

"I think when some people on the far right start seeing the benefits of what Hyundai is doing, they're going to start to see things a little differently," said Tollison, who previously worked as an aide to former Republican Representative Jack Kingston of Savannah, and before that for Democratic U.S. Senator Sam Nunn. "I don't know if they're going to change their minds completely, but they're going to be more understanding."

There are other promising signs that the investments and jobs coming with the clean economy boom may be helping thaw the partisan divide when it comes to clean energy and climate action.

In March 2023, two weeks after the U.S. House passed its ill-fated legislation to repeal the IRA, Florida Atlantic University (FAU) polled more than 1,400 Floridians about climate change. Virtually all respondents (90 percent) said they believe climate change is happening, with 65 percent (including 49 percent of GOP voters) attributing the causes to human actions. The poll also found that nearly 55 percent of Floridians—including 40 percent of Republicans—said they supported the federal IRA, leading FAU researchers to conclude that climate change "is no longer an effective partisan wedge issue."[52]

George Riley, former executive director of the Republican Party of Florida, agreed. "As the 2024 election cycle begins and Republican candidates come to Florida to court voters, they would be wise to include clean energy in their speeches," Riley wrote in a piece that appeared in the *Tampa Bay Times* shortly after the FAU survey was released.[53] He is now Florida director of Conservatives for Clean Energy. Not only are Florida conservatives supportive of expanding technologies like solar and wind, Riley wrote, they "are growing more and more alarmed about how climate change impacts them and are looking to leaders who will address those concerns."

Another poll, by the Rainey Center Freedom Project, also found that a strong majority of Republican voters across the country support clean energy, including solar, wind, nuclear, and hydrogen. Taken about a month after the passage of the IRA, that poll also showed widespread support for tax credits for residential solar, battery storage, and energy-efficient appliances.

Rainey Center researchers said there were several major takeaways from the polling, but one was most important, and most hopeful. "There is clearly fertile ground for Republicans and Democrats to come together on clean energy and climate solutions," researchers Sarah E. Hunt and Michael Dorsey wrote in an opinion piece in *The Hill*.[54] "There is a chance for new, strategic cross-partisan alliances to deliver a new, clean energy economy."

If there's anything about climate change that Republicans and Democrats can agree on, it's about the jobs and other economic benefits that can come with shifting to clean energy and clean transportation. Just ask conservative Republican Governor Eric Holcomb of Indiana, one of the reddest states in the country and one of the biggest users of fossil fuels for electricity.

In November 2022, Holcomb flew sixteen hours from Indianapolis to Sharm el-Sheikh, Egypt, to attend the twenty-seventh United Nations climate summit. He was one of only a few Republican elected officials who attended the international summit—but don't mistake him for some sort of tree-hugging climate champion. During the Trump administration, Holcomb supported the repeal of the federal Clean Power Plan that was designed to clean up fossil fuel plants. He also publicly cheered Trump's decision to pull America out of the Paris climate agreement.[55]

As Holcomb explained to *Politico*, he was at the international climate summit in Egypt to meet with and recruit makers of electric and other clean vehicles to his state. "I want to make sure that our automobile industry is flourishing, not just tomorrow, but 10 years from now, 20 years from now," he told the publication.[56]

Back home, Holcomb was hammered by some of his fellow Republicans. Former Indiana congressman David McIntosh, president of the ultraconservative Club for Growth, accused Holcomb in a scathing opinion piece of embracing the "woke programs" coming out of the international climate conference to the detriment of Indiana's economy and its residents.[57]

But it turns out Holcomb was on the right track.

In the months following his trip to the climate summit, at least four EV companies announced new plants or expansions in Indiana. A subsidiary of South Korean company Soulbrain Holdings said it would invest $75 million to build a new seventy-five-employee battery parts factory in Kokomo.[58] Netherlands-based Stellantis said it would invest $155 million and create 265 new jobs at three Indiana factories that make electric drivetrains for new EV versions of Jeeps, Ram trucks, and other vehicles.[59] Oregon-based Entek announced a new $1.5 billion, 640-employee factory in Terre Haute that will make materials for lithium-ion batteries used in EVs and for energy storage. And General Motors announced a $45 million expansion of its aluminum die-casting factory in Bedford to support expected demand for new electric versions of its Chevrolet Silverado and GMC Sierra pickup trucks.[60]

The arrival of the clean economy in Indiana was validation of Holcomb's belief that acting on climate change doesn't have to be a losing proposition for Republicans.

"It's not either the economy or the environment," Holcomb told *Politico*. "It can be both."

CHAPTER 11

Remaking the Country

"We Think This Is Big"

Savannah is Georgia's oldest city.

History flows through its streets like a damp summer breeze through the moss in its century-old live oak trees. The past is present everywhere, from Oglethorpe Square, named after the colonial governor of Georgia who founded the city in 1733, to Colonial Park Cemetery, where tombstones mark the final resting place of soldiers and families from the Revolutionary War, as well as Declaration of Independence signer Button Gwinnett, namesake of the state's second-biggest county.

Rice and cotton were once the foundation of Savannah's economy. Later, it was people. About two miles from Oglethorpe Square is the site of one of the largest slave auctions in U.S. history. During two horrific days in March 1859, more than 435 men, women, and children were sold to Southern plantation owners, bitterly breaking up so many African families that it became known as "the weeping time."[1] Descendants of some of those enslaved people are still a part of Savannah. About 52 percent of the city's population is Black or African American; 39 percent is white.

Today, much of Savannah's economy is connected to the transportation industry. Private jet maker Gulfstream Aerospace Corporation is headquartered here, employing more than 11,000 workers.[2] The Port of Savannah, one of the fastest-growing container terminals in America,

employs another 1,400 people. About three hundred residents work at
Great Dane Trailers, which makes refrigerated trucks.

Soon, the next evolution in transportation could create more jobs in
the Savannah region than all of those employers combined, reshaping the
community in ways never imagined and putting it at the forefront of the
clean economy.

Between Hyundai and all of its suppliers, more than 13,000 Savan-
nah-area residents will soon be employed doing something completely
new for the region: Making EVs and the parts that go in them. Following
Hyundai, parts maker Ecoplastic Corporation announced 450 jobs in
nearby Register, Georgia. Seoyon E-HWA, which makes seats, head-
liners, and door trim, announced a 740-employee factory in the town
of Rincon. Driveshaft and axle maker Seohan Auto announced another
180 jobs at a $72 million factory in Liberty County. Hyundai Mobis,
which makes everything from electronic airbags and headlight control
systems, announced a 1,600-employee plant in Bryan County.[3]

"In a single month, Georgia's economic development community . . .
announced more than 1,900 new jobs for hardworking Georgians, with
the bulk of those jobs related to the Hyundai Metaplant," Georgia Governor Kemp said after announcing in March 2023 that Hyundai parts
supplier PHA would create four hundred new jobs and invest $67 mil-
lion in the Savannah area.[4] "We are witnessing unprecedented economic
growth coming to this region."

The region is gearing up to meet that unprecedented growth in myriad ways. Since it opened its doors in 1929, Savannah Technical College
has prepared residents for work. During World War II, it taught classes
on how to make military equipment. Later, its most popular classes
included truck driving and health care.[5] In 2023, in partnership with
Hyundai, Savannah Tech announced an entirely new EV production and
technician program. Students who earn a certificate from the program
will be trained to go directly to work at the new EV factory. "Literally,
after the press release on it, I had four different students call me at home
at night like, 'Hey, what do I need to do to get in this?'" Anthony Hobbs,
head of the automotive department at Savannah Tech told WTOC
11 News.[6]

So many new jobs connected to Hyundai and its suppliers are being created that there's no way they can all be filled by locals, with or without Savannah Tech and other community colleges. Local officials know there are not even enough available workers within a sixty-mile radius to fill all the jobs being created. "We know we can't find completely all the workforce we need here," said Tollison of the Savannah Economic Development Authority. "We do envision a lot of local hires but we know we've got to go outside if we're going to be successful." With scores of other new EV and clean energy companies flocking not only to Georgia but throughout the Southeast, that means going way far outside. Tollison's economic development group has identified ten cities and regions across America where it plans to launch robust marketing campaigns to try and convince workers to move to Savannah. "We could go up to Buffalo, New York, and say, 'Tired of your winters? Come to Savannah,'" he said. Other cities and regions of the country where manufacturing has been on the decline also might be ripe for recruiting new transplants to Savannah.

On the other side of Georgia, solar panel manufacturer Qcells also is scrambling for workers. When the company opened its first factory in Dalton in January 2019, the local unemployment rate was about 6.3 percent. With a booming economy driven by the influx of clean energy companies into Georgia and surrounding states, the unemployment rate was about half that by the time the company started building its second plant and preparing to break ground on other factories in Dalton and in Cartersville. To try and find the workers it needs, Qcells starts connecting with prospective employees when they're young—very young.

"We start at middle school," said Lisa Nash, general manager for human resources at the Dalton factory.[7] The company hosts summer camps for aspiring young solar workers and engineers, and apprenticeship programs for older kids. "We want to get them interested in manufacturing as early as we can," she said. About 80 percent of Dalton-area students don't go to college, Nash said, making the solar panel factory a good alternative. But "we're creating jobs faster than we're creating people," she said. "It's a big issue."

In addition to thousands of new jobs making solar panels and other clean energy equipment, more than 27,000 new jobs have been created in

EV and battery manufacturing factories in Georgia since 2000, according to state estimates. The state is at "the epicenter of the industrial revolution of our time," with EVs leading the way, Georgia Governor Kemp said.[8] Today, Georgia may be known as the "Peach State," but someday soon it might as well be known as the "EV State."

Already, they're renaming roads after the companies transforming Georgia's economy in ways not seen since Reconstruction. For years, Steve Reynolds Industrial Parkway was the name of one of the most important roads in the town of Commerce, four hours northeast of Savannah. Steve Reynolds was a native of Commerce who grew up working in the peach business and also the petroleum distribution industry. He later went on to become a state senator and chair of the legislature's Transportation Committee before serving two decades as a member of the Georgia Transportation Board. Eighteen-wheelers roll up and down the road named after him night and day, filling up at the Love's Truck Stop across from a rusted water tower before hauling goods from the Ollie's Bargain Outlet distribution center and a GE appliance distribution center to the rest of the Southeast via nearby Interstate 85. In January 2022, a new company came to town unlike any other since the town was incorporated, back in the middle of the U.S. Civil War.[9] South Korea's SK On opened a $2.6 billion EV battery factory on Steve Reynolds Industrial Parkway across the street from Ollie's distribution center, creating nearly three thousand local jobs for Georgians making batteries for Ford's F-150 Lightning and Volkswagen's ID.4. The battery plant is one of several SK On went on to announce in Georgia. A year later, at a ceremonial ribbon cutting outside the Commerce factory, local leaders officially renamed Steve Reynolds Boulevard to SK Boulevard. "This is an incredible investment for our community," proclaimed Mayor J. Clark Hill.[10] "We are so thankful they chose to locate here in Commerce."

Along with the factory, new restaurants with names like Seoul Garden and Mr. K's Korean BBQ have opened up in Commerce. In nearby Athens, Fook's Foods and the Orient Market Asian grocery stores are busier than ever. And in a place where Confederate battle flags and Trump 2024 banners hang proudly outside some homes, there's another flag on the side of the newly renamed SK Boulevard: A Korean flag, flapping high, right next to a U.S. flag and a Georgia state flag at the entrance to the battery plant.

Similar transformations are happening all across America. They're bringing new opportunities to cities and counties left behind by the industries of America's past, connecting them to the rest of the world and the economy of the future, and remaking the country, sometimes in unusual ways that could've never been imagined.

Near Charleston, West Virginia, Savion Energy is building what is expected to be the state's biggest solar farm at the site of the bankrupt Hobet coal mine, creating more than 250 local construction jobs and injecting $320 million into the local economy.[11] Not too far away, in the town of Marlowe, a subsidiary of FirstEnergy is building a solar farm on the ground that previously was used to store hazardous coal ash left from years of burning coal in a nearby power plant.

On the flat Kansas plains between Lawrence and Kansas City, at the site of a former military ammunition factory built after Japan bombed Pearl Harbor, a Japanese manufacturer—Panasonic—is building a $4 billion lithium-ion battery plant expected to create more than four thousand good-paying jobs. The factory will forever change the town of DeSoto, Kansas (population 6,400), adding traffic, congestion, and other problems. But it will also put the rural community at the leading edge of making some of the most consequential products in the clean energy age. It will also provide new opportunities for workers and families searching for ways to keep their kids from leaving the area for careers elsewhere. It won't be the first economic earthquake to shake up sleepy DeSoto. When the Sunflower Army Ammunition Plant opened there in May 1942, thousands of Kansans rolled into town looking for work, many sleeping at night in temporary tent cities after spending their days manufacturing smokeless gunpowder and rocket propellants to fight the country that today is home to the company that will become DeSoto's biggest employer by far.[12]

In Adams County, Colorado, not far from a ninety-year-old petroleum refinery that is one of the worst polluters in the nation, a solar company from India is helping build America's new clean energy economy. Kolkata, India-based Vikram Solar plans to hire nine hundred

Coloradans at an average salary of $70,000 a year to make solar panels at a factory in the town of Brighton. Not long ago, the town north of Denver was home to little more than ranches and farms. Now, it's becoming an international clean energy hotspot.[13] In addition to Vikram's solar panel factory—its first in the United States—Brighton is home to a 1,100-employee wind turbine parts factory operated by Denmark-based Vestas Winds Systems. Since 2010, workers at the hulking Vestas plant have made nacelles, the cone-shaped hearts of wind turbines that house generators, gears, and electric equipment that make them work. After the passage of the federal clean energy laws, Vestas announced it would invest $40 million and hire between eight hundred and one thousand workers to expand the Brighton plant and also a blade factory in Windsor, Colorado. Vestas North America President Laura Beane credited both the IRA and Colorado's clean energy policies for driving demand and making the expansion possible.[14]

The new and expanding clean energy factories are a striking dichotomy to the tangle of pollution-belching pipes and smokestacks protruding from the old Suncor petroleum refinery just twenty minutes or so south. The refinery, in operation since the 1930s, is one of the dirtiest oil and gas operations in the country. In 2016, the zip code where it sits was deemed the most polluted zip code in America.[15] Four years later, the state of Colorado fined the plant $9 million for air pollution violations.[16]

While solar and wind help replace lost fossil fuel jobs in Colorado and West Virginia, it's another battery factory helping recharge a town in New York's Hudson Valley that was once at the center of the global technology space before it fell into a sharp spiral of decline.

For more than thirty years, IBM's complex in Kingston, New York, was the birthplace of some of the most advanced products of its time. The first electric typewriters were made there in the 1950s, and later, some of the world's first mainframe computers and digital telephone equipment. During the Cold War, IBM in Kingston helped develop and deploy the national network of computers at the core of the country's efforts to monitor and respond to a Soviet nuclear attack. At its peak, IBM Kingston employed more than seven thousand workers. Once known as "TechCity," the complex at its height was responsible for 12 percent of the entire economy in the surrounding county of Ulster.[17] Kingston was the epitome of a company town. Employees who worked alongside each other Monday through Friday in their requisite white shirts and ties for men and skirts or dresses for women changed into bathing suits and tennis outfits and reconnected over tennis and swimming at the IBM Recreational Center or Salvucci's restaurant out on Route 28 for cocktails and pasta.[18]

The stereotypical suburban serenity was shattered in the 1990s. After a series of layoffs, IBM closed the Kingston operation in 1994, shuttering buildings, padlocking gates, and abandoning the complex forever. The state and city floated ideas to reinvigorate the complex time after time—as a tech hub, as a manufacturing site, as an artist community, as a film studio. Nothing really stuck. Eventually, some of the buildings that didn't crumble on their own were demolished, creating a new problem: Many were filled with asbestos and other toxins. Big hills of hazardous debris were scattered across the property, covered in plastic sheeting and surrounded by red caution tape warning people to stay out or risk cancer. Not exactly a great curb appeal for prospective buyers. Like the IBM complex, much of Kingston fell on hard times. In the 1960s, nearly 30,000 people called the town home. By 1990, the population was down to 23,000.[19]

Finally, that's changing. In January 2023, long-duration battery storage company Zinc8 announced it was moving its headquarters from Vancouver, Canada, to a site at the former TechCity, now known as iPark87, after the interstate highway along one of its borders. Aided by a $9 million state grant and federal tax credits, the company plans to build a $68 million manufacturing plant and headquarters on the site, creating as many as five hundred new jobs and once again breathing activity and new life into the old IBM complex. Company CEO Ron McDonald, who spent ten years in the Canadian parliament before getting into private industry, credited federal and state policies for convincing the company to move to the United States. "I follow policy, and I follow leadership," McDonald said in announcing his company's plans at a press conference with New York Governor Kathy Hochul.[20]

For Hochul, climate change is personal. She grew up on the shores of Lake Erie, watching emissions from Bethlehem Steel mills cloud the sky. "I thought as a child the sky was supposed to be orange because that was the color of the smoke coming out of the smokestacks," she said. During her first week on the job as the state's governor in August 2021, two back-to-back hurricanes slammed into the Northeast, causing massive flooding in New York City. A year later, her hometown of Buffalo—a place that knows about snow—got walloped with one of the biggest snowstorms in its history, dumping more than five feet of snow on the region, leaving 1,600 homes without power and leading to the deaths of forty people.[21]

Zinc8's plans for Kingston, the governor said, are indicative of how public policy can help reinvigorate local communities, address climate change, and create jobs, opportunities, and new tax revenues all at once. "This is really bringing new life, a rebirth" to the region, Hochul said. "We're taking a former site, investing in it, bringing resources here and embracing this phenomenal opportunity."[22]

Not unlike when IBM was the crown jewel of Kingston, the clean energy and clean transportation factories now coming to New York and just about every other state in America are creating ripple effects throughout the entire economy. And—whether or not people like solar or wind or EVs or believe in science or climate change—the impacts of this are filtering down throughout the entire economy. Construction workers building a new factory need a place to stay and tools and equipment to build it. Once operational, a factory needs suppliers for everything from heavy equipment to paper clips. Workers need homes. And when they clock out at the end of a shift, they want dinner or maybe a drink at the local bar. Even if companies initially get tax breaks to move to a community, payroll taxes help states and cities pay for everything from police and parks to streetlights to schools. There's a multiplier effect for every investment in a local economy. None is higher than for manufacturing. For every $1 invested in a factory, another $2.60 or so is added to the overall economy.[23]

Perhaps no place in America stands to benefit more from the clean economy revolution than Imperial Valley, California, or as some are now calling it, Lithium Valley. Located east of San Diego, the region is one of the poorest, unhealthiest, and environmentally hazardous communities in the country. More than 22 percent of the population of Imperial County lives in poverty, nearly double the national rate.[24] The region has one of the highest childhood asthma rates in the country. It ranks number eighteen in the nation for air particle pollution and number thirteen for high ozone days. Often, the air is a brown haze, made thick by dust kicked up from local farms; pollution from cars and trucks speeding along Interstate 8 and idling at the Mexico border nearby; and smokestack emissions from factories on either side of the border that settle in low-lying Imperial Valley with no place to go.[25] Adding to the air pollution is toxic dust from the shrinking and polluted Salton Sea, an environmental disaster filled with chemicals from decades of runoff from the industrial farming operations that surround it. Shallow and landlocked, much of the 340-square-mile Salton Sea is like a chemical-filled toilet that can't be flushed. Its salty, stagnant waters are smelly in the searing desert heat, and its toxicity regularly leads to mass kill-offs of birds, fish, and other wildlife.

It is the Salton Sea, or rather what's beneath it, that could also turn this area into a veritable twenty-first-century gold mine. Imperial Valley is home to what could be one of the biggest lithium deposits in the world. By some estimates, there could be as much as 18 million metric tons of lithium beneath the valley and below the Salton Sea.[26] If state and private companies can figure out how to extract that lithium in an environmentally sensitive way, it could forever change the economy and the future of Imperial—aka Lithium—Valley.

"We think this is big," California Governor Gavin Newsom told President Biden and other participants at a White House meeting on critical materials in America.[27] "And if it's as big as it appears to be, this is a game changer."

Hand in hand with private industry, California is placing big bets on Lithium Valley in hopes it can lead America's EV and battery storage industry, make the country more competitive with foreign suppliers, and bring new good-paying jobs and economic opportunities to an area that sorely needs them. In 2022, Governor Newsom signed legislation directing $5 million to support lithium development efforts in the region, on top of $27 million invested by the California Energy Commission into programs researching how to best extract and process lithium produced from geothermal brine below the Salton Sea and surrounding areas.[28] The state also invested $80 million to expand science, math, and engineering programs related to lithium at San Diego State University's campus in Imperial Valley.[29] To create a road map for the future of the industry in the state, Governor Newsom and the legislature created a special blue-ribbon commission that held more than twenty public hearings to gather input from local communities, tribes, businesses, environmental groups, and others.[30]

In reality, companies have been harvesting lithium in Imperial Valley for decades, and the region is already a unique leader in the renewable energy business. Imperial Valley is the second-biggest source of geothermal energy in the country. Visiting there is like stepping into some sort of Mad Max movie set. It's hot, dry, and dirty; the flat horizon is broken up by massive, rusting geothermal plants with twisted pipes and hulking towers that jut up from the desert. Great plumes of steam fill the air as the plants suck boiling brine from miles below the earth's surface and use it to power generators that produce electricity carried by power lines to as far away as Sacramento and Arizona.

Flowing through those billions of gallons of brine used to produce electricity are loads of lithium. Traditionally, the eleven geothermal plants operating around the Salton Sea simply pumped the liquid back into the ground like giant recirculating fountains without ever extracting lithium or anything else from it as it passed through the pipes.[31]

Given the surge in demand and prices for lithium—in 2022 it sold for as much as $37,000 per metric ton—some big-time players are trying to change that. For more than forty years, Berkshire Hathaway, the holding company controlled by celebrated investor Warren Buffett, has operated ten geothermal plants in Imperial Valley. "Right now we are pumping 50,000 gallons per minute of lithium-rich brine to the surface," said Alicia Knapp, president and CEO of Berkshire's BHE Renewables subsidiary.[32] "Because there is no proven, viable commercial technology, we are pumping it right back into the ground."

In 2020, supported by $20 million in state and federal grants, BHE Renewables launched a pilot project to figure out how to separate and extract lithium from brine as it is pumped through its plants. If successful, the company and others like it could create thousands of new jobs, bring billions of dollars in new investments, and attract other new companies and jobs to the area, not unlike what Hyundai is doing in Savannah.

Another company, Controlled Thermal Resources (CTR), wants to build an entire clean energy campus in Imperial Valley. It would include its geothermal plant, unaffectionately but fittingly known as Hell's Kitchen, as well as a lithium processing plant, a battery "gigafactory," and related businesses. In 2021, CTR and its Australian parent company received a major boost when General Motors announced a multimillion-dollar investment in the company and an agreement to get first dibs on lithium it produces at the Salton Sea. Two years later, automaker Stellantis announced a separate, $100 million deal with CTR to procure lithium from Hell's Kitchen for its EV lineup, which includes Jeep, Dodge Ram, Chrysler, and others.[33] Meanwhile, a company launched by the founder of Italian battery maker Italvolt, working with CTR, announced plans to build a $4 billion, 2,500-employee plant in Imperial Valley that could produce enough batteries to power 650,000 EVs every year.[34]

"With the right support, California is set to become the world's leader in sustainable and highly efficient lithium production," CTR CEO Rod Colwell said at a press conference with Governor Newsom at the company's Hell's Kitchen operation.[35] "Making electric vehicles even cleaner is something we can all get behind and be proud of."

If the business and government investments in Lithium Valley pay off, it could mean new jobs for residents. It could also mean new tax revenues for schools and parks and streetlights in a place that needs them. And it could help reinvigorate a community accustomed to poverty and environmental degradation.

It's a story that locals have heard before, however.

Silvia Paz is the executive director of Alianza Coachella Valley, a nonprofit that works on environmental justice and other community issues in the region. She is keeping a close eye on Lithium Valley. Paz also was the chair of the state's blue ribbon commission on Lithium Extraction.

"When our community hears about the excitement around lithium, there's cautious optimism. It's a community that has seen unfilled promises before," Paz said at the White House meeting.[36] "Could this be a game changer? Yes, it could—if done right."

Like Imperial Valley, the clean economy promises to benefit other parts of rural America in a big way. According to an E2 economic analysis, about one in four large-scale clean energy projects announced in the first year of the IRA is located in a demographically rural area. These projects are expected to inject $20 billion in investments, create more than 67,000 new jobs, and generate almost $5 billion in local, state and federal tax revenues that will benefit rural America. For rural communities, clean energy projects—whether new local factories or solar and wind installations on farms—can be a lifeline to the new economy.[37]

Some parts of rural America don't think it's worth it, however. Near the town of Rutledge, about an hour east of Atlanta, Rivian Automotive Inc., in 2021, announced plans for a $5 billion, 7,500-employee factory to make electric trucks and SUVs. On its surface, it would seem to be an ideal location for the plant. In addition to the huge and growing ecosystem of EV and battery companies reshaping the state, the idea of building fancy electric pickup trucks and SUVs in a place that likes fancy pickup trucks and SUVs seems like a match made in automobile heaven. Except for many residents of Rutledge, it seems more like hell. The company's announcement was greeted not with open arms, but with protests and "We Oppose Rivian" yard signs. At a regional development authority meeting, more than two hundred local residents filled a room and told authorities that the massive plant Rivian was planning would change their rural community too much.[38] "This place has been a bubble . . . and you all are going to ruin that," resident Chelsea Whitley said, according to the *Morgan County Citizen* newspaper. "This place is a gem, and (Rivian) will change everything."

About 220 miles down Interstate 16 in Savannah, the story is a little different.

Of course, some people don't want Hyundai and all the companies that have followed it negatively changing their city and its rich history. But many more want the positive benefits that come with it. Before Hyundai announced it was coming to Savannah in the spring of 2022, home values were falling and unemployment was rising. A year later, median prices were up more than 10 percent at a time when prices in other markets across the country were in decline. By comparison, home prices during the same period fell by 3 percent in Atlanta and by 6 percent in Jacksonville, Florida, another coastal city two hours to the south.[39] The economic prospects in Savannah turbocharged the commercial real estate market too. The influx of EV companies helped make Savannah the hottest industrial market in the country in 2022, according to real estate firm Colliers.[40]

Jobs at the new Hyundai factory are expected to average around $58,000 a year, 15 percent higher than the average salary of $50,400 in Savannah in 2023. In a place where both the local unemployment rate and the local poverty rate in recent years have typically been almost twice as high as the rest of the country, the addition of thousands of new jobs is welcome. If the cure for poverty is jobs, *Savannah Morning News* columnist Adam Van Brimmer opined, "Hyundai may be that panacea."[41]

Panacea or not, rural and lower-income areas in Republican-led red states are definitely seeing the bulk of the benefits from the clean economy revolution. Two-thirds of clean energy investments announced since the IRA have gone to counties with lower-than-average weekly wages, and 66 percent have gone to counties with lower-than-average college graduation rates, according to the Treasury Department.[42] The majority of those counties are in Republican-led red states, which have suffered the most from poverty, a lack of job opportunities, low education levels, and a dearth of innovation capital in recent years. According to E2's analysis, nearly 60 percent of major clean energy projects announced since the IRA have gone to Republican congressional districts.[43]

The fact that every Republican in Congress voted against the policy that's now benefiting their states the most created a political paradox. But that was okay with the administration, recalled former national climate advisor Gina McCarthy, because the president always said he wanted to be a president for all Americans, not just those in his political party. And to rebuild an economy "from the bottom up and the middle out," as Biden liked to say, the benefits of his policies had to flow to the places they were most needed. "It was following the sorts of values that President Biden was insisting on," said McCarthy..[44]

For his part, Biden understood the political calculus. Democrats who were responsible for passing all his climate and clean energy policies would quite naturally expect the benefits of those policies to flow to their states. Conversely, bringing new jobs, opportunities, and benefits to red states could help win over some Republicans. Either way, he saw his plans as a once-in-a-generation opportunity to remake the economy for *all* of America—Republicans, Democrats, and Independents, in blue states, red states, and purple states.

"Some analysis has said that the laws I've signed are going to do more to help red America than blue America," Biden said at a July 2023 speech in South Carolina at the new factory of Enphase Energy, a solar battery equipment manufacturer.[45] "Well, that's okay with me, because we're all Americans. My view is: Wherever the need is most, that's the place we should be helping.

"The progress we're making is good for all Americans, all of America," he added.

In a different speech at a different clean energy project, just one week earlier, Georgians got a different take from a different politician.

Even though his state benefited more than any other from the Biden climate and clean energy programs, Georgia Governor Kemp refused to give the administration any credit, instead bashing the programs that are enabling all the growth in his state.

"Georgia's electric mobility boom is taking place because our state is second to none for companies looking to invest, relocate, expand, and innovate—not because the federal government continues to put their thumb on the scale, favoring a few companies over the industry as a whole," Kemp said at a speech in the town of Bainbridge announcing a new four-hundred-employee, $800 million synthetic graphite factory by battery company Anovion Technologies. He didn't mention that Anovion was building the plant with the help of a $117 million grant from the Department of Energy's battery advancement program and that the company also would benefit from other federal tax breaks created by the Biden administration's policies.[46]

Kemp and Biden weren't the only ones giving speeches about clean energy and EVs in the summer of 2023. So was Donald Trump, in his campaign to regain the White House for a second term.

In a video released by his campaign in July 2023, Trump ignored the EV manufacturing boom in Georgia and other states completely, claiming falsely once again that federal clean vehicle policies were killing American auto manufacturing. Either oblivious or unconcerned with the reality that U.S. manufacturing was in the middle of its biggest expansion in recent history and that voters in Republican states were benefiting the most, he promised to end the federal clean energy policies driving that expansion if elected.

"Biden is killing American consumers, and also killing U.S. manufacturing," Trump claimed. "If Biden's assault is not stopped, the American auto production will be totally dead. That's why I'm going to terminate these green new deal atrocities on day one."[47]

CHAPTER 12

Reshaping the World

"One of the Most Transformative Economic Opportunities in Modern History"

CAR COMPANIES FROM KOREA, VIETNAM, AND GERMANY. SOLAR PANEL and wind turbine makers from India, Denmark, and Korea. Battery manufacturers from Japan, China, and Canada. Lithium and hydrogen companies from Australia, Norway, and the Netherlands.

The clean economy revolution is bringing new opportunities and foreign investments to communities all across the United States. Beyond U.S. borders, it's also doing something else. It's forcing other nations to double down on their investments in clean energy to keep up with America. It's transforming the global manufacturing sector. It's making countries more secure and less dependent on oil-state oligarchies like Russia. And it's reinvigorating the global fight against climate change, resurrecting hope for the possibility that we might be able to avert some of its worst impacts.

In 2022, the amount of foreign direct investment in the United States nearly quadrupled to $411 billion, the highest amount in five years and a dramatic reversal from the sharp declines during the Trump administration.[1] In a survey of two hundred U.S. subsidiaries of foreign companies by the Global Business Alliance, company executives said they were most encouraged by investments into U.S. infrastructure and the semiconductor industry and the "reshoring" of supply chains away from China.[2]

Clean energy projects are helping lead the way. Of the two-hundred-plus major clean energy projects announced in America in the first year after the IRA was signed into law, about half were by foreign-based companies or joint ventures involving foreign companies.[3] South Korea led the international parade to America with nearly fifteen announcements, mainly in the EV and solar space. But money flowed from some unexpected countries as well. A Mexico-based glass company, Vitro, announced it was building a $94 million factory in the Pennsylvania town of Cochranton to supply solar panel maker First Solar.[4] Instead of taking jobs south of the border, the company said it would hire 130 workers in America for the plant. Another Mexican company, ProlecGE, announced it would invest nearly $29 million and hire more than 150 workers to expand a plant in Shreveport, Louisiana, where it makes electrical transformers for solar and wind farms.[5] In Tennessee, Australian-based EV charging company Tritium announced plans for a 750-employee factory in the city of Lebanon, while in Memphis, a Portuguese industrial company teamed up with a Brazilian steelmaker to announce a new 130-employee factory to build equipment for solar company Nextracker Inc.[6]

Up in Michigan, meanwhile, a Norwegian company announced in May 2023 that it would build what it claims will be one of the world's biggest factories for electrolyzers used to make hydrogen. Nel Hydrogen's $400 million factory is expected to create five hundred new jobs.[7] Company CEO Håkon Volldal said he decided to open the factory, its second in the United States, because of the new federal policies and tax credits made available through the IRA. "I can tell you as a European, it does work," Volldal said at a press conference with U.S. Commerce Secretary Gina Raimondo and Michigan Governor Gretchen Whitmer, who recruited the company to her state during a trade mission to Europe four months earlier.[8] "Some of our largest orders are now coming from the United States, and we as a supplier want to be close to our customers," he said. According to Volldal, Nel Hydrogen will manufacture more electrolyzers at the Michigan factory than are produced in all of Europe, making it one of the largest—if not the largest—factory of its kind.[9]

In Buckeye, Arizona, KORE Power Inc. is building a battery factory based on Asian technology. That factory, which is backed by an $850 million loan from the Department of Energy, is expected to create about seven hundred construction jobs and another 1,250 manufacturing jobs when it opens in 2025.[10] KORE plans to base the assembly lines and processes for the Arizona plant after a factory in Jiaozuo, China, that's operated by partner Do-Fluoride Chemicals (DFD) which currently produces the company's batteries under contract.[11]

Clean energy opponents and some politicians have raised concerns about using taxpayer dollars to support factories and other operations that involve companies from foreign nations, especially China. No project has come under more scrutiny than Ford's agreement with China-based CATL—the biggest battery maker in the world—to build a factory in Marshall, Michigan. Shortly after the agreement was announced, the Republican-led House Select Committee on the Chinese Communist Party opened an investigation into CATL's ties to the Chinese Communist Party and its use of forced labor and also scrutinized the Biden administration's role in the agreement. In September 2023, Ford announced it was pausing construction on the $3.5 billion factory amid the investigation and a strike by the United Auto Workers union.[12]

The problem with trying to limit federal investments and tax credits to U.S.-based clean energy companies is that U.S. companies are just too far behind their foreign competitors. America simply dragged its feet so long on climate and clean energy policies that other countries were able to zoom ahead. Unfortunately, while Donald Trump and other politicians were doubling down on twentieth-century energy sources, keeping Americans dependent on oil and gas and promising they'd somehow resurrect the coal industry, China and other countries were investing in factories to build batteries, solar panels, electric vehicles, and other goods to power the world in the twenty-first century. American companies are beginning to get back in the game, but it will take time to recover lost ground. Until then, "frankly I just don't think we're going to be able to meet the president's (climate and clean energy) goals without foreign direct investment in the United States," Jigar Shah, director of the Energy Department's Loan Programs Office said at an event sponsored by the nonprofit Resources for the Future. "So we're not shying away from that investment, but we do have to do it properly."[13]

In the case of the Department of Energy's $850 million investment in KORE Power, for instance, Shah said the agency closely reviewed and scrutinized the contracts and agreements between the company and China-based DFD. Of particular concern was ensuring that DFD can't take KORE's intellectual property or transfer U.S. loans back to China if something goes wrong. "We're bringing technology back from China," Shah said. "We're putting it back into the United States, and we're manufacturing it here."[14] The investment in the Arizona factory also made sense to the Department of Energy for other reasons. Since the area where it's located is considered to be a disadvantaged area, it aligns with the Biden administration's Justice40 initiative, which calls for 40 percent of Department of Energy loans to go to such areas. Surrounding Maricopa County also is home to several tribal communities, aligning with the Biden administration's Justice40 Initiative.

Manufacturing goods in America based on foreign technology is a huge change. For decades, the story of American technology has gone like this: U.S. entrepreneurs and companies invent the technology. They ship the manufacturing—and the jobs—to other countries where they can make things cheaper. Eventually, foreign companies replicate the made-in-America technology and end up taking over markets.

What has changed, remarkably, is that it is now cheaper to make many clean energy products and the parts that go in them in America than it is to make them in foreign countries. The cost of making solar panels in the United States is 30 percent cheaper than making them overseas when tax credits from the IRA are included, according to a study by Princeton and Dartmouth universities.[15] Similarly, the costs of just about every component used in a wind turbine, from tower to blade to nacelle, is now cheaper to make in America when federal tax benefits are figured in, according to researchers. As automakers are proving, tax credits and other incentives coupled with cheaper shipping and supply chain costs can make it less expensive to build EVs in America than to make them in Mexico or Asia and ship them to the United States.

Like with batteries, China is the undisputed world leader in solar panel manufacturing, controlling two-thirds of the global market.[16] Yet as with batteries, China is now investing in factories in the United States to make solar panels too. After the passage of the IRA, at least three Chinese companies announced plans to build solar panel factories in America.[17] In 2023, Hounen Solar announced its $33 million, two-hundred-employee plant in Orangeburg, South Carolina. JA Solar said it would build a six-hundred-employee factory in Arizona. The world's biggest panel maker, LONGi Solar, announced in March 2023 that it and US partner Invenergy would build a $200 million factory in Pataskala, Ohio, that will employ an estimated 850 workers and become the single-biggest solar panel factory in the country. Just a few years earlier, it would have been unfathomable for a Chinese company to open a factory in America. The expected U.S. demand for solar panels wasn't big enough without certainty over tax credits for solar installations. Operating costs were prohibitive. And the Trump administration was outwardly hostile toward foreign countries, particularly China.

In addition to bringing foreign investments to America, federal support for clean energy is helping keep American companies from moving overseas. In June 2022, when it looked like the Biden administration's clean energy plans were dead, the biggest U.S.-based solar manufacturer, First Solar, announced it was shelving plans to build a new factory in the United States. The uncertainty and mixed signals about tax incentives and trade policies were just too much, the company said.[18] Instead, First Solar said it would build a factory in India or Europe. Two months later, the IRA was signed into law. Three months after that, in November 2022, First Solar announced it would build a new factory in Alabama, investing $1.1 billion into the state and creating more than seven hundred new jobs.[19]

To be sure, clean energy is driving growth in manufacturing not just in the United States, but everywhere. "The energy world is at the dawn of a new industrial age—the age of clean energy technology manufacturing," Fatih Birol, executive director of the International Energy Agency (IEA) wrote in the organization's 2023 Energy Technology Perspectives report.[20] The agency predicts that global clean energy manufacturing will triple and that clean energy manufacturing jobs will more than double by 2030. The difference is that—unlike previously—the United States now is back in the game and is helping to shape it. While the IEA predicts that China will likely continue to dominate this new industrial age, the United States is seeing a manufacturing renaissance. Construction spending on manufacturing buildings in the United States in 2023 doubled to a record high, driven largely by investments in battery, automobile, and semiconductor factories. The growth in the United States came as new factory construction in other countries—most notably Japan and Germany—was flat or declining, according to the U.S. Department of the Treasury.[21] U.S. employment in manufacturing jobs, meanwhile, hit its highest level in fifteen years in 2023. And that was before all the new factories announced in the wake of the IRA opened their doors.[22]

The manufacturing renaissance in America is reshaping the global economy in other ways, too. Making more goods in the United States, whether electric automobiles or solar panels and batteries, helps reduce the nation's trade deficit. It reduces supply chain shortages. It increases international business opportunities. It holds manufacturers to American environmental and workplace standards, setting a new bar for other countries. And it improves national security by making America less dependent on foreign countries.

"Clean energy presents one of the most transformative economic opportunities in modern history," said Treasury Secretary Janet Yellen. The Inflation Reduction Act is a historic environmental law, she said, "but it's also a generational economic law."[23]

Of course, other countries recognize this historic opportunity as well. It's hard not to. Transitioning the world's economy to net-zero emissions by 2050—a goal almost every country in the world agreed to as part of the 2015 Paris Climate Agreement[24]—will take a lot more solar panels, EVs, and other clean energy products. Just to get on track to meet that goal, the number of EVs on the world's roads needs to increase sixfold by 2030, according to the IEA.[25] Renewable energy needs to double by then. The number of electrolyzers used to create hydrogen needs to increase by 40 percent. And the number of electric-powered heat pumps needs to increase by 60 percent.

Setting goals and making projections is one thing. Taking action is another. When the United States finally passed the IRA and other climate and clean energy policies in 2021–2022, it was as if a sleeping giant awoke. Other countries first screamed and shouted and complained—and then took action. America was finally leading again. If they didn't want to get stepped on, other countries had to follow. "The Inflation Reduction Act, in my view, is the most important climate action after the Paris 2015 agreement," Birol said at the World Economic Forum in Davos, Switzerland in January 2023. Also sparking action, especially in Europe, was Russia's February 2022 invasion of Ukraine, which sent gas prices soaring and reminded the world that reliance on fossil fuels controlled largely by one hostile country is a bad idea.

The European Union (EU) responded by rolling out its Green Deal Industrial Plan and Net Zero Industry Act, designed to inject billions of euros for clean energy projects and companies. The plan also provided a blueprint for speeding up permitting for clean energy projects; reforming electricity markets to make renewables more accessible to more people and ensuring European countries can obtain rare earth materials needed to make clean energy products.[26] The policies built on earlier clean economy programs including the European Green Deal, a broad initiative that helped direct about one-third of the EU's roughly €2 trillion COVID-19 economic recovery package to clean energy investments, and the REPowerEU plan designed to rapidly reduce the continent's reliance on Russian gas and reach its goals to reduce greenhouse gas emissions by 55 percent by 2030.

In Canada, where the Justin Trudeau government warned the United States not to start a global "carbon-subsidy war" with the IRA and other programs, the government reacted with C$80 billion in tax credits and other investments into clean energy to keep the country from falling behind the United States.[27] The Canadian plan is similar to the U.S. plan. It includes a 30 percent tax credit on the purchase of manufacturing equipment for renewable and clean energy projects and a 15 percent tax credit for clean energy and storage and gas-fired generation projects, as long as the emissions from those gas projects are abated. The plan also includes other tax breaks and incentives to expand hydrogen, carbon capture, and geothermal energy. It also includes plans to upgrade Canada's electric grid to meet the country's goal of having a net-zero emissions electricity grid by 2035.[28]

In Japan, which accused the United States of protectionism for excluding foreign-made automobiles from EV tax credits, the government rolled out its Green Transformation Act, which includes new incentives and the sale of government bonds designed to drive $1.1 trillion in cleaner energy investments. The plan has a major focus on renewable energy and energy efficiency and also outlines goals to reduce emissions from ships and aviation by shifting to hydrogen and ammonia-based fuels. But it also pushes the country to increase its dependence on natural gas and restart nuclear power development.[29]

Australia's response to the United States' action committed AUS $15 billion to its National Reconstruction Fund, which includes $3 billion for renewable and low-emissions energy, $1 billion for advanced manufacturing projects, and $500 million for climate-friendly agriculture, forestry, and fisheries projects.

In India, meanwhile, the government expanded its Production Linked Incentive programs to include $2.4 billion in incentives for solar panel production and projects. The country's push for solar resulted in a record number of solar installations in 2022 and is attracting international manufacturers, including U.S.-based First Solar, which in 2023 opened a $684 million factory in the state of Tamil Nadu.[30] India also plans to invest as much as $2.6 billion in incentives for battery production and $3.5 billion to boost production of electric and hydrogen-powered vehicles.[31]

Smaller developing nations whose mineral resources are key to batteries and other clean energy products also are positioning themselves to be a bigger part of the clean energy revolution and protect their countries from being used just for mining. Countries including Indonesia, Namibia, and Zimbabwe have banned exports of raw and unprocessed materials like nickel, lithium, cobalt, and graphite, according to the *Wall Street Journal*.[32] The countries don't just want companies to mine the materials, destroy their lands, and leave with profits; they want them to build processing plants and other related operations to create jobs and drive bigger investments within their borders. Other nations, including Chile and Mexico, are imposing greater government control over lithium reserves to limit exploitation by foreign companies and secure a bigger piece of the clean economy for their citizens. "What's generally driving this is fairly basic and straightforward," Cullen Hendrix, a senior fellow for the Peterson Institute for International Economics, told the *Journal*. "It's a desire to capture a larger share of the benefits of the green-energy transition."

And then there's China. No nation has captured a larger share of the clean economy transition. The country that already invests more in clean energy and already controls more of the market for solar, EVs, batteries, and other clean energy goods responded to the United States and other countries' clean economy ambitions by investing even more in its own. In 2022, China led the world in clean energy investments, sinking $546 billion into new solar, wind, EVs, storage, and other clean energy sectors, according to BloombergNEF.[33] In its 2020 five-year plan, China said it will double its production of renewable energy and get 50 percent of its electricity from renewables by 2025 by investing even more into wind, solar, big hydro and storage, and micro-grids, especially in rural areas.[34] Already, China's clean energy investments dwarf those of any other country. The United States was a very distant second in 2022, with about $141 billion in clean energy spending—or about a quarter of what China laid out for clean energy. While the dramatic growth in U.S. battery, solar, and EV factory investments captured headlines domestically, more than 90 percent of manufacturing investments globally in 2022 were in China, according to BloombergNEF, with battery and battery-related component factories leading the way.

Led by China and supported by policy changes by governments around the globe, a record $1.1 trillion was invested in clean energy in 2022, according to BloombergNEF. It marked an inflection point for clean energy in more than dollars. "Investment in clean energy technologies is on the brink of overtaking fossil fuel investments, and won't look back," said Albert Cheung, head of global analysis at BloombergNEF.[35] Even so, he added, the world needs to do more—much more—to reduce the impacts of climate change. If it does, the benefits to private industry and communities in America and every other country will continue to accrue. "These investments will drive short-term job creation and help to address medium-term energy security objectives," Cheung said in a statement. "But much more investment is needed to get on track for net zero in the long term."

According to BloombergNEF, the world needs to triple its annual investments in clean energy to get on a trajectory of net-zero emissions by 2050. Like with a retirement account or savings plan, investing early is important. By BloombergNEF's estimates, the world must invest an annual average of $4.55 trillion in the next decade alone to stay on track for its 2050 goals.[36] It's a dizzying amount, equal to the GDP of France and Italy combined. Just to ensure there are enough materials to meet 2050 net-zero goals, huge investments need to be made in clean energy materials mining, processing, and manufacturing—the basic cornerstones of the clean economy. The IEA estimates the world needs to invest an average of $270 billion per year between 2023–2025 into clean energy supply chains to meet 2050 net-zero goals. That's nearly seven times the average amount invested in clean energy supply chains in past years.[37] More public investment will encourage more private investment. If today's global clean energy market is worth $23 trillion, as the International Finance Corporation estimates, tomorrow's market could be exponentially bigger.[38]

Still, the policies passed and investments made by countries in recent years put clean energy and the world in a better place than it's been in a very long time. The wave of clean energy investments sweeping the globe brings with it new opportunities, jobs, and energy security. Global competition will continue to bring prices down for everything from solar panels to EVs, and foster innovation and new technology we can't even imagine yet. All of this will help reduce greenhouse gas emissions, curb the impacts of climate change, and leave a cleaner, healthier planet for future generations.

America, at least for now, is at the center of it all.

Epilogue

"Now Is Not the Time to Go Backward"

MY FIRST JOB AFTER GRADUATING FROM COLLEGE IN 1988 WAS AS A business reporter at the *Greenville News* in South Carolina.

Located along Interstate 85 between Charlotte and Atlanta, Greenville was still a textile town back then, holding on by a thread to an industry steadily moving overseas while desperately searching for a new future. Most of the stories I wrote for the newspaper were about layoffs and bank closures, as the country was in the middle of the savings and loan crisis. The city reflected its economy. Downtown was dominated by empty storefronts and smoke shops. About the only restaurants on Main Street were Kay's Kitchen, where you could get a cafeteria-style plastic plate of fried chicken, overcooked green beans, and mashed potatoes, or if you were feeling adventurous and it happened to be payday, the Red Baron, a kitschy German-style place whose sandwich specialties included its signature Red Baron (corned beef and red cabbage) and the Big Dolly (turkey breast, ham, and ranch-style dressing).

Thirty-three years after leaving Greenville, I returned for the first time as part of my reporting work for this book.

My mind was blown at how the city had changed.

Greenville today is one of the most beautiful and vibrant cities in the American South. Downtown is now dominated by picturesque Falls Park, a grassy, tree-lined natural frame for the waterfalls of the Reedy River that were hidden by kudzu and briars and a since-removed road that ran through the middle of it all back when I lived there. The old *Greenville News* building was replaced by the Peace Center, a renowned performing arts venue and home to the Greenville Symphony Orchestra and the International Ballet. Kay's Kitchen and the Red Baron are gone. Now there's Trappe Door, which specializes in hand-pulled Belgian beers and mussels served four ways, and Between the Trees, a restaurant in the five-star Grand Bohemian hotel, where you can order Carolina bison tenderloin and lobster beignets while watching the water slip over the rocky falls.

Ask anybody what led to Greenville's renaissance and they'll likely say two names: Michelin and BMW.

French tire maker Michelin moved its North American headquarters to Greenville in 1985 and expanded several times since, including building a state-of-the-art research center where researchers are trying to meet a corporate goal of making 100 percent sustainable tires, and a three-million-square-foot, LEED Gold-certified distribution center where forklifts are powered by hydrogen fuel cells. Michelin is the world's biggest tire supplier for EVs. About 80 percent of the tires you see on EVs are Michelins, according to the company.[1]

BMW picked neighboring Spartanburg for its first factory outside of Germany in 1992. It would soon become the automaker's biggest factory in the world, with 11,000 workers producing more than 1,500 vehicles every single day. Soon they will all be electric, powered by batteries built at a new three-hundred-worker factory that will solidify the region as BMW's North American EV hub.[2]

BMW and Michelin aren't just the embodiment of the epic evolution of Greenville and surrounding communities. They're also at the core of a statewide transformation that has unexpectedly made South Carolina a leader in the clean economy revolution. In just one year, between August 2022 and August 2023, companies announced at least eighteen major clean energy projects and $11 billion in investments in South Carolina, ranging from lithium processing plants to solar wafer factories to new EV and battery factories. Only one other state, neighboring Georgia, attracted more new clean energy projects in that time—and just barely with nineteen announcements. It's been the biggest economic boom in the history of either state.

After nearly forty years as a business and political journalist and later, as executive director of a national business organization, I know why this is happening.

It's because of policy.

It was policy passed by the late Republican South Carolina Governor Carroll Campbell while I was a cub reporter in Greenville, including billions in state and local government incentives, that convinced Michelin and BMW to come to greater Greenville and forever change the region's future. It is policy passed by President Biden and Congress, along with hundreds of billions in federal incentives, that is now convincing record numbers of clean energy and clean transportation companies to build and expand at a pace like we could've never imagined, forever changing the future our nation and civilization writ large.

We are in the middle of an economic and environmental transformation like no one has ever seen before. South Carolina and many other states are reaping the benefits.

But here's the thing.

We are also on the verge of squandering it all.

Right after America passed its trifecta of climate and clean energy policy—the IRA, the Infrastructure Investment and Jobs Act, and the CHIPS and Science Act—opponents sprang into action to kill it all. Not because these policies aren't working. They are, whether you measure success by jobs, by foreign and domestic investment, by American competitiveness, by foreign trade, by reduced carbon emissions, or yes, even by lower inflation. I heard optimism like I've never heard before in the voices of the people I talked to across the country for this book: Newly hired solar panel factory workers in Georgia. Clean energy entrepreneurs in Colorado and Illinois. Economic development officials in South Carolina. As one battery factory executive in Georgia told me, "Without the IRA, this all goes away."

The reason opponents are trying to make these policies go away has nothing to do with making America great or stronger or more competitive, and everything to do with politics, pure and simple.

We cannot let politics kill the biggest American business revolution in generations.

If ever there was a time when we needed to tame the ugly beast of partisan politics, it's now. The opportunity for a cleaner, more resilient, more equitable, and more competitive economy is on our front doorstep. The howling specter of climate change and the prospect of increasingly unlivable parts of our planet are pounding at the back door.

As I write this, the world just suffered through its hottest month on record. The average high in Arizona in July 2023 was a record 114.7 degrees Fahrenheit, with nineteen consecutive days of temperatures 110 degrees or higher. The East Coast coughed and wheezed through weeks of smoke from Canadian wildfires. Off the coast of Florida, the Atlantic Ocean topped 101 degrees, among the highest temperatures ever recorded in the ocean. Humanity is in hot water. A month after the mainland experienced its hottest month on record, the deadliest U.S. wildfire in over a century tore through the Hawaiian island of Maui, killing more than one hundred people, causing billions of dollars in damage, and quite literally sending much of the region's tourism-heavy economy up in smoke. San Diego, where I live, is supposed to have the best weather in the country. It's supposed to be a climate change refuge. But a once-in-a-century hurricane just hammered the Baja coastline before dumping more rain on Southern California communities than they historically see in a year. As two of my daughters began college, one had to attend classes virtually because of flooding in San Diego. The other had to wear a mask and stay inside because western wildfires made the air too unhealthy to breathe in Portland, Oregon. This is the world we are leaving our children.

Partisan politics is the biggest threat to policies that can lessen these impacts of climate change while boosting American jobs and the economy. We've already seen the impacts of politics in Congress, in state-houses in places like Texas, and on the campaign trail.

But other threats loom too.

Workforce availability is a big one. Clean energy companies are creating millions of new jobs at a time when unemployment is already near rock-bottom lows, thanks to the red-hot economy. Now that the policy problem is solved, companies I spoke with said their biggest issue is finding enough workers for their factories and projects. We must ensure we have a pipeline of available workers to build this new clean economy, or it won't happen.

Yes, we need to expand union apprenticeship programs and pay good wages and benefits. We also need to change our perspectives on how and where we get workers to fill the coming job boom. That means developing high school curricula that give students a path not just to college after graduation, but also to good-paying careers in clean energy. It means not just locking up convicted criminals and forgetting about them until they hit the streets again, but expanding prison training programs to prepare them for clean energy jobs, and reducing stigmas around hiring ex-cons. It means reexamining immigration policies. At a time we need all the workers we can get, we need to move past the idea that American-born workers are losing all their jobs to immigrants. Tens of thousands of potential workers are hoping, wishing, and praying every day to find jobs in America. We now have more jobs than we have workers. We need to fill those jobs.

Implementation is another huge hurdle. It's one thing to pass laws and set aside money; it's another to implement those laws and make sure the money is going to the right places. In the spring of 2023, I spoke to a group of local government workforce and economic development leaders about community grants and other investments expected to come to them from the federal climate and clean energy laws. Overwhelmingly, I heard they had no idea how to handle the funding that was beginning to flow their way. Biden administration officials, or whoever succeeds them, have a lot of work to do. Local communities and regions expect federal direction and help and need their support.

Misinformation is a tremendous threat, as already evidenced by Donald Trump's falsehoods about clean energy and EVs on the campaign trail, and previously, while in office. It's not just politicians. It's big-monied fossil fuel interests and lobbyists, and politically focused groups that care more about winning elections in the short term than creating a sustainable future for America. In Ohio, a dark money group with ties to the gas industry, along with the conservative American Legislative Exchange Council, or ALEC, pushed through legislation that legally redefined gas as "green energy," helping ensure it will be considered more favorably in state energy plans.³ In California, a lobbyist with ties to the petroleum industry was caught saying he was trying to change the wording of a bill with the expressed intent of misleading lawmakers and environmentalists that using carbon dioxide to stimulate more oil production from wells was a good solution for climate change when in fact producing and using more oil is a driver of climate change.⁴ And then there are groups like the Heritage Foundation and its Project 2025 playbook, which calls for the immediate repeal of the IRA and the bipartisan infrastructure bill, quite literally lumping them and the expansion of clean energy in with drag queens, pornography, communism, and drugs as threats to the foundation and future of America.⁵

Abject nationalism is a problem. Of course we all wish U.S.-based companies could reap 100 percent of the benefits from America's clean energy revolution. Regrettably, some of the same flag-waving politicians who told Americans they were going to make America run on coal again while letting foreign countries and companies take the lead in the clean economy are now suggesting foreign clean energy companies shouldn't get tax breaks for investing in America. But isn't it better for foreign companies to invest and create jobs in America, rather than take American jobs and move them overseas?

Government isn't the solution to climate change, expanding clean energy, or just about anything else. But it must be *part* of the solution. When it comes to changes as monumental as transforming our transportation system, our energy system, our manufacturing sector, and ensuring it's all done with equity, there's no way businesses alone can do it. Biden administration officials are accurate when they say the clean economy revolution is government enabled, but private-sector-powered.

In 2000, the organization I lead, E2, was founded to make the business and economic case for the California clean car standards, the first-ever greenhouse gas tailpipe emissions vehicle limits in the world. E2's founders—investors and business leaders from across the economy and throughout the state—admittedly didn't know much about automobiles or petroleum or greenhouse gases. But they did know about business, investing, and innovation. And they knew that government policy could send the right market signals to industry to invest, expand,

and innovate to meet expected demand—especially when those market signals came from the government in a state like California, the nation's single-biggest automobile market, and on its own the world's fifth-largest economy.

They were right. Despite opponents' fire-and-brimstone predictions that such policies would kill the auto industry and the economy, the exact opposite happened. The clean car standards that E2's founders and members pushed for in Sacramento helped turbocharge an entirely new market for vehicles that pollute less and go farther on a gallon of gasoline. It led to the evolution of hybrid vehicles, and later, EVs. It prompted states across the country, and ultimately the federal government, to adopt similar emissions standards that paved the way for the continued evolution of EVs that today are transforming the nation's transportation sector.

Years later, E2 helped spearhead business support for California's Global Warming Solutions Act. Before President Biden took office, it was the most significant climate policy every passed in America. Governor Schwarzenegger and legislative leaders who drafted the law noted the importance of business voices in making the case for policies that are good for our economy and our environment. As with the clean car standards, California's groundbreaking climate policies made the state the nation's leader in clean energy jobs, investments, and innovation.

The lesson learned was that we must speak up for the things we want; for the brighter, cleaner future we know is possible. The clean economy boom and the investments and jobs pouring into communities nationwide are signposts on a path to a better tomorrow—as long as we don't stop or turn back. Clean energy businesses are innovating, investing, expanding, and hiring new workers at a pace faster than just about any other industry in America. They're also helping address the climate crisis, creating a healthier future for our children, and making America less dependent on foreign suppliers, whether it's the Middle East for oil and gas or China and Asia for batteries, solar panels, and EVs.

Why in the world would we want to stop all of that?

Some say we shouldn't be spending taxpayer money to address climate change and expand clean energy. At another time, others said the same about railroads, highways, space travel, and the research that led to the internet.

Some say foreign companies shouldn't get tax breaks or other benefits for investing in America. Problem is, America's past inaction is what let foreign companies take the lead in the clean economy in the first place. We need to regain that lead.

Some say we should leave it all to businesses and free enterprise, and that the government should butt out. But the biggest challenges in the country—much less the planet—simply can't be solved by business alone. Without government leadership and smart policies, we wouldn't have landed on the moon. We wouldn't have extended railways to the West or highways to every state or the Internet to every computer and phone in the world.

As always, this is a path that will be tough and long. But with every new record heat wave, wildfire, storm, or drought; with every new billion-dollar clean energy investment, and every new job created in solar, wind, battery, or EV factory, we know it's the right thing to do.

Now is not the time to go backward.

We're just getting started.

NOTES

CHAPTER 1

1. American Battlefield Trust, "Kings Mountain," https://www.battlefields.org/learn/revolutionary-war/battles/kings-mountain#:~:text=The%20fierce%20firefight%20at%20Kings,of%20the%20tide%20of%20success.%22.

2. "Albemarle Corporation Announces New U.S. Lithium Mega-Flex Processing Facility in South Carolina," 2023, *PR Newswire*, https://www.prnewswire.com/news-re-leases/albemarle-corporation-announces-new-us-lithium-mega-flex-processing-facili-ty-in-south-carolina-301778807.html.

3. Turbyfill, Diane, "Federal Money to Boost Proposed Lithium Mine," *The Shelby Star*, October 21, 2022, www.shelbystar.com/story/news/2022/10/21/federal-money-to-boost-proposed-kings-mountain-lithium-mine/69574679007.

4. Albemarle Corporation, "Albemarle Kings Mountain Town Hall March 2022," YouTube, June 6, 2022, www.youtube.com/watch?v=FlPiJ1EgsVU.

5. "Albemarle Corporation Announces New U.S. Lithium Mega-Flex Processing Facility in South Carolina," 2023, *PR Newswire*, https://www.prnewswire.com/news-re-leases/albemarle-corporation-announces-new-us-lithium-mega-flex-processing-facili-ty-in-south-carolina-301778807.html.

6. Clean Economy Works, "IRA One-Year Review 2023," E2, https://e2.org/reports/clean-economy-works-2023/.

7. E2 Clean Economy Works Announcements, 2023, E2, https://e2.org/announcements.

8. "Randolph County (1779)—North Carolina History Project," North Carolina History Project, March 16, 2016, northcarolinahistory.org/encyclopedia/randolph-county-1779.

9. Daniel Crews, "Toyota Gearing Up to Start Hiring for Manufacturing Plant at Greensboro-Randolph Megasite," WFMY News 2, March 17, 2023, https://www.wfmynews2.com/article/news/local/toyota-gearing-up-to-start-hiring-for-manufacturing-plant-at-the-greensboro-randolph-megasite-toyota-battery-manufacturing-jobs/83-8d5f8d27-1ef3-481f-b994-106f150508fa.

10. "New York Green Hydrogen Facility," n.d., Air Products, https://www.airproducts.com/energy-transition/new-york-green-hydrogen-facility.

11. Marcus McIntosh, 2022, "Wind Turbine Blade Produc-tion to Resume at Iowa Plant," KCCI, https://www.kcci.com/article/wind-turbine-blade-production-resume-at-iowa-plant/41868795.

12. Katie Sloan, "First Solar Plans $1.1B Solar Module Manufacturing Facility in Northern Alabama," REBusinessOnline, November 2022, rebusinessonline.com/first-solar-plans-1-1b-solar-module-manufacturing-facility-in-northern-alabama.

13. Jon Whiteaker, "Invenergy and LONGi Partner for Ohio Solar Panel Factory," Investment Monitor, March 23, 2023, www.investmentmonitor.ai/news/invenergy-and-longi-partner-for-ohio-solar-panel-factory.

14. QcellS.com, https://qcells.com/us/stay-in-the-loop/trending-news-detail?newsId=NEW220526083613042.

15. "Marjorie Taylor Greene Mocked for Suggesting Solar and Wind Energy Don't Work at Night," *The Independent*, August 15, 2022, www.independent.co.uk/climate-change/news/marjorie-taylor-greene-solar-energy-b2145521.html. NowThis Earth, "Marjorie Taylor Greene Thinks Global Warming Is Good for Us," *YouTube*, June 16, 2022, www.youtube.com/watch?v=4xa8ZxE_ics.

16. AJC.com, "The Jolt: Kemp Looking for Legacy with EV Expansion in Georgia," https://www.ajc.com/politics/politics-blog/the-jolt-kemp-looking-for-legacy-with-ev-expansion-in-georgia/H24XOY52AJEAFKDS46BWXXWW7M/.

17. Goldman Sachs, "The US Is Poised for an Energy Revolution," April 17, 2023. https://www.goldmansachs.com/intelligence/pages/the-us-is-poised-for-an-energy-revolution.html

18. EFI Digital, "EFI Analysis Projects Inflation Reduction Act Impacts," EFI Foundation, December 2022, energyfuturesinitiative.org/insights/efi-analysis-projects-inflation-reduction-act-impacts.

19. Steve Hanley, "One-Third of All Electricity Will Come from Renewables by 2030," CleanTechnica, July 14, 2023, https://cleantechnica.com/2023/07/14/one-third-of-all-electricity-will-come-from-renewables-by-2030/; BloombergNEF. "Global Low-Carbon Energy Technology Investment Surges Past $1 Trillion for the First Time, BloombergNEF," BloombergNEF, January 25, 2023, about.bnef.com/blog/global-low-carbon-energy-technology-investment-surges-past-1-trillion-for-the-first-time; Stuart Stone, "Staggering: US on Cusp of 600 GW Clean Energy Boom," Greenbiz, April 27, 2023. https://www.greenbiz.com/article/staggering-us-cusp-600-gw-clean-energy-boom.

20. "Global Low-Carbon Energy Technology Investment Surges Past $1 Trillion for the First Time, BloombergNEF," BloombergNEF, January 25, 2023, about.bnef.com/blog/global-low-carbon-energy-technology-investment-surges-past-1-trillion-for-the-first-time.

21. Brian Kennedy et al., "Majorities of Americans Prioritize Renewable Energy, Back Steps to Address Climate Change, Pew Research Center," Pew Research Center Science and Society, June 28, 2023, www.pewresearch.org/science/2023/06/28/majorities-of-americans-prioritize-renewable-energy-back-steps-to-address-climate-change.

22. Rob Nikolewski, "Electric Cars: More Consumers Now Want to Buy Them, Survey Says," *San Diego Union-Tribune*, July 8, 2022, www.sandiegouniontribune.com/business/energy-green/story/2022-07-07/electric-cars-growing-number-of-consumers-now-interested-in-buying-them-survey-says.

23. Lauren Sforza, "Majority Expecting 'Significant Negative Effect' from Climate Change: Poll," *The Hill*, 19 July 2023, thehill.com/policy/energy-environment/4106224-majority-expecting-significant-negative-effect-from-climate-change-poll.

24. Josh Saul, "Goldman Sees Biden's Clean-Energy Law Costing US $1.2 Trillion," Bloomberg.com, March 23, 2023, www.bloomberg.com/news/articles/2023-03-23/goldman-sees-biden-s-clean-energy-law-costing-us-1-2-trillion.

25. "Remarks by President Biden on the Inflation Reduction Act and Bidenomics, Milwaukee, WI," the White House, August 2023, www.whitehouse.gov/briefing-room/speeches-remarks/2023/08/15/remarks-by-president-biden-on-the-inflation-reduction-act-and-bidenomics-milwaukee-wi/#:~:text=We're%20going%20to%20have,it's%20that%20trickle%2Ddown%20economics.

26. "IFC Report Identifies More Than $29 Trillion in Climate Investment Opportunities in Cities by 2030," pressroom.ifc.org/all/pages/PressDetail.aspx?ID=25011.

27. Sarah McFarlane, "The Battery Pioneer Who, at Age 96, Keeps Going and Going," *Wall Street Journal*, August 9, 2018, www.wsj.com/articles/the-battery-pioneer-who-at-age-96-keeps-going-and-going-1533807001.

28. Jason Peace Remarks on E2 Press Conference Call, August 16, 2023, https://www.youtube.com/watch?v=GMmCUzxiKX8

29. "Executive Summary—The Role of Critical Minerals in Clean Energy Transitions—Analysis—IEA," n.d., International Energy Agency, https://www.iea.org/reports/the-role-of-critical-minerals-in-clean-energy-transitions/executive-summary.

30. Ana Swanson and Chris Buckley, "Red Flags for Forced Labor Found in China's Car Battery Supply Chain," *New York Times*, November 4, 2022, www.nytimes.com/2022/06/20/business/economy/forced-labor-china-supply-chain.html.

31. "Albemarle Corporation Selects Mecklenburg County for Advanced Lithium Technology Park," Mecklenburg County News Releases, December 13, 2022, news.mecknc.gov/news/albemarle-corporation-selects-mecklenburg-county-advanced-lithium-technology-park.

32. White House, "Remarks as Prepared for Delivery by Senior Advisor John Podesta on the Biden-Harris Administration's Priorities for Energy Infrastructure Permitting Reform," the White House, May 2023, www.whitehouse.gov/briefing-room/speeches-remarks/2023/05/10/remarks-as-prepared-for-delivery-by-senior-advisor-john-podesta-on-the-biden-harris-administrations-priorities-for-energy-infrastructure-permitting-reform.

33. Interview with Rodriguez at Kings Mountain site, March 23, 2023.

34. "How Does the Environmental Impact of Mining for Clean Energy Metals Compare to Mining for Coal, Oil and Gas?," MIT Climate Portal, climate.mit.edu/ask-mit/how-does-environmental-impact-mining-clean-energy-metals-compare-mining-coal-oil-and-gas.

35. Mary Hui and Clarisa Diaz, "EVs Are Far Cleaner Than Gas-Powered Cars—Even If Batteries Require More Mining," Quartz, 3 Mar. 2023, qz.com/electric-vehicles-cleaner-battery-mining-1850129845.

36. Michael Thomas, "A Fossil Fuel Economy Requires 535x More Mining Than a Clean Energy Economy," March 29, 2023, www.distilled.earth/p/a-fossil-fuel-economy

-requires-535x#:~:text=But%20how%20does%20it%20compare,economy%20would
%20require%20in%202040.

37. "Excerpt: 'Railroaded' by Richard White," Scribd, www.scribd.com/document
/57550652/Excerpt-Railroaded-by-Richard-White#.

38. https://www.youtube.com/watch?v=goh2x_G0ct4

39. "Remarks as Prepared for Delivery by U.S. Energy Secretary Jennifer M. Granholm at the 2022 Sydney Energy Forum," Energy.gov, www.energy.gov/articles/remarks
-prepared-delivery-us-energy-secretary-jennifer-m-granholm-2022-sydney-energy
-forum.

CHAPTER 2

1. "FACT SHEET: Biden-Harris Administration Celebrates Historic Progress
in Rebuilding America Ahead of Two-Year Anniversary of Bipartisan Infrastructure Law," 2023, The White House, https://www.whitehouse.gov/briefing-room/
statements-releases/2023/11/09/fact-sheet-biden-harris-administration-celebrates-his-
toric-progress-in-rebuilding-america-ahead-of-two-year-anniversary-of-bipartisan-in-
frastructure-law.

2. https://twitter.com/jim_jordan/status/1392099930978803717

3. US Senator John Barrasso, "Barrasso: Biden's Proposal Builds Back Worse." *News
Releases, United States Senator John Barrasso*, www.barrasso.senate.gov/public/index.cfm
/2021/3/barrasso-biden-s-proposal-builds-back-worse.

4. Houston Keene, "Lindsey Graham Warns Build Back Better 'Spending Orgy' Is
'Paving a Path to Socialism,'" *Fox News*, December 10, 2021, www.foxnews.com/politics/
lindsey-graham-build-back-better-spending-path-socialism.

5. Interview with Gina McCarthy, June 16, 2023.

6. "Chairman Yarmuth's Floor Remarks in Support of the Build Back Better," House
Budget Committee Democrats, February 14, 2023, democrats-budget.house.gov/news/
press-releases/chairman-yarmuth-s-floor-remarks-support-build-back-better-act.

7. "Billion-Dollar Weather and Climate Disasters, National Centers for Environmental Information (NCEI)," NCEI.Monitoring.Info@noaa.gov, www.ncei.noaa.gov/access
/billions.

8. Bryan Metzger, "Mitch McConnell Says the Final Version of the Democrats' 'Build
Back Better' Bill Will Be 'Written by Joe Manchin and Kyrsten Sinema,'" Business
Insider, November 12, 2021, www.businessinsider.com/mitch-mcconnell-build-back
-better-joe-manchin-kyrsten-sinema-reconciliation-2021-11.

9. Emma Ockerman, "Of Course Joe Manchin Drives a Maserati," Vice News, https:
//www.vice.com/en/article/qjb4g7/joe-manchin-drives-maserati.

10. Tony Romm, "Manchin Says He 'Cannot Vote' for Democrats' $2 Trillion Spending
Package, Drawing Sharp White House Rebuke," *Washington Post*, December 31, 2021,
www.washingtonpost.com/us-policy/2021/12/19/manchin-build-back-better-biden.

11. Trevor Hunnicutt, "Manchin Blames White House Staff for Breakdown in Biden
Bill Talks," Reuters, December 21, 2021, www.reuters.com/world/us/manchin-says-white
-house-staff-drove-him-reject-bidens-social-policy-plan-2021-12-20.

12. Clare Foran et al., "Manchin Delivers Grim News for Biden's Build Back Better Plan: 'It's Dead,'" CNN, February 2, 2022, www.cnn.com/2022/02/01/politics/manchin -build-back-better-dead/index.html.

13. Leslie Kaufman, Jennifer A. Dlouhy, Ari Natter, Sana Pashankar, and Janet Paskin, 2022, "President Biden's Climate Ambitions Are All But Dead," Bloomberg.com, https://www.bloomberg.com/news/features/2022-04-27/ president-biden-s-climate-ambitions-are-all-but-dead.

14. Schumer remarks at White House Inflation Reduction Act event, August 16, 2023.

15. "Annual 2021 Drought Report," 2022, National Centers for Environmental Infor- mation, https://www.ncei.noaa.gov/access/monitoring/monthly-report/drought/202113.

16. Meeting with Senator Carper at E2 event in Silicon Valley, April 22, 2022.

17. Mariko Paulson, "The Impact of the Build Back Better Act (H.R. 5376) on Infla- tion," Penn Wharton Budget Model, April 2022, budgetmodel.wharton.upenn.edu/is- sues/2021/12/17/build-back-better-act-hr-5376-inflation.

18. Akshat Rathi and Jennifer A. Dlouhy, "Bill Gates, Joe Manchin, and How Biden's Inflation Reduction Act Almost Failed," Bloomberg.com, August 17, 2022, www .bloomberg.com/news/features/2022-08-16/how-bill-gates-lobbied-to-save-the-climate -tax-bill-biden-just-signed.

19. Bill Gates discussion at Cascadia Innovation Corridor conference, September 2022.

20. "Breaking: Manchin Puts Final Nail in the Biden Agenda Coffin," July 15, 2022, https://thehill.com/hilltv/rising/3560851-rising-july-15-2022/.

21. https://twitter.com/SenSchumer/status/1533787856258355201

22. Mountain Valley Pipeline Project, https://www.mountainvalleypipeline.info.

23. https://twitter.com/SenTinaSmith/status/1552414678214664193

24. Brian Schwartz, "How Wall Street Wooed Sen. Kyrsten Sinema and Preserved Its Multibillion-dollar Carried Interest Tax Break," CNBC, August 10, 2022, www.cnbc .com/2022/08/09/how-wall-street-wooed-sen-kyrsten-sinema-and-preserved-its-multi -billion-dollar-carried-interest-tax-break.html.

25. "Manchin Bill to Close Carried Interest Tax Loophole, Eliminate Tax Breaks for Wall Street Investment Managers," US Senator Joe Manchin of West Virginia, May 12, 2021, www.manchin.senate.gov/newsroom/press-releases/manchin-bill-to-close-carried -interest-tax-loophole-eliminate-tax-breaks-for-wall-street-investment-managers.

26. Joan Meiners, "Will Kyrsten Sinema See the New Climate and Inflation Bill as a Good Deal for Arizona?" *Arizona Republic*, August 3, 2022, www.azcentral.com/story /news/local/arizona-environment/2022/08/03/how-arizona-sen-sinema-vote-climate -inflation-bill/10205938002.

27. www.msn.com/en-us/news/politics/schumer-defends-dropping-carried-interest -tax-change-to-win-over-sinema/ar-AA10lv01.

28. Schumer remarks at White House Inflation Reduction Act event, August 16, 2023.

CHAPTER 3

1. Robinson Meyer, "Why the CHIPS and Science Act Is a Climate Bill," *The Atlantic*, September 12, 2022, www.theatlantic.com/science/archive/2022/08/chips-act-climate -bill-biden/671095.

2. "How Much Did the Apollo Program Cost?" n.d., The Planetary Society, https://www.planetary.org/space-policy/cost-of-apollo.

3. Richard F. Weingroff, n.d., "Federal-Aid Highway Act of 1956: Creating The Interstate System | FHWA," Federal Highway Administration, https://highways.dot.gov/public-roads/summer-1996/federal-aid-highway-act-1956-creating-interstate-system.

4. Bill Dupor, 2021, "How Recent Fiscal Interventions Compare with the New Deal," Federal Reserve Bank of St. Louis, https://www.stlouisfed.org/publications/regional-economist/third-quarter-2021/how-recent-fiscal-interventions-compare-new-deal.

5. David Leonhardt, "An Exit Interview with Brian Deese," *New York Times*, February 22, 2023, www.nytimes.com/2023/02/22/briefing/brian-deese-exit-interview.html.

6. Kate Gordon speech to Climate Leadership Conference, Los Angeles, May 12, 2023.

7. Interview with Gina McCarthy, June 16, 2023.

8. Billion-Dollar Weather and Climate Disasters, National Centers for Environmental Information (NCEI), www.ncei.noaa.gov/access/billions.

9. "The US Is Poised for an Energy Revolution," Goldman Sachs, April 17, 2023, www.goldmansachs.com/intelligence/pages/the-us-is-poised-for-an-energy-revolution.html.

10. "The US Is Poised for an Energy Revolution," 2023, Goldman Sachs, https://www.goldmansachs.com/intelligence/pages/the-us-is-poised-for-an-energy-revolution.html.

11. www.documentcloud.org/documents/23257578-ira-a-tipping-point-in-climate-action-1.

12. "Inflation Reduction Act Guidebook," White House, https://www.whitehouse.gov/wp-content/uploads/2022/12/Inflation-Reduction-Act-Guidebook.pdf.

13. "Remarks as Prepared for Delivery by Secretary Jennifer Granholm at CERAWeek 2023," Energy.gov, www.energy.gov/articles/remarks-prepared-delivery-secretary-jennifer-granholm-ceraweek-2023.

14. Interview with Betty Jaing, January 11, 2023.

15. Interview with Robert Howey at Qcells factory, Dalton, Georgia, July 12, 2023.

16. Kelly Pickerel, "REC Silicon to Lay Off 100 Employees at Washington Polysilicon Production Facility," Solar Power World, August 30, 2022, www.solarpowerworldonline.com/2018/07/rec-silicon-to-lay-off-100-employees-at-washington-polysilicon-production-facility.

17. "Hanwha Pledges Commitment to Build a Fully American Solar Supply Chain," Hanwha Solutions, March 23, 2022, https://www.prnewswire.com/news-releases/hanwha-pledges-commitment-to-build-a-fully-american-solar-supply-chain-301508928.html.

18. Interview with Scott Moskowitz, March 27, 2023.

19. "Levelized Cost of Energy," www.lazard.com/perspective/levelized-cost-of-energy-levelized-cost-of-storage-and-levelized-cost-of-hydrogen.

20. Nicole Pollack, "On Competitiveness with Renewables, Dry Fork Station Stands Alone, Report Finds," *Casper Star Tribune*, June 5, 2023, https://trib.com/business/energy/on-competitiveness-with-renewables-dry-fork-station-stands-alone-report-finds/article_e3f156d0-a1bd-11ed-b2af-2b07fe94961a.html.

21. Roberto Baldwin et al., "EV vs. Gas: Which Cars Are Cheaper to Own?" *Car and Driver*, December 7, 2022, www.caranddriver.com/shopping-advice/a32494027/ev-vs -gas-cheaper-to-own.

22. "EFI Analysis Projects Inflation Reduction Act Impacts," EFI Foundation, December 2022, energyfuturesinitiative.org/insights/efi-analysis-projects-inflation-re-duction-act-impacts.

23. "IRA Jobs Factsheet," Blue Green Alliance, https://www.bluegreenalliance.org/wp -content/uploads/2022/08/BGA-IRA-Jobs-Factsheet-8422_Final.pdf.

24. "Jobs, Emissions, and Economic Growth—What the Inflation Reduction Act Means for Working Families," n.d., EFI Foundation, https://efifoundation.org/wp-con-tent/uploads/sites/3/2023/03/NDC-Report-January-17-v2.pdf.

25. Interview with Dave Foster, February 13, 2023.

CHAPTER 4

1. Timeline History of Natural Gas and Oil Tax Provisions, IPPA, http://www.ipaa .org/wp-content/uploads/2016/12/2009-04-TimelineHistoryofNaturalGasandOilTaxP rovisions.pdf.

2. Environmental and Energy Study Institute (EESI), "Fact Sheet, Fossil Fuel Subsi-dies: A Closer Look at Tax Breaks and Societal Costs," 2019, www.eesi.org/papers/view/ fact-sheet-fossil-fuel-subsidies-a-closer-look-at-tax-breaks-and-societal-costs.

3. Interview with Michael Rucker, February 23, 2023.

4. "The Inflation Reduction Act and the Path to a Net Zero America," Princeton University Zero Lab, https://cpree.princeton.edu/sites/g/files/toruqf651/files/documents /2022-09-12%20-%20Inflation%20Reduction%20Act%20and%20Path%20to%20Net -Zero.pdf.

5. "Global Energy Perspective 2022," McKinsey & Company, April 26, 2022, www .mckinsey.com/industries/oil-and-gas/our-insights/global-energy-perspective-2022.

6. State of California, "Milestone: 1 in 4 New Cars Sold in California Were Zero-Emission," California Governor, August 2, 2023, www.gov.ca.gov/2023/08 /02/milestone-1-in-4-new-cars-sold-in-california-were-zero-emission/#:~:text =California%20Governor-,MILESTONE%3A%201%20in%204%20New%20Cars,in %20California%20Were%20Zero%2DEmission&text=SACRAMENTO%20%E2%80 %93%20In%20a%20historic%20first,two%20years%20ahead%20of%20schedule.

7. EEITV, "Elon Musk and EEI Chair Pedro J. Pizarro, President and CEO, Edi-son International at EEI 2023," YouTube, June 23, 2023, www.youtube.com/watch?v =t_WFsgjqpOU; Tim Higgins, "Elon Musk's Latest Mission: Rev Up the Electricity Industry," *Wall Street Journal*, July 29, 2023, www.wsj.com/articles/elon-musks-latest -mission-rev-up-the-electricity-industry-1583a184.

8. The Inflation Reduction Act and the Path to a Net Zero America."

9. "WINDExchange: Production Tax Credit and Investment Tax Credit for Wind Energy," windexchange.energy.gov/projects/tax-credits#:~:text=The%20Production%20 Tax%20Credit%20(PTC,facility%20is%20placed%20into%20service.

10. Diana DiGangi, "New Clean Energy Investments Have Topped $40B since the IRA Passed, Report Says," Utility Dive, December 15, 2022, www.utilitydive.com/news/ira-clean-energy-investments-billions-solar-manufacturing/638809.

11. "Energy Transition Investment Trends 2023," BloombergNEF, https://assets.bbhub.io/professional/sites/24/energy-transition-investment-trends-2023.pdf.

12. "Clean Economy Works, Tracking New Clean Energy Projects across U.S.," April 24, 2023, e2.org/announcements; "Clean Energy Investing in America," ACP, August 7, 2023, cleanpower.org/investing-in-america.

13. Interview with Jon Carson, July 25, 2023.

14. "Solar Market Insight Report 2022 Year in Review," SEIA, www.seia.org/research-resources/solar-market-insight-report-2022-year-review.

15. Frank Andorka, "Origis Energy Completes Georgia's Second-Largest Solar Installations," Solar Power World, February 10, 2014, www.solarpowerworldonline.com/2014/02/origis-energy-completes-georgias-second-largest-solar-installations.

16. "Origis Announces New $750 Million Construction Warehouse Facility," Origis Energy, August 16, 2023, https://www.prnewswire.com/news-releases/origis-energy-announces-new-750-million-construction-warehouse-facility-301901412.html.

17. Diana DiGangi, "First Solar Brings US Manufacturing Investment to $4B after Selling Out of Panels through 2025," Utility Dive, February 1, 2023, www.utilitydive.com/news/first-solar-billion-domestic-manufacturing-ira-ohio/641692/#:~:text=First%20Solar%20is%20investing%20%241.3,out%20of%20product%20through%202026.

18. "Wind Blade Manufacturer TPI Plans to Reopen Newton Plant. But New Jobs Might Be Months Away," Des Moines Register, November 4, 2022, www.desmoinesregister.com/story/money/business/2022/11/04/tpi-composites-newton-iowa-10-year-lease-reopen-plant/69619151007.

19. "Siemens to Reopen Wind Plants in Kansas and Iowa," Oklahoma Energy Today, March 13, 2023, www.okenergytoday.com/2023/03/siemens-to-reopen-wind-plants-in-kansas-and-iowa/?utm_source=rss&utm_medium=rss&utm_campaign=siemens-to-reopen-wind-plants-in-kansas-and-iowa#:~:text=The%20%E2%80%9Chibernation%E2%80%9D%20Siemens%20Gamesa%20Renewable,of%20slow%20wind%20turbine%20orders.

20. Jenkins speech, Center for Policy Research on Energy and the Environment (C-PREE), cpree.princeton.edu/events/2022/inflation-reduction-act-and-path-net-zero-america.

21. "Wind Power Risks Becoming Too Cheap, Says Top Turbine Maker," Reuters, November 24, 2021, www.reuters.com/markets/commodities/wind-power-risks-becoming-too-cheap-says-top-turbine-maker-2021-11-24.

22. "Fact Sheet: Biden-Harris Administration Announces New Actions to Expand U.S. Offshore Wind Energy," the White House, September 2022, www.whitehouse.gov/briefing-room/statements-releases/2022/09/15/fact-sheet-biden-harris-administration-announces-new-actions-to-expand-u-s-offshore-wind-energy.

23. Wayne Parry, "US Gives Go-Ahead for Orsted's New Jersey Offshore Wind Farm to Start Construction," AP News, July 5, 2023, apnews.com/article/offshore-wind-orsted-new-jersey-boem-approved-047f15b29fee4e951fb2fa64a923c646.

24. Josh Saul, Will Mathis, and Rachel Morison, "Planet Saving Wind Farms Fall Victim to Global Inflation Fight," Bloomberg News, March 10, 2023, www.bloomberg.com/news/articles/2023-03-10/offshore-wind-farms-face-fresh-hurdles-around-the-world-because-of-inflation?leadSource=uverify%20wall.

25. Lawrence Berkeley Lab, "Queued Up: Characteristics of Power Plants Seeking Transmission Interconnection," Electricity Markets and Policy Group, emp.lbl.gov/queues.

26. Lawrence Berkeley Lab, "Generation, Storage, and Hybrid Capacity in Interconnection Queues," Electricity Markets and Policy Group, emp.lbl.gov/generation-storage-and-hybrid-capacity.

27. Brad Plumer, "Wind and Solar Energy Projects Risk Overwhelming America's Antiquated Electrical Grids," *New York Times*, June 20, 2023, www.nytimes.com/2023/02/23/climate/renewable-energy-us-electrical-grid.html.

28. Evan Raskin, "California Breaks Record by Achieving 100% Renewable Energy for the First Time," Earth Day, August 2022, www.earthday.org/california-breaks-record-by-achieving-100-renewable-energy-for-the-first-time/#:~:text=June%2010%2C%202022,for%20the%20first%20time%20ever.

29. California ISO, "Managing Oversupply," www.caiso.com/informed/Pages/ManagingOversupply.aspx.

30. Lights on California, "What Is an RTO," April 2023, lightsonca.org/what-is-an-rto.

31. "Fact Sheet: The Bipartisan Infrastructure Deal," the White House, March 2023, www.whitehouse.gov/briefing-room/statements-releases/2021/11/06/fact-sheet-the-bipartisan-infrastructure-deal.

32. "Big but Affordable Effort Needed for America to Reach Net-Zero Emissions by 2050, Princeton Study Shows," Princeton University, December 15, 2020, www.princeton.edu/news/2020/12/15/big-affordable-effort-needed-america-reach-net-zero-emissions-2050-princeton-study.

33. Chloe Holden, "The Price of a Fully Renewable US Grid: $4.5 Trillion," Wood Mackenzie, July 1, 2019, www.greentechmedia.com/articles/read/renewable-us-grid-for-4-5-trillion.

34. Leonard Susskind et al., "Sources of Opposition to Renewable Energy Projects in the United States," *Energy Policy* 165 (June 2022): 112922. https://doi.org/10.1016/j.enpol.2022.112922.

35. "Big but Affordable Effort Needed."

36. Daniel Moore, "Why a US Transmission Line Planned 17 Years Ago Still Isn't Built," Bloomberg.com, March 15, 2023, www.bloomberg.com/news/features/2023-03-15/why-a-us-transmission-line-planned-17-years-ago-still-isn-t-built.

37. "Pattern Shares Anticipated Economic Impact from SunZia Transmission, Wind Projects," North American Windpower, April 2023, nawindpower.com/pattern-shares-anticipated-economic-impact-from-sunzia-transmission-wind-projects.

38. "Bringing It Home: Manufacturing," *Washington Post Live*, March 21, 2023.

39. "Remarks as Prepared for Delivery by Senior Advisor John Podesta on the Biden-Harris Administration's Priorities for Energy Infrastructure Permitting Reform," the White House,, May 2023, www.whitehouse.gov/briefing-room/speeches-remarks

/2023/05/10/remarks-as-prepared-for-delivery-by-senior-advisor-john-podesta-on-the
-biden-harris-administrations-priorities-for-energy-infrastructure-permitting-reform.

40. "Fact Sheet: Biden-Harris Administration Outlines Priorities for Building America's Energy Infrastructure Faster, Safer, and Cleaner," the White House, May 2023, www .whitehouse.gov/briefing-room/statements-releases/2023/05/10/fact-sheet-biden-harris -administration-outlines-priorities-for-building-americas-energy-infrastructure-faster -safer-and-cleaner.

41. "Congress Passes Inflation Reduction Act," *Permitting Dashboard*, www.permits .performance.gov/fpisc-content/congress-passes-inflation-reduction-act.

42. "Remarks as Prepared for Delivery by Senior Advisor John Podesta on the Biden-Harris Administration's Priorities for Energy Infrastructure Permitting Reform," the White House, May 2023, www.whitehouse.gov/briefing-room/speeches-remarks /2023/05/10/remarks-as-prepared-for-delivery-by-senior-advisor-john.

43. "Webcast: Federal Infrastructure Permitting—FAST-41 Reforms and What's Next on Capitol Hill," Gibson Dunn, February 21, 2023, www.gibsondunn.com/webcast -federal-infrastructure-permitting-fast-41-reforms-and-whats-next-on-capitol-hill.

CHAPTER 5

1. Motorward, "General Motors Keynote, CES 2022," *YouTube*, January 6, 2022, www .youtube.com/watch?v=rDAwAeSVljY.

2. "GM Authority: GM Stock Value Sets New Record," https://gmauthority.com/blog /2022/01/gm-stock-value-sets-new-record-following-mary-barras-ces-2022-keynote -speech/.

3. Owen Edwards, n.d., "The Death of the EV-1 | Science," *Smithsonian Magazine*, https://www.smithsonianmag.com/science-nature/the-death-of-the-ev-1-118595941.

4. "General Motors Responds on Electric Vehicles," *Wall Street Journal*, August 12, 2022, www.wsj.com/articles/general-motors-gm-ev-electric-vehicle-cars-auto-industry -11660247608?mod=article_inline.

5. "BEV Models Currently Available in the US," *EVAdoption*, March 4, 2023, evadoption.com/ev-models/bev-models-currently-available-in-the-us/#:~:text- t=As%20of%20March%203%2C%202023%20there%20are%2040%20battery%2Delec- tric,models%20available%20in%20the%20US.

6. "Clean Economy Works: IRA One-Year Review," E2, August 17, 2023, e2.org/reports/clean-economy-works-2023.

7. Colin McKerracher, "Electric Car Sales Top $1 Trillion in Wake-Up Call for Automakers," *Bloomberg.com*, February 14, 2023, www.bloomberg.com/news/articles/2023-02 -14/electric-vehicle-sales-top-1-trillion-in-wake-up-call-for-carmakers#xj4y7vzkg.

8. "Ford to Lead America's Shift to Electric Vehicles with New Mega Campus in Tennessee and Twin Battery Plants in Kentucky; $11.4B Investment to Create 11,000 Jobs and Power New Lineup of Advanced Evs," Ford Media Center, September 27, 2021, https://media.ford.com/content/fordmedia/fna/us/en/news/2021/09/27/ford-to-lead -americas-shift-to-electric-vehicles.html.

9. "LPO Announces Conditional Commitment for Loan to BlueOval SK to Further Expand U.S. EV Battery Manufacturing Capacity," *Energy.gov*, www.energy.gov/lpo

/articles/lpo-announces-conditional-commitment-loan-blueoval-sk-further-expand-us
-ev-battery.

10. "Stanton, TN," www.realtor.com/realestateandhomes-search/Stanton_TN/
overview.

11. "BlueOval City," Ford, https://corporate.ford.com/operations/blue-oval-city.html.

12. "How VW Paid $25 Billion for Dieselgate—and Got off Easy," *ProPublica*, March
2, 2020, www.propublica.org/article/how-vw-paid-25-billion-for-dieselgate-and-got-off
-easy.

13. "Scout Motors Selects South Carolina," SC Governor's Office, https://governor
.sc.gov/news/2023-03/scout-motors-selects-south-carolina-production-site-plans-create
-4000-jobs.

14. "Scout Motors Selects South Carolina," https://governor.sc.gov/news/2023-03/
scout-motors-selects-south-carolina-production-site-plans-create-4000-jobs;

Keith Naughton, "VW's Scout Brand Builds $2 Billion Electric Vehicle Plant with
IRA Funds," *Bloomberg.com*, March 21, 2023, www.bloomberg.com/news/articles/2023
-03-20/vw-sees-biden-backed-support-for-ev-manufacturing-as-gold-rush.

15. Dan Mihalascu, "EVs Made Up 5.6 Percent of US Car Market in 2022 Driven by
Tesla," *InsideEVs*, February 20, 2023, insideevs.com/news/653395/evs-made-up-5point6-
percent-of-overall-us-car-market-in-2022-driven-by-tesla.

16. "Tesla Model Y Second Only to Ford F-150 as Best-Selling Vehicle in US,"
InsideEVs, June 19, 2023, insideevs.com/news/672690/tesla-model-y-second-only-ford-
f-150-best-selling-vehicle-us.

17. Ella Nilsen, "EPA Proposes New Tailpipe Rules That Could Push EVs to Make
Up Two-Thirds of New Car Sales in US by 2032," *CNN*, April 22, 2023, amp.cnn.
com/cnn/2023/04/12/politics/car-pollution-standards-electric-vehicles-biden-climate/
index.html. Ira Boudway, "More Than Half of US Car Sales Will Be Electric by 2030,"
Bloomberg.com, September 20, 2022, www.bloomberg.com/news/articles/2022-09-20/
more-than-half-of-us-car-sales-will-be-electric-by-2030.

18. Mark Kane, "California: Plug-In Car Sales Surged to 24% Market Share
in Q4 2022," *InsideEVs*, February 10, 2023, insideevs.com/news/651899/cali-
fornia-plugin-car-sales-2022q4/#:~:text=California%3A%20Plug%2DIn%20
Car%20Sales,Market%20Share%20In%20Q4%202022. "Advanced Clean Fleets
Regulation Summary," California Air Resources Board, May 17, 2023, ww2.arb.
ca.gov/resources/fact-sheets/advanced-clean-fleets-regulation-summary#:~:-
text=State%20and%20local%20agencies.,are%20zero%2Demission%20by%20
2027.

19. "Advanced Clean Fleets Regulation Summary."

20. "Hyundai Motor Group," Georgia Department of Economic Development, www
.georgia.org/hyundaimotorgroup.

21. Russ Num, "Hyundai Gets $1.8B in Aid to Build Electric Cars in Georgia," AP
News, July 22, 2022, apnews.com/article/technology-georgia-electric-vehicles-savan-
nah-f86760ac7a198c589a7ef1dd97b83c27.

22. Alexa St. John, "Biden Wants EV Chargers on Every 50 Miles of Highway. That
Misses a Key Piece of the Electrification Puzzle," Business Insider, February 15, 2023,

www.businessinsider.com/ev-charging-highway-network-plan-tesla-biden-white-house
-home-2023-2.

23. "Fact Sheet: Biden-Harris Administration Announces New Standards and Major Progress for a Made-in-America National Network of Electric Vehicle Chargers," the White House, February 2023, www.whitehouse.gov/briefing-room/ statements-releases/2023/02/15/fact-sheet-biden-harris-administration-announces-new -standards-and-major-progress-for-a-made-in-america-national-network-of-electric -vehicle-chargers.

24. "US Electric Vehicle Charging Market Growth by 2030," PricewaterhouseCoopers, www.pwc.com/us/en/industries/industrial-products/library/electric-vehicle-charging -market-growth.html.

25. "US Electric Vehicle Charging Market Growth by 2030."

26. Federal Highway Administration, State Motor Vehicle Registrations, by Years, https://www.fhwa.dot.gov/ohim/summary95/mv200.pdf.

27. "The History of Fuel Retailing," www.convenience.org/Topics/Fuels/The-History -of-Fuels-Retailing.

28. "Plug in America," http://pluginamerica.org/wp-content/uploads/2023/05/2023 -EV-Survey-Final.pdf.

29. Ryan Fisher, "Electric Car-Charging Investment Soars Driven by EV Growth, Government Funds," *Bloomberg.com*, August 18, 2022, www.bloomberg.com/news/articles /2022-08-16/car-charging-investment-soars-driven-by-ev-growth-and-government -funds.

30. "ChargePoint Secures Additional $127 Million in Funding," *ChargePoint*, www .chargepoint.com/about/news/chargepoint-secures-additional-127-million-funding.

31. "EV Charging Company EnviroSpark Secures $15 Million in Total Funding, Led by Investments from Ultra Capital and Top Ga. Business Leaders," EnviroSpark, December 14, 2022, www.prnewswire.com/news-releases/ev-charging-company-envirospark -secures-15-million-in-total-funding-led-by-investments-from-ultra-capital-and-top -ga-business-leaders-301703312.html.

32. "Itselectric Raises $2.2M Pre-Seed Funding Round to Close the Urban EV Charging Gap," Itselectric, March 7, 2023, www.prnewswire.com/news-releases /itselectric-raises-2-2m-pre-seed-funding-round-to-close-the-urban-ev-charging-gap -301764039.html.

33. "Leading the Charge: Walmart Announces Plan to Expand Electric Vehicle Charging Network," Corporate US, April 6, 2023, corporate.walmart.com/news-room/2023/04/06/leading-the-charge-walmart-announces-plan-to-expand-electric-ve-hicle-charging-network.

34. "Charging," Rivian, rivian.com/experience/charging.

35. "Electrify America Raises $450 Million—Siemens Becomes a Minority Shareholder; Company Intensifies Commitment to Rapid Deployment of Ultra-Fast Charging," Electrify America, media.electrifyamerica.com/en-us/releases/190.

36. Steven Loveday et al., "A Comprehensive Guide to U.S. EV Charging Networks," *U.S. News & World Report*, January 2023, cars.usnews.com/cars-trucks/advice/ev-charging-stations.

37. Interview with Ariel Fan.

38. David Rempel, Carleen Cullen, Mary Matteson Bryan, and Gustavo Vianna Cezar, "Reliability of Open Public Electric Vehicle Direct Current Fast Chargers," University of California, Berkeley, https://arxiv.org/ftp/arxiv/papers/2203/2203.16372.pdf.

39. www.chargerhelp.com.

40. "Biden-Harris Administration Making $100 Million Available to Improve EV Charger Reliability," US Department of Transportation, September 13, 2023, https://highways.dot.gov/newsroom/biden-harris-administration-making-100-million-available-improve-ev-charger-reliability.

41. "Frito-Lay Transforms California Facility into Showcase for Sustainability," January 18, 2023, www.prnewswire.com/news-releases/frito-lay-transforms-california-facility-into-showcase-for-sustainability-301725247.html.

42. National Grid. "Electric Highways Study: Summary Sheet," November 2022, https://www.nationalgrid.com/document/148621/download.

43. "The Tesla Semi Is Finally Here," CNBC, February 18, 2023, www.cnbc.com/video/2023/02/18/the-tesla-semi-is-finally-here.html.

CHAPTER 6

1. "Trane Technologies Surpasses Department of Energy Requirements," Business Wire, November 3, 2022. https://www.businesswire.com/news/home/20221103005955/en/Trane-Technologies-Surpasses-U.S.-Department-of-Energy-Requirements-for-High-Efficiency-Cold-Climate-Heat-Pump.

2. "What Is a Heat Pump? History and Information about Heat Pump Technology," Finn Geotherm, August 9, 2023, finn-geotherm.co.uk/the-history-of-heat-pumps/#:~:text=The%20first%20heat%20pump%20as,dry%20salt%20in%20salt%20marshes.

3. "How a Heat Pump Works," IEA, www.iea.org/reports/the-future-of-heat-pumps/how-a-heat-pump-works.

4. "How to Find the Best Hybrid Heat Pump Water Heater," December 2022, carbonswitch.com/heat-pump-water-heater-buyers-guide/#:~:text=Heat%20pump%20water%20heaters%20are%20generally%204x%20more%20efficient%20than,you%20between%20%243%2C000%20and%20%244%2C000.%E2%80%99%20192.%20%20MIT%20Technology%20Review:%20Everything%20you%20need%20to%20know%20about.

5. Casey Crownhart, "Everything You Need to Know about the Wild World of Heat Pumps," MIT Technology Review, February 17, 2023, www.technologyreview.com/2023/02/14/1068582/everything-you-need-to-know-about-heat-pumps.

6. "Why the Building Sector?" architecture2030.org/why-the-building-sector/#:~:text=The%20built%20environment%20generates%2040,for%20an%20additional%2013%25%20annually. "EPA.GOV," https://www.epa.gov/system/files/documents/2021-12/section-2-building-performance-standards_2-12-2021_v2.pdf.

7. "Bringing Infrastructure Home," Rewiring America, www.rewiringamerica.org/policy/bringing-infrastructure-home-report.

8. "Energy Information Administration (EIA)—Commercial Buildings Energy Consumption Survey (CBECS)" www.eia.gov/consumption/commercial.

9. "Chart: Americans Bought More Heat Pumps Than Gas Furnaces Last Year," *Canary Media*, February 10, 2023, www.canarymedia.com/articles/heat-pumps/chart -americans-bought-more-heat-pumps-than-gas-furnaces-last-year.

10. "Global Heat Pump Sales Continue Double-Digit Growth," *IEA*, www.iea.org/ commentaries/global-heat-pump-sales-continue-double-digit-growth.

11. "Pumpspiration Pump: Chic—Test Drive a Heat Pump," www.pumpchic.com/ pumpspiration.

12. https://twitter.com/mikefsway/status/1503362924529823756

13. "Heat Pumps Are Sexy Short-Sleeve Unisex T-Shirt," Energy Alabama, July 28, 2023, energyalabama.org/product/heat-pumps-are-sexy-short-sleeve-unisex-t-shirt.

14. "Biden-Harris Administration Announces $250 Million to Accelerate Electric Heat Pump Manufacturing Across America," Energy.gov, www.energy.gov/articles/biden -harris-administration-announces-250-million-accelerate-electric-heat-pump.

15. https://www.fox13memphis.com/news/carrier-looking-to-fill-hundreds-of-full -time-jobs/article_7b02f606-4e2c-56fe-89de-b03842eea34c.html

16. "Carrier Announces Portfolio Transformation to Create Global Leader in Intelligent Climate and Energy Solutions," April 25, 2023, www.prnewswire.com/news-releases /carrier-announces-portfolio-transformation-to-create-global-leader-in-intelligent -climate-and-energy-solutions-301807509.html.

17. Chris Bryant, "Energy Transition: Who Wants to Become a Heat-Pump Billionaire?" Bloomberg.com, May 17, 2023, www.bloomberg.com/opinion/articles/2023-05-17 /energy-transition-who-wants-to-become-a-heat-pump-billionaire.

18. "12.80.010 Findings and Purpose," Berkeley Municipal Code, berkeley.municipal. codes/BMC/12.80.010.

19. Susie Cagle, "Berkeley Became First US City to Ban Natural Gas. Here's What That May Mean for the Future," *The Guardian*, August 26, 2021, www.theguardian.com/ environment/2019/jul/23/berkeley-natural-gas-ban-environment.

20. Alex Ayers, "Changing Heat Pump Demand in California," HARDI, https:// efiling.energy.ca.gov/Lists/DocketLog.aspx?docketnumber=22-DECARB-01

21. "California Ban on Gas Appliances Starts with Jan. 1 'All Electric' Rule," gvwire.com/2022/12/16/california-ban-on-gas-appliances-starts-with-jan-1-all-elec-tric-rule/#:~:text=1%20'All%20Electric'%20Rule,-Published&text=New%20homes%20 and%20buildings%20that,by%20the%20California%20Energy%20Commission.

22. State of California, https://www.gov.ca.gov/wp-content/uploads/2022/07/07.22 .2022-Governors-Letter-to-CARB.pdf?emrc=1054d6

23. US Courts for the Ninth Circuit: California Restaurant Association v. City of Berkeley 21–16278, https://www.ca9.uscourts.gov/cases-of-interest/california-restaurant -association-v.city-of-berkeley/

24. "Zero Emission Building Ordinances," BDC, June 20, 2023, buildingdecarb.org/zeb-ordinances.

25. Jennifer Peltz, "NYC Moves to Stop New Buildings from Using Natural Gas," AP News, December 16, 2021, apnews.com/article/climate-technology-business-environ-ment-and-nature-new-york-ef51dcf3091a497a2d0fef28d4308ea2.

26. "LA Bans Natural Gas in New Buildings," *Grist*, January 6, 2023, grist.org/beacon/la-bans-natural-gas-in-new-buildings.

27. Isabella Breda, 2023, "WA Adopts New Rules to Phase Out Fossil Fuels in New Construction," *Seattle Times*, https://www.seattletimes.com/seattle-news/environment/wa-adopts-new-rules-to-phase-out-fossil-fuels-in-new-construction.

28. Anna Phillips, "N.Y. Ditches Gas Stoves, Fossil Fuels in New Buildings in First Statewide Ban in U.S.," *Washington Post*, May 7, 2023, www.washingtonpost.com/climate-environment/2023/05/03/newyork-gas-ban-climate-change.

29. "DOE Releases New Report on Anniversary of Inflation Reduction Act Detailing How POTUS' Investing in America Agenda Will Strengthen U.S. Economy by 2030," Energy.gov, www.energy.gov/articles/doe-releases-new-report-anniversary-inflation-reduction-act-detailing-how-potus-investing#:~:text=WASHINGTON%2C%20D.C.%20%E2%80%94%20Today%2C%20on,the%20U.S.%20Energy%20Economy%20and.

30. RMI, New York: Single-Family Homes, https://rmi.org/wp-content/uploads/dlm_uploads/2020/10/eeb_nyc.pdf.

31. RMI, Austin: Single Family Homes, https://rmi.org/wp-content/uploads/dlm_uploads/2020/10/eeb_all_cities.pdf.

32. E2, "Building Opportunity: New York," https://e2.org/wp-content/uploads/2022/04/Building-Opportunities-NY-Decarbonization.-Apr-2022.-E2.pdf

33. E2, "Building Opportunity: Chicago," https://e2.org/wp-content/uploads/2023/01/E2CleanBuildingsCH-FS-22-12-A_04.pdf

34. Interview with Steve Eubanks, Henderson, North Carolina, July 15, 2023.

35. "Introducing Trane Technologies," *Trane Technologies Blog*, February 2023, blog.tranetechnologies.com/en/home/sustainable-investing/introducing-trane-technologies.html.

36. https://www.linkedin.com/in/dave-regnery-ab91aa10/details/experience/

37. Trane Transcript. CITI Conference, https://s2.q4cdn.com/950394465/files/doc_downloads/2022/03/Trane-Transcript-Citi-Conference-February-2022.pdf.

38. Trane Technologies, "Trane Technologies CEO Dave Regnery Discusses Climate Change," YouTube, 9 Nov. 9, 2021, www.youtube.com/watch?v=xLA9s2jjl2g.

39. Trane Technologies, "Trane Technologies CEO Dave Regnery."

40. "Heat Pump Water Heaters," Energy.gov, www.energy.gov/energysaver/heat-pump-water-heaters#:~:text=How%20They%20Work&text=Heat%20pump%20water%20heaters%20use,like%20a%20refrigerator%20in%20reverse.

41. "Heat Pump Water Heaters—Game Changers in Efficiency," CleanTechnica, April 28, 2020, cleantechnica.com/2020/04/26/heat-pump-water-heaters-game-changers-in-efficiency.

42. "Residential Heat Pump (Hybrid) Water Heater Market, Production, and Trade," US International Trade Commission, https://www.usitc.gov/publications/332/executive_briefings/ebot_residential_heat_pump_hybrid_water_heaters.pdf; carbonswitch.com/heat-pump-water-heater-buyers-guide/#:~:text=Heat%20pump%20water%20heaters%20are%20generally%204x%20more%20efficient%20than,you%20between%20%243%2C000%20and%20%244%2C000.

43. "Commercial Heat Pump Water Heater," Rheem Manufacturing Company, www.rheem.com/commercialheatpumpwaterheater/?utm_source =commercialheatpumpwaterheater&utm_medium=vanityURL&utm_campaign =vanityURL.

44. "Heat Pump Water Heater," Rewiring America, www.rewiringamerica.org/app/ira -calculator/information/heat-pump-water-heater.

45. Kaddie Sharpe, "Brewer Company's Expansion Will Bring Jobs to Bangor," March 3, 2023, www.wabi.tv/2023/03/03/brewer-companys-expansion-will-bring-job-bangor.

46. https://twitter.com/RonnyJacksonTX/status/1612839703018934274

47. "New Study Finds Research on Natural Gas Cooking and Asthma Fails to Demonstrate Causal Relationship," American Gas Association, May 4, 2023, www.aga .org/news/news-releases/new-study-finds-research-on-natural-gas-cooking-and-asthma -fails-to-demonstrate-causal-relationship. Hiroko Tabuchi, "In the Fight Over Gas Stoves, Meet the Industry's Go-To Scientist," *New York Times*, January 30, 2023, www .nytimes.com/2023/01/29/climate/gas-stove-health.html.

48. Aaron Gell, "Gas Stove Ban Panic Could Fuel Induction Range Growth," Bloomberg.com, March 9, 2023, www.bloomberg.com/news/features/2023-03-09/gas -stove-ban-panic-could-fuel-induction-range-growth.

49. "Induction Cooktops Market Size, Share and Trends Analysis Report by Product (Built-in, Free-Standing), by Application (Household, Commercial), by Distribution Channel (Online, Specialty Stores), and Segment Forecasts, 2021–2028," www .grandviewresearch.com/industry-analysis/induction-cooktops-market.

50. "2021–2022 Residential Induction Cooking Tops," Energy Star, www.energystar .gov/partner_resources/brand_owner_resources/spec_dev_effort/2021_residential_ induction_cooking_tops.

51. "Impulse Launches with $20M Series A to Accelerate Electrification with Next-Gen Home Appliances," Impulse Blog, www.impulselabs.com/blog/impulse-labs -series-a-annoucement.

52. https://www.channingcopper.com/products/pre-order

53. "Invisacook Induction Cooktop," Design Delivered LA, invisacook.shop/?useYB=1.

54. https://e4thefuture.org/wp-content/uploads/2022/12/EE-Jobs-in-America_All -States_2022.pdf

55. "Updated Inflation Reduction Act Modeling," Energyinnovation.org, https:// energyinnovation.org/wp-content/uploads/2022/08/Updated-Inflation-Reduction-Act -Modeling-Using-the-Energy-Policy-Simulator.pdf.

56. "Energy Efficiency Jobs in America 2022," E4TheFuture, https://e4thefuture.org/ wp-content/uploads/2022/12/EE-Jobs-in-America_All-States_2022.pdf..

Chapter 7

1. "DOE National Laboratory Makes History by Achieving Fusion Ignition," Energy.gov, www.energy.gov/articles/doe-national-laboratory-makes-history-achieving -fusion-ignition.

2. Ben Brasch et al., "U.S. Lab Says It Repeated Fusion Energy Feat—With Higher Yield," *Washington Post*, August 7, 2023, www.washingtonpost.com/climate-solutions /2023/08/06/nuclear-fusion-net-energy-gain-higher-yield.

3. "From the FIA," Fusion Industry Association, May 30, 2023, www .fusionindustryassociation.org/about-fusion-industry.

4. "Technology," CFS, cfs.energy/technology.

5. https://www.helionenergy.com/our-technology/

6. https://www.zapenergy.com/how-it-works

7. James Temple, "This Startup Says Its First Fusion Plant Is Five Years Away. Experts Doubt It," *MIT Technology Review*, May 9, 2023, www.technologyreview.com/2023/05 /10/1072812/this-startup-says-its-first-fusion-plant-is-five-years-away-experts-doubt -it.

8. "Small Modular Reactors," www.iaea.org/topics/small-modular-reactors.

9. "Voygr Power Plants," https://www.nuscalepower.com/en/products/voygr-smr -plants.

10. "CFPP—Carbon Free Power Project," www.cfppllc.com.

11. "Utah Cities Are Sticking with Their Nuclear Power Plan after a Hefty Price Jump," *Salt Lake Tribune*, March 7, 2023, www.sltrib.com/renewable-energy/2023/03/03 /utah-cities-are-sticking-with.

12. Cat Clifford, "America's First New Nuclear Reactor in Nearly Seven Years Starts Operations," CNBC, July 31, 2023, www.cnbc.com/2023/07/31/vogtle-unit-3-nuclear -reactor-long-delayed-starts-delivering-power.html.

13. "Scaling Green Hydrogen in a Post-IRA World," Rhodium Group, March 16, 2023, rhg.com/research/scaling-clean-hydrogen-ira.

14. Emily Pontecorvo, "Why the 'Swiss Army Knife' of Climate Solutions Is So Controversial," *Grist*, October 2021, grist.org/energy/why-the-swiss-army-knife-of-climate-solutions-is-so-controversial.

15. "Green Hydrogen Market Size, Share and Trends Analysis Report by Technology (PEM Electrolyzer, Alkaline Electrolyzer), by Application (Power Generation, Transportation), by Distribution Channel, by Region, and Segment Forecasts, 2022–2030," www .grandviewresearch.com/industry-analysis/green-hydrogen-market.

16. "The Clean Hydrogen Opportunity for Hydrocarbon-Rich Countries," November 23, 2022, www.mckinsey.com/industries/oil-and-gas/our-insights/the-clean-hydrogen -opportunity-for-hydrocarbon-rich-countries?cid=other-eml-alt-mkq-mck&hlkid =72e14398152440cba5313793e6ac78eb&hctky=14558187&hdpid=3ab51353-88d4 -437c-8542-3d4bec465fac%E2%80%99.

17. "Financial Incentives for Hydrogen and Fuel Cell Projects," Energy.gov, www .energy.gov/eere/fuelcells/financial-incentives-hydrogen-and-fuel-cell-projects.

18. "IRA Clean Hydrogen Tax Credit: Debunking Five Myths," April 24, 2023, www .nrdc.org/bio/pete-budden/ira-clean-hydrogen-tax-credit-debunking-five-myths.

19. Letter to Department of Energy Sec. Jennifer Granholm, "Don't Believe the 'Hydrogen Hype'—Reject All Applications for Department of Energy Regional Clean Hydrogen Hubs," August 22, 2023, https://www.biologicaldiversity.org/programs/ climate_law_institute/pdfs/National-Hydrogen-Letter-8_22_23.pdf.

20. Ian Palmer, "Here's How Oil and Gas Companies Are Jumping on Hydrogen, but Is It Over-Rated," *Forbes*, 8 June 2023, www.forbes.com/sites/ianpalmer/2023/06/08/heres-how-oil-and-gas-companies-are-jumping-on-hydrogen-but-is-it-over-rated/?sh=19fb74f932e3.

21. "ADVANCED CLEAN ENERGY STORAGE," n.d., Department of Energy, https://www.energy.gov/lpo/advanced-clean-energy-storage.

22. IPP Renewed—Intermountain Power Agency, www.ipautah.com/ipp-renewed.

23. "US Dept. of Energy Awards Delta Hydrogen Project $504 Million Loan Guarantee," *Millard County Chronicle Progress*, May 4, 2022, millardccp.com/featured-local-news/54-featured-news/6535-us-dept-of-energy-awards-delta-hydrogen-project-504-million-loan-guarantee.

24. "DOE Announces First Loan Guarantee for a Clean Energy Project in Nearly a Decade," Energy.gov, www.energy.gov/articles/doe-announces-first-loan-guarantee-clean-energy-project-nearly-decade.

25. Molly Burgess, "Air Products to Build Alberta's First Commercial-Scale Hydrogen Station," Gasworld, May 2, 2023, www.gasworld.com/story/air-products-to-build-albertas-first-commercial-scale-hydrogen-station.

26. Air Products, "Seifi Ghasemi in Conversation with Reuters BreakingViews on Hydrogen's Role in the Energy Transition," YouTube, January 31, 2022, www.youtube.com/watch?v=tJjQlSN6Vu8.

27. Frontier Solar Holdings, July 29, 2020, frontiersolarholdings.com.

28. "$4B Hydrogen Production Facility Planned for Idled Oklaunion Site," *Southwest Ledger*, December 23, 2022, www.southwestledger.news/news/4b-hydrogen-production-facility-planned-idled-oklaunion-site.

29. Reuters, "LIVE: Air Products CEO Seifi Ghasemi Talks to Reuters," YouTube, January 25, 2022, www.youtube.com/watch?v=UKCTVPYd240.

30. www.facebook.com/watch/live/?ref=watch_permalink&v=938372253190277

31. Ben Tracy and Analisa Novak, "Cement Industry Accounts for about 8% of CO2 Emissions. One Startup Seeks to Change That," CBS News, January 22, 2023, www.cbsnews.com/news/cement-industry-co2-emissions-climate-change-brimstone.

32. https://www.mhi.com/products/engineering/co2plants_process.html; "Additional Selections for Funding Opportunity Announcement 2515," Energy.gov, www.energy.gov/fecm/additional-selections-funding-opportunity-announcement-2515.

33. https://springmillstatepark.com/gus-grissom-memorial/

34. "Additional Selections for Funding Opportunity Announcement 2515."

35. "Carbon Removal in the Bipartisan Infrastructure Law and Inflation Reduction Act," World Resources Institute, www.wri.org/update/carbon-removal-BIL-IRA.

36. "Biden-Harris Administration Announces Up to $1.2 Billion for Nation's First Direct Air Capture Demonstrations in Texas and Louisiana," Energy.gov, August 11, 2023, https://www.energy.gov/articles/biden-harris-administration-announces-12-billion-nations-first-direct-air-capture.

37. "Oil Industry Sees a Vibe Shift on Climate Tech," *Politico*, March 8, 2023, www.politico.com/news/2023/03/08/oil-industry-shift-climate-tech-00085853.

38. Interview with Vikram Aiyer, May 16, 2023.

39. https://calpinecarboncapture.com/calpine-blue-planet-transform-captured-carbon-into-high-grade-limestone/

40. https://www.businesswire.com/news/home/20220908005446/en/CarbonCapture-Inc.-Announces-Five-Megaton-Direct-Air-Capture-and-Storage-Project-in-Wyoming

41. Interview with Matthew Bright, CarbonCapture director of external affairs, May 11, 2023.

42. Justine Calma, "Microsoft Inks Another Deal to Capture and Store Its Carbon Emissions Underground," The Verge, March 22, 2023, www.theverge.com/2023/3/22/23651587/microsoft-climate-tech-startup-carboncapture-wyoming.

43. "California Can Pave the Way on Decarbonizing Cement," December 14, 2022, www.nrdc.org/bio/christina-theodoridi/california-can-pave-way-decarbonizing-cement; Nadia Lopez, "Climate-Friendly Cement? California Takes on a High-Carbon Industry," CalMatters, June 29, 2022, calmatters.org/environment/2022/06/california-cement-carbon-climate.

44. Irina Ivanova, "Texas Winter Storm Costs Could Top $200 Billion—More Than Hurricanes Harvey and Ike," CBS News, February 25, 2021, www.cbsnews.com/news/texas-winter-storm-uri-costs.

45. Cameron Murray, "Eolian Claims First Use of Inflation Reduction Act Standalone ITC for 200MW Battery Storage Projects," Energy-Storage.News, March 2023, www.energy-storage.news/eolian-claims-first-use-of-inflation-reduction-act-standalone-itc-for-200mw-battery-storage-projects.

46. L. P. Eolian, "Eolian Closes First-of-Its-Kind Standalone Battery Energy Storage Tax Equity Financing," February 13, 2023, www.prnewswire.com/news-releases/eolian-closes-first-of-its-kind-standalone-battery-energy-storage-tax-equity-financing-301745302.html. Accessed August 24, 2023.

47. "Gas and Power Forward Curves," n.d., S&P Global, https://www.spglobal.com/commodityinsights/en/products-services/electric-power/gas-and-power.

48. "Annual and Q4 2022 Funding and M&A Report for Storage, Grid and Efficiency," Mercom Capital Group, January 24, 2023, mercomcapital.com/product/annual-q4-2022-funding-ma-report-for-storage-grid-efficiency.

49. "Biden-Harris Administration Announces Nearly $350 Million For Long-Duration Energy Storage Demonstration Projects," 2022, Department of Energy, https://www.energy.gov/articles/biden-harris-administration-announces-nearly-350-million-long-duration-energy-storage.

50. "White Pine Pumped Storage Project," www.whitepinepumpedstorage.com; "Giant 1GW Pumped-hydro Energy Storage Project Enters Final Review," Canary Media, March 9, 2023, www.canarymedia.com/articles/hydropower/giant-1gw-pumped-hydro-energy-storage-project-enters-final-review.

51. "Pumped Storage Hydropower," rPlus Energies, www.rplusenergies.com/pumped-storage-hydropower.

52. "Biden-Harris Administration Announces $325 Million For Long-Duration Energy Storage Projects to Increase Grid Resilience and Protect America's Communities," Department of Energy, https://www.energy.gov/articles/

biden-harris-administration-announces-325-million-long-duration-energy-storage-projects.

53. Alex DeMarban, "Plan for $330M Energy Storage Project in Healy Moves Forward," *Anchorage Daily News*, September 27, 2023, https://www.adn.com/business-economy/energy/2023/09/26/plan-for-330m-energy-storage-project-in-healy-moves-forward/#:~:text=The%20project%20will%20use%20a,electricity%20using%20a%20heat%20engine; Julian Spector, "Long Duration Storage Gets Big Boost with $325M from DOE," Canary Media, September 22, 2023. https://www.canarymedia.com/articles/long-duration-energy-storage/long-duration-storage-gets-big-boost-with-325m-from-doe; "Biden-Harris Administration Announces $325 Million for Long-Duration Energy Storage Projects," Energy Department, September 22, 2023, https://www.energy.gov/articles/biden-harris-administration-announces-325-million-long-duration-energy-storage-projects.

54. Kirsti Marohn, "'Rusty' Batteries Could Hold Key to Minnesota's Carbon-Free Power Future," MPR News, August 3, 2023, www.mprnews.org/story/2023/02/10/rusty-batteries-could-hold-key-to-carbonfree-power-future.

55. Brad McElhinny, "Form Energy Says $760 Million Project Will Pay Off for West Virginia," WV MetroNews, February 6, 2023, wvmetronews.com/2023/01/31/form-energy-says-760-million-project-will-pay-off-for-west-virginia; "Form Energy to Build Facility in West Virginia Steel Town," December 28, 2022, https://www.thecentersquare.com/west_virginia/article_0bfcbf5c-862f-11ed-b3aa-77ebc98d248e.html.

56. "Gov. Justice Announces Form Energy Will Site First American Battery Manufacturing Plant in Weirton," governor.wv.gov/News/press-releases/2022/Pages/Gov.-Justice-announces-Form-Energy-will-site-first-American-battery-manufacturing-plant-in-Weirton.aspx.

57. David Iaconangelo and Brian Dabbs, "DOE Awards Loan for Massive 'Virtual Power Plant' Project," EE News, April 21, 2023, https://www.eenews.net/articles/doe-awards-loan-for-massive-virtual-power-plant-project/.

58. "LPO Offers First Conditional Commitment for a Virtual Power Plant," Department of Energy, April 20, 2023, https://www.energy.gov/lpo/articles/lpo-offers-first-conditional-commitment-virtual-power-plant-sunnovas-project-hestia.

59. Telephone interview with Jigar Shah, November 21, 2022.

CHAPTER 8

1. "History of East Palo Alto," County of San Mateo, California, www.smcgov.org/district-4-warren-slocum/history-east-palo-alto#:~:text=The%20crack%20epidemic%20decimated%20the,a%20population%20of%20just%2024%2C000.

2. 2023 Silicon Valley Index, Joint Venture Silicon Valley, https://jointventure.org/download-the-2023-index.

3. 2023 Silicon Valley Index.

4. 2023 Silicon Valley Index.

5. "New Berkeley Lab Report on Solar-Adopter Income and Demographic Trends," Electricity Markets and Policy Group, emp.lbl.gov/news/new-berkeley-lab-report-solar-adopter-2.

6. "Tesla Model 3 Demographics: Income, Age, Gender and More," Hedges and Company, February 2022, hedgescompany.com/blog/2019/03/tesla-model-3-demographics-income.

7. "About Us, People of Red Mountain," peopleofredmountain.com/about-us.

8. "Remarks by President Biden at Signing of an Executive Order on Racial Equity," the White House, January 2021, www.whitehouse.gov/briefing-room/speeches-remarks /2021/01/26/remarks-by-president-biden-at-signing-of-an-executive-order-on-racial -equity/#:~:text=And%20I%20firmly%20believe%20the,of%20America%20for%20every %20American.

9. Email interview with Tom Soto, September 2023.

10. "Knight Diversity of Asset Managers Research Series: Industry," Knight Foundation, December 2, 2021. https://knightfoundation.org/reports/knight-diversity-of-asset -managers-research-series-industry/#fn-1.

11. Jake Rosenfeld and Meredith Kleykamp, "Organized Labor and Racial Wage Inequality in the United States," *American Journal of Sociology* (March 2012), https://www .journals.uchicago.edu/doi/10.1086/663673.

12. Kate Gordon speech at Climate Leadership Summit, Los Angeles, May 12, 2023.

13. https://www.herox.com/InclusiveEnergyInnovationPrize; https://www .feedthesecondline.org/programs/getlitstaylit

14. Interview with Ajulo Othow, May 31, 2023.

15. "Help Wanted: Diversity in Clean Energy," E2.org, September 9, 2021, https:// e2.org/wp-content/uploads/2021/09/E2-ASE-AABE-EEFA-BOSS-Diversity-Report -2021.pdf.

16. Emma Foehringer Merchant, "US Solar Industry's Top Jobs Remain Dominated by White Men," Wood Mackenzie, May 7, 2019, www.greentechmedia.com/articles/read /us-solar-industrys-top-jobs-remain-dominated-by-white-men.

17. "Black Founders Still Raised Just 1% of All VC Funds in 2022," January 6, 2023, techcrunch.com/2023/01/06/black-founders-still-raised-just-1-of-all-vc-funds- in-2022/?guccounter=1#:~:text=In%20total%2C%20U.S.%20Black%20found- ers,Let's%20break%20this%20down.

18. Sara Silano, "Women Founders Get 2% of Venture Capital Funding in U.S.," Morningstar, Inc., March 6, 2023, www.morningstar.com/alternative-investments/ women-founders-get-2-venture-capital-funding-us.

19. Interview with Tonya Hicks, June 23, 2023.

20. Interview with Devin Hampton, June 28, 2023.

21. "About the Greenhouse Gas Reduction Fund | US EPA," 2023, Environmental Protection Agency, https://www.epa.gov/greenhouse-gas-reduction-fund/ about-greenhouse-gas-reduction-fund.

22. "EPA Releases Framework for the Implementation of the Greenhouse Gas Reduction Fund as Part of President Biden's Investing in America Agenda," U.S. EPA, April 19, 2023, www.epa.gov/newsreleases/epa-releases-framework-implementation-greenhouse -gas-reduction-fund-part-president.

23. "EPA Releases Framework."

24. Kison Patel, "15 Top Venture Capital Firms in the World (2023 Updated)," Deal-room.net, July 3, 2023, dealroom.net/blog/top-venture-capital-firms. Accessed August 24, 2023.

25. Michael Regan discussion at NRDC Green Leaders for Change meeting, Washington, April 26, 2023.

26. "Environmental Justice History," Energy.gov, https://www.energy.gov/lm/environmental-justice-history#:~:text=The%20initial%20environmental%20justice%20spark,of%20toxic%20waste%20along%20roadways.

27. Michael Regan discussion at NRDC."

28. "Best and Worst States for Climate Change," Policygenius, www.policygenius.com/homeowners-insurance/best-and-worst-states-for-climate-change/#:~:text=2.-,Mississippi,in%20a%20low%20emissions%20future.

29. Kyle Solar and Clio Admin., "Tacony Plantation," Clio: Your Guide to History, September 12, 2018, Accessed June 13, 2023. www.theclio.com/entry/13611

30. "First to Tell the Truth," NPCA.org., Fall 2022, https://www.npca.org/articles/3269-first-tell-the-truth.

31. "Natchez, MS-LA," Data USA, datausa.io/profile/geo/natchez-ms-la.

32. Energy.gov. https://www.energy.gov/sites/default/files/2022-10/DOE%20BIL%20Battery%20FOA-2678%20Selectee%20Fact%20Sheets%20-%201_2.pdf

33. Office of Governor, John Bel Edwards,_https://gov.louisiana.gov/index.cfm/newsroom/detail/3860.

34. Office of Governor, John Bel Edwards.

35. Marc Wiley, "These Are the Worst States for Electric Vehicle Ownership," Motor-Biscuit, April 2023, www.motorbiscuit.com/avoid-worst-states-ev-ownership-plan-buy-electric-vehicle; Scooter Doll, "Current EV Registrations in the US: How Does Your State Stack Ip and Who Grew the Most YOY?" Electrek, August 2022, electrek.co/2022/08/24/current-ev-registrations-in-the-us-how-does-your-state-stack-up.

CHAPTER 9

1. "Where Our Oil Comes From," U.S. Energy Information Administration (EIA), www.eia.gov/energyexplained/oil-and-petroleum-products/where-our-oil-comes-from.php.

2. Adrian Hedden, "Oil and Gas Revenue at an All-time High in New Mexico. Industry Touts Growth," *Carlsbad Current-Argus*, September 21, 2022, www.currentargus.com/story/news/2022/09/21/oil-and-gas-revenue-on-new-mexico-state-land-grows-to-2-billion/69504732007.

3. Michael Gerstein, "Report Oil and Gas Interests Spent $11.5M in New Mexico Politics in Recent Years," *Santa Fe New Mexican*, March 31, 2020, https://www.santafenewmexican.com/news/legislature/report-oil-and-gas-interests-spent-11-5m-in-new-mexico-politics-in-recent-years/article_42b86826-7362-11ea-b076-0f1eeb8d01f9.html.

4. Interview with Stephanie Garcia Richard, November 29, 2022.

5. Billy Ludt, "26-MW Solar Project under Construction on New Mexico State Trust Land," Solar Power World, October 20, 2022, www.solarpowerworldonline.com/2022/10/solar-project-under-construction-on-new-mexico-state-trust-land.

6. NM State Land Office, "Land Office Brings in Record-Shattering $2.4 Billion," October 5, 2022, www.nmstatelands.org/2022/10/05/land-office-brings-in-record-shattering-2-4-billion.

7. California Air Resources Board. "AB 32 Global Warming Solutions Act," https://ww2.arb.ca.gov/resources/fact-sheets/ab-32-global-warming-solutions-act-2006.

8. "Clean Jobs America," E2, https://e2.org/wp-content/uploads/2022/08/E2-FS-2022-Clean-Jobs-America.pdf.

9. E2 interview (by Nicole Lederer) with Governor Schwarzenegger at E2 20th Anniversary celebration, October 5, 2021.

10. E2 interview (by Nicole Lederer) with Governor Schwarzenegger..

11. "State Renewable Portfolio Standards and Goals," August 23, 2023, www.ncsl.org/energy/state-renewable-portfolio-standards-and-goals#:~:text=Thirty%20states%2C%20Washington%2C%20D.C.%2C,opposing%20trends%20in%20recent%20years; "Table of 100% Clean Energy States," Clean Energy States Alliance, February 9, 2023, www.cesa.org/projects/100-clean-energy-collaborative/guide/table-of-100-clean-energy-states.

12. ACEEE, "State Scorecard Rank," database.aceee.org/state-scorecard-rank.

13. ACEEE, "State Scorecard Rank," database.aceee.org/state-scorecard-rank.

14. Massachusetts Clean Energy Center, "2022 Massachusetts Clean Energy Industry Report," 2022, https://www.masscec.com/sites/default/files/documents/2022%20Massachusetts%20Clean%20Energy%20Industry%20Report_Final.pdf.

15. Sabrina Shankman, "Baker Signs Major Climate Bill into Law," BostonGlobe.com, August 12, 2022, www.bostonglobe.com/2022/08/11/science/baker-signs-major-climate-bill-into-law.

16. United Nations Treaty Collection, Chapter XXVII Environment, Paris Agreement: https://treaties.un.org/Pages/ViewDetails.aspx?src=TREATY&mtdsg_no=XXVII-7-d&chapter=27&clang=_en, p. 351. https://www.usclimatealliance.org/publications/2018/1/4/ca-governor-brown-ny-governor-cuomo-and-wa-governor-inslee-announce-formation-of-us-climate-alliance.

17. Office of Governor Edmund G. Brown Jr., "CA Gov. Brown, NY Governor Cuomo and WA Gov. Inslee Announce Formation of US Climate Alliance," June 1, 2017, https://www.ca.gov/archive/gov39/2017/06/01/news19818/index.html.

18. United States Climate Alliance, "2022 Annual Report," https://static1.squarespace.com/static/5a4cfbfe18b27d4da21c9361/t/632879f89c4448476bd312ad/1663597050469/USCA_2022+Annual+Report-Final_20220915-low+res.pdf.

19. Inslee speech at Climate Leadership Conference, Los Angeles, May 12, 2023.

20. https://www.eviation.com/wp-content/uploads/2022/09/Eviation-First-Flight-Press-Release-9.27.22.docx-1.pdf

21. "University Hydrogen Successfully Completes First Flight of Hydrogen Regional Airliner," Businesswire, March 2, 2023, https://www.businesswire.com/news/home

/20230302005768/en/Universal-Hydrogen-Successfully-Completes-First-Flight-of
-Hydrogen-Regional-Airliner.

22. "Sustainable Aviation Fuel Credit," Internal Revenue Service, www.irs.gov/credits
-deductions/businesses/sustainable-aviation-fuel-credit.

23. Cantwell speech at NRDC Action Fund dinner, Washington, D.C., April 25, 2023.

24. https://news.alaskaair.com/newsroom/alaska-airlines-makes-significant
-investment-in-sustainable-aviation-fuel/

25. Dominic Gates, "New $800M Sustainable Aviation Fuel Plant Planned for Wash-
ington State," *The Seattle Times*, May 19, 2023, www.seattletimes.com/business/boeing
-aerospace/new-800m-sustainable-aviation-fuel-plant-planned-for-washington-state.

26. Douglas P. Woodward, "Assessing Economic Development Incentives: Lessons from BMW," *National Tax Association Proceedings* 87(1994), www
.jstor.org/stable/42912346?read-now=1&seq=3#page_scan_tab_contents; Andy
Levine, "BMW and South Carolina: The Big Deal That Almost Never Happened," Development Counsellors International (DCI), June 18, 2018,
aboutdci.com/2017/07/bmw-south-carolina-big-deal-that-almost-never-happened.

27. "Economist: BMW Plant Spartanburg Adds $26.7 Billion to SC's Economy.
Here's How," *Spartanburg Herald-Journal*, March 22, 2023, www.goupstate.com/story
/news/local/2023/03/22/bmw-plant-spartanburg-billions-to-south-carolina-economy
/70028044007.

28. "BMW Group Announces $1.7 Billion (USD) Investment to Build Electric
Vehicles in the US," BMW, October 19, 2022, https://www.bmwgroup-werke.com/
spartanburg/en/news/2022/BMW-Group-Electrification-Plans-Press-Release.html.

29. "Envision AESC to Establish Florence County Electric Vehicle Gigafactory,"
South Carolina Governor's Office, December 6, 2022, https://governor.sc.gov/news/2022
-12/envision-aesc-establish-florence-county-electric-vehicle-battery-gigafactory.

30. "Clean Economy Works," E2, https://e2.org/announcements/.

31. "Governor Puts His Weight behind Electric Vehicle Industry," GSA Business
Report, October 14, 2022, https://gsabusiness.com/news/automotive/82700.

32. Interview with John Lummus, July 14, 2023.

33. Interview with Trip Tollison, July 21, 2023.

34. "Georgia Gov. Kemp Signs Tax Exemption, State Budget into Law at Hyundai
EV Plant Site," *Savannah Morning News*, May 5, 2023, www.savannahnow.com/story/
news/2023/05/05/georgia-governor-bryan-kemp-signing-ceremony-hyundai-metaplant
-bryan/70187060007. "Announced HMGMA Suppliers—Savannah Harbor-Interstate
16 Corridor," Savannah Joint Development Authority, www.savannahjda.com/hmgma
-suppliers.

35. "Hyundai Motor Group and LG Energy Solution to Establish Battery Cell Manufacturing Joint Venture in the U.S.," Hyundai Motors, May 26, 2023, www.hyundai
.com/worldwide/en/company/newsroom/hyundai-motor-group-and-lg-energy-solution
-to-establish-battery-cell-manufacturing-joint-venture-in-the-u.s.-0000017038.

36. "Economic Development Agreement," State of Georgia, May 2, 2022, https://www
.georgia.org/sites/default/files/2022-05/jda-rivian_-_economic_development_agreement
.pdf.

37. "Kia Unveils New Electric Vehicle Fleet to Be Manufactured at Georgia Plant," WSB-TV Channel 2, Atlanta, April 5, 2023, www.wsbtv.com/news/local/atlanta/kia-unveils-new-electric-vehicle-fleet-with-interior-made-partially-recycled-materials/7KKM7RE6EZDB3KGSGP55R3QACU.

38. "Governor Walz Signs Bill Moving Minnesota to 100 Percent Clean Energy by 2040," Michigan Commerce Department, February 7, 2023, https://mn.gov/commerce/news/?id=17-563384.

39. Dan Kraker, 2023, "State Lawmakers Agree to 'Historic' Environment and Climate Bill," *MPR News*, https://www.mprnews.org/story/2023/05/18/state-lawmakers-agree-to-historic-environment-and-climate-bill.

40. "How Did Minnesota Pass a 100 Percent Clean Electricity Standard? We Talked to the Experts," Evergreen Action, February 16, 2023, www.evergreenaction.com/blog/how-did-minnesota-pass-a-100-percent-clean-electricity-standard-we-talked-to-the-experts.

41. "New York Passes First Statewide Ban on Gas in New Buildings," Canary Media, May 3, 2023, www.canarymedia.com/articles/fossil-fuels/new-york-passes-first-statewide-ban-on-gas-in-new-buildings.

42. Susan Arbetter, "New York Advocates Push 'All-Electric Building Act' as a Response to the High Costs of Heating Oil," Spectrum News 1 Central NY, November 29, 2022, spectrumlocalnews.com/nys/central-ny/politics/2022/11/28/new-york-advocates-push-the—all-electric-building-act-.

43. "Building Opportunity: New York," E2, https://e2.org/wp-content/uploads/2022/04/Building-Opportunities-NY-Decarbonization.-Apr-2022.-E2.pdf.

44. "Mayor De Blasio Signs Landmark Bill to Ban Combustion of Fossil Fuels in New Buildings," The Official Website of the City of New York, December 22, 2021, www.nyc.gov/office-of-the-mayor/news/852-21/mayor-de-blasio-signs-landmark-bill-ban-combustion-fossil-fuels-new-buildings.

45. "Mayor De Blasio Signs Landmark Bill."

46. "Mayor Adams Announces $4 Billion Plan to Make New Schools All-Electric, Electrify 100 Existing Schools," The Official Website of the City of New York, October 28, 2022, www.nyc.gov/office-of-the-mayor/news/787-22/mayor-adams-4-billion-plan-make-new-schools-all-electric-electrify-100-existing#/0.

47. "California's Energy Efficiency Success Story," NRDC, July 2013, https://www.nrdc.org/sites/default/files/ca-success-story-FS.pdf.

48. "California Energy Efficiency Jobs in America," E4theFuture and E2, 2022, https://e4thefuture.org/wp-content/uploads/2022/12/California_2022.pdf.

49. "Appliance Efficiency Program: Outreach and Education," California Energy Commission, www.energy.ca.gov/programs-and-topics/programs/appliance-efficiency-program-outreach-and-education; "Our History," Energy Star, www.energystar.gov/about/how_energy_star_works/history.

50. "PHL to Test New Electric Locomotive at California Ports," Progressive Railroading, www.progressiverailroading.com/mechanical/news/PHL-to-test-new-electric-locomotive-at-California-ports--69186.

51. Ben Klayman, "GM to Supply Electric Batteries, Hydrogen Fuel Cell Systems for Wabtec Locomotive," Reuters, June 15, 2021, www.reuters.com/business/sustainable-business/gm-supply-electric-batteries-hydrogen-fuel-cell-systems-wabtec-locomotive-2021-06-15.

52. Laine Randolph remarks at E2 Celebration of Climate Action event in San Francisco, September 27, 2022.

CHAPTER 10

1. "Republican Party of Texas Resolution on Fossil Fuels," Republican Party of Texas, March 17, 2023, texasgop.org/fossilfuelsresolution.

2. Russell Gold, "The Texas GOP's War on Renewable Energy," *Texas Monthly*, May 9, 2023, www.texasmonthly.com/news-politics/texas-republican-war-on-renewable-energy.

3. Erin Douglas, "Texas Power Outage: Why Natural Gas Went Down during the Winter Storm," *The Texas Tribune*, February 20, 2021, www.texastribune.org/2021/02/16/natural-gas-power-storm.

4. "Texas Senate Passes Anti-Renewable Energy Legislation," Environment Texas, April 5, 2023, environmentamerica.org/texas/media-center/texas-senate-passes-anti-renewable-energy-legislation; Miranda Willson and Jason Plautz, "Could Texas Lawmakers End the State's Renewable Boom?" E&E News by Politico, May 2023, www.eenews.net/articles/could-texas-lawmakers-end-the-states-renewable-boo; "Texas SB1303, 2023–2024, 88th Legislature," LegiScan, legiscan.com/TX/text/SB1303/id/2722272.

5. Texas Senate Committee on Business and Commerce hearing, March 28, 2023, https://tlcsenate.granicus.com/MediaPlayer.php?clip_id=17514.

6. "Go to Texas to See the Anti-Green Future of Clean Energy," *The Economist*, January 12, 2023, www.economist.com/business/2023/01/12/go-to-texas-to-see-the-anti-green-future-of-clean-energy.

7. Texas Senate Committee on Business and Commerce hearing.

8. Texas Senate Committee on Business and Commerce hearing.

9. Doug Lewin, "Is the Texas Power Grid Fixed Yet?" The Texas Energy and Power Newsletter, May 30, 2022, https://www.douglewin.com/p/is-the-texas-power-grid-fixed-yet.

10. Ed Hirs, "Why the Texas Power Market Failed," Yale Insights, March 2021, insights.som.yale.edu/insights/why-the-texas-power-market-failed.

11. R. A. "Jake" Dyer, "New Report: TCAP Updates Signature History of Deregulation Chronology," Texas Coalition for Affordable Power, September 27, 2019, tcaptx.com/industry-news/new-report-tcap-updates-signature-history-of-deregulation-chronology.

12. Dyer, "New Report."

13. Thad Warren, "6 Largest Wind Farms in Texas [2023]," EnergyBot, July 2023, www.energybot.com/blog/biggest-wind-farms-in-texas.html#:~:text=While%20Texas%20is%20known%20for,largest%20contributor%20in%20the%20world.

14. EIA Independent Statistics and Analysis, U.S. Energy Information Administration, June 15, 2023, www.eia.gov/state/analysis.php?sid=TX.

15. "Intellectual Gladiator—Steve Wolens," *Texas Monthly*, July 1, 1999, www.texasmonthly.com/news-politics/intellectual-gladiator-steve-wolens.

16. "President Bush Attends Washington International Renewable Energy Conference 2008," the White House, March 20, 2008. georgewbush-whitehouse.archives.gov/news/releases/2008/03/20080305.html.

17. "ACP 2022 Annual Report: A Historic Year for Clean Energy," American Clean Power, May 10, 2023, cleanpower.org/resources/acp-annual-report-2022.

18. E2, "Clean Jobs America," https://e2.org/wp-content/uploads/2022/08/E2-FS-2022-Clean-Jobs-America.pdf.

19. John Fitzgerald Weaver, "Wind and Solar Energy Saved Texans $11 Billion in 2022," *PV Magazine USA*, May 12, 2023, pv-magazine-usa.com/2023/05/12/wind-and-solar-energy-saved-texans-11-billion-in-2022/#:~:text=A%20detailed%20examination%20of%20the,300%25%20increase%20from%20previous%20years.

20. Jimmy Cloutier, "GOP Accepted Millions from Oil and Gas Ahead of Texas Primary," OpenSecrets News, March 2022, www.opensecrets.org/news/2022/03/gop-candidates-accepted-millions-from-oil-and-gas-ahead-of-texas-primary.

21. Paul Krugman, "Why Texas Republicans Are Targeting Renewable Energy," *New York Times*, May 30, 2023, www.nytimes.com/2023/05/30/opinion/texas-wind-renewable-energy.html

22. State of Wyoming, 67th Legislature. SJ0004—Phasing Out New Electric Vehicle Sales by 2035. https://wyoleg.gov/Legislation/2023/SJ0004

23. Bryan Pietsch, "Wyoming GOP Lawmaker Pushes Electric-Car Ban, Then Says He Didn't Mean It," *Washington Post*, January 17, 2023, www.washingtonpost.com/climate-environment/2023/01/17/wyoming-ban-electric-vehicles-cars-2035.

24. Jake Zuckerman, "Ten Ohio Counties Ban Wind, Solar Projects under New State Law," *Ohio Capital Journal*, August 23, 2022, https://ohiocapitaljournal.com/2022/08/23/nine-ohio-counties-ban-wind-solar-projects-under-new-state-law/.

25. David Roberts, "Ohio Just Passed the Worst Energy Bill of the 21st Century," Vox, July 27, 2019, www.vox.com/energy-and-environment/2019/7/27/8910804/ohio-gop-nuclear-coal-plants-renewables-efficiency-hb6.

26. "Former Ohio House Speaker Sentenced to 20 Years in Prison for Leading Racketeering Conspiracy Involving $60 Million in Bribes," June 29, 2023, www.justice.gov/usao-sdoh/pr/former-ohio-house-speaker-sentenced-20-years-prison-leading-racketeering-conspiracy.

27. "Jury Convicts Former Ohio House Speaker, Former Chair of Ohio Republican Party of Participating in Racketeering Conspiracy," March 9, 2023, www.justice.gov/usao-sdoh/pr/jury-convicts-former-ohio-house-speaker-former-chair-ohio-republican-party; Kathiann M. Kowalski, "What's Next in Ohio's Ongoing HB 6 Scandal?" Energy News Network, March 13, 2023, energynews.us/newsletter/%E2%9A%A1-whats-next-in-ohios-ongoing-hb-6-scandal.

28. Molly Taft, "Ron Desantis Signs a Bill That Mandates Cities Keep Using Fossil Fuels," *Gizmodo*, June 28, 2021, gizmodo.com/ron-desantis-signs-a-bill-that-mandates-cities-keep-usi-1847176182.

29. Florida House of Representatives, CS/CS/HB839 (2021), https://www.myfloridahouse.gov/Sections/Bills/billsdetail.aspx?BillId=71648&SessionId=90.

30. Ari Natter, "DeSantis Says No Thanks to $377 Million in US Energy Funds," *Bloomberg News*, July 11, 2023. Florida House of Representatives, CS/CS/HB839 (2021), https://www.myfloridahouse.gov/Sections/Bills/billsdetail.aspx?BillId=71648 &SessionId=90.

31. Hannah Northey and Timothy Cama, "How a Republican President Could Hobble the Climate Law," *Politico*, August 16, 2023, https://www.politico.com/news/2023/08 /16/how-a-republican-president-could-hobble-the-climate-law-00111555.

32. Kevin Breuniger, "Tim Scott Praises the Laffer Curve as He Vows to Make Trump-Era Tax Cuts Permanent," CNBC, September 14, 2023, https://www.cnbc.com /2023/09/14/scott-vows-to-make-trump-tax-cuts-permanent-axe-bidens-inflation-law .html.

33. E2, Clean Economy Now, August 16, 2023, https://e2.org/announcements/.

34. HR 2811, Limit Save, Grow Act, https://www.govinfo.gov/content/pkg/BILLS -118hr2811ih/pdf/BILLS-118hr2811ih.pdf.

35. Kaitlin Lewis, "These Four Republicans Voted against Debt Limit Bill," *Newsweek*, April 27, 2023, www.newsweek.com/these-four-republicans-voted-against-debt-limit -bill-1796935

36. "Debt Limit," U.S. Department of the Treasury, August 16, 2023, home.treasury. gov/policy-issues/financial-markets-financial-institutions-and-fiscal-service/debt-limit.

37. Lisa Mascaro et al., "Biden and McCarthy Reach a Final Deal to Avoid US Default and Now Must Sell It to Congress," AP News, June 21, 2023, apnews.com/article/debt-limit-deal-biden-mccarthy-default-01657c829be119850cd65ab9ffb0626a.

38. HR 3938, Build It in America Act, https://www.congress.gov/bill/118th-congress /house-bill/3938/text.

39. Kashmira Gander, "Donald Trump Bashes Solar Power and 'Windmills': 'When the Wind Doesn't Blow, Turn off the Television Darling.'" *Newsweek*, March 21, 2019, www.newsweek.com/donald-trump-criticizes-solar-power-windmills-turn-television -1370707.

40. E2, Clean Economy Works, https://e2.org/announcements/; Lauren Sforza, "Trump Takes Aim at EV Industry During Speech to Michigan Republicans," *The Hill*, June 26, 2023, https://thehill.com/blogs/blog-briefing-room/4067252-trump -takes-aim-at-ev-industry-during-speech-to-michigan-republicans/.

41. Peter Wade, "Trump Trashes Electric Vehicles Standing in Front of GOP Governor Who Supports Them," *Rolling Stone*, January 28, 2023, www.rollingstone.com/politics /politics-news/trump-trashes-electric-vehicles-mcmaster-1234670312.

42. "Project 2025, Presidential Transition Project," www.project2025.org.

43. Lisa Friedman, "A Republican 2024 Climate Strategy: More Drilling, Less Clean Energy," *New York Times*, August 7, 2023, www.nytimes.com/2023/08/04/climate/ republicans-climate-project2025.html; Dharna Noor, "'Project 2025': Plan to Dismantle US Climate Policy for Next Republican President," *The Guardian*, July 27, 2023, www .theguardian.com/environment/2023/jul/27/project-2025-dismantle-us-climate-policy -next-republican-president.

44. "Executive Order No. 2022–31," SC.gov. Office of the Governor, October 12, 2022, https://governor.sc.gov/sites/governor/files/Documents/Executive-Orders/2022

-10-12%20FILED%20Executive%20Order%20No.%202022-31%20-%20Establishing
%20Electric%20Vehicle%20Initiatives%20%26%20Interagency%20Working%20Group
.pdf.

45. "Gov. Henry McMaster Launches State's First Electric Vehicle Website," SC.gov.
Office of the Governor, February 10, 2023, https://governor.sc.gov/news/2023-02/gov
-henry-mcmaster-launches-states-first-electric-vehicle-website.

46. Interview with Bob Inglis, July 28, 2023.

47. Solar Panels, www.bmwgroup-werke.com/spartanburg/en/responsibility/corporate
-sustainability/solar-panels.html.

48. Information from Plugshare USA, ChargePoint, and US Census.

49. Conservatives for Clean Energy SC and Red Oak Strategic, "South Carolina
Statewide Survey," November 9, 2021, https://cleanenergyconservatives.com/wp-content
/uploads/2021/11/FINAL-NOVEMBER-9_SC_CCE_Survey_Analysis_202111091
.pdf.

50. "Not Just an Ugly Industrial Site: Hyundai Officials Unveil Site Design for
EV Factory," *Savannah Morning News*, https://finance.yahoo.com/news/not-just-ugly
-industrial-hyundai-091555289.html?guce_referrer=aHR0cHM6Ly93d3cuZ29vZ2xlL
mNvbS8&guce_referrer_sig=AQAAAG-VddbDhR1VYaxW2X72HlhF0LYJ8thk8db
YCe_KmmvKlzRSbPtw5GwzeTL2YhVfSjHH47r21ueaHMZv0IfaiQ1kPquM5V8P
0nQUQ5O7SRTC9yEty3J0svBftb7SuZaerOOv2bC3wDNCmTnaiqJatAGnlPpglHr
-GcHBcYPr47Qn

51. Interview with Tollison, July 21, 2023.

52. Gisele Galoustian, "Climate Change Concern in Florida Linked with Recent
Extreme Weather," Florida Atlantic University, May 10, 2023, www.fau.edu/newsdesk/
articles/climate-survey-extreme-weather.php.

53. George Riley, "Here's Why Florida Republicans Are Starting to Embrace Clean
Energy," *Tampa Bay Times*, June 2, 2023, www.tampabay.com/opinion/2023/06/02/heres
-why-florida-republicans-are-starting-embrace-clean-energy-column.

54. Sarah E. Hunt and Michael Dorsey, "Republican Voters Support Clean
Energy: It's Time to Find Common Ground," *The Hill*, November 3, 2022, the-
hill.com/opinion/energy-environment/3717570-republican-voters-support-clean-ener-
gy-its-time-to-find-common-ground.

55. Maureen Groppe, "Gov. Eric Holcomb Applauds Trump Attack on Climate
Rules," *IndyStar*, March 28, 2017, www.indystar.com/story/news/politics/2017/03/28/
holcomb-applauds-trump-attack-climate-rules/99735174.

56. "A Red-State Governor Walks into a COP," *Politico*, November 15, 2022, www
.politico.com/newsletters/the-long-game/2022/11/15/a-red-state-governor-walks-into
-a-cop-00066950.

57. David McIntosh, "Op/Ed: Holcomb Flip Flop? He's at COP27 after Praising
Reversal of Climate Change Rules," *IndyStar*, November 11, 2022, www.indystar.com
/story/opinion/2022/11/11/eric-holcomb-indiana-governor-un-cop27-climate-change
-conference/69635144007.

58. Alex Brown, "EV Battery Supplier Expanding to Kokomo," Inside Indiana Business, December 13, 2022, https://www.insideindianabusiness.com/articles/ev-battery -supplier-expanding-to-kokomo

59. Breana Noble, "Stellantis to Invest $155M in Indiana for Electric Drive Units," *Detroit News*, February 28, 2023, www.detroitnews.com/story/business/autos/chrysler /2023/02/28/stellantis-investment-kokomo-indiana-electric-drive-units/69952883007.

60. "GM to Invest $45M at Bedford Casting Operations to Expand Capacity for EV Drive Unit Castings," *Green Car Congress*, November 20, 2022, www.greencarcongress. com/2022/11/20221119-bedford.html.

CHAPTER 11

1. Kristopher Monroe, "The Weeping Time," *The Atlantic*, September 22, 2014, www .theatlantic.com/business/archive/2014/07/the-weeping-time/374159.

2. Savannah Chamber of Commerce. "Major Employers," Savannah Chamber, February 27, 2023, www.savannahchamber.com/economic-development/major-employers.

3. Savannah Harbor-Interstate 16 Corridor Joint Development Agency, https:// www.savannahjda.com/hmgma-suppliers/; E2, Clean Economy Works, https://e2.org/ announcements/states/georgia/.

4. "Hyundai Supplier PHA to Create over 400 Jobs in Chatham County," State of Georgia, March 6, 2023, https://www.georgia.org/press-release/hyundai-supplier-pha -create-over-400-jobs-chatham-county.

5. Mary Dowling Cook, "Savannah Technical College," New Georgia Encyclopedia, September 9, 2013, https://www.georgiaencyclopedia.org/articles/education/savannah -technical-college/.

6. Kyle Jordan, "Skilled to Work: Savannah Tech Launching New Electric Vehicle Program." May 23, 2023, WTOC 11, https://www.wtoc.com/2023/05/23/skilled-work -savannah-tech-launching-new-electric-vehicle-program/.

7. Interview with Lisa Nash, July 12, 2023.

8. "Gov. Kemp: EV Parts Supplier NVH Korea to Create Over 160 Jobs, Invest $72M in Henry County," Georgia Department of Economic Development, June 22, 2023. gov- .georgia.gov/press-releases/2023-06-22/gov-kemp-ev-parts-supplier-nvh-korea-create- over-160-jobs-invest-72m.

9. City of Commerce, https://commercega.hosted.civiclive.com/living_here/history_of _commerce.

10. SK Battery America Inc., Facebook.com., post, July 20, 2023.

11. Amanda Barber and Lane Ball, "Former Hobet Mine Site to Become WV's Largest Solar Field," 13 News, April 5, 2022, https://www.wowktv.com/news/local/former -hobet-mine-site-to-become-wvs-largest-solar-field/.

12. JoCoMuseum, "Sunflower Army Ammunition Plant: A City Unto Itself," *JoCoHistory Blog*, December 26, 2018, jocohistory.wordpress.com/2014/02/18/sunflow- er-army-ammunition-plant-a-city-unto-itself.

13. "Solar Manufacturer Announces Plans for Brighton Location," Colorado Community Media, June 22, 2023, https://ccm.creativecirclemedia.com/stories/solar -manufacturer-announces-plans-for-brighton-location,438514?

14. https://us.vestas.com/en-us/careers/Colorado-Manufacturing-Investment

15. Jessica A. Knoblauch, "A Giant Oil Refinery Wants to Hide Its Role in Creating the Nation's Most Polluted ZIP Code," *Earthjustice*, October 2022, earthjustice.org/article/a-giant-oil-refinery-wants-to-hide-just-how-dirty-it-makes-the-nation-s-most-polluted-zip-code.

16. "State Health Department Announces an Historic $9 Million Enforcement Package," Department of Public Health and Environment, cdphe.colorado.gov/press-release/state-health-department-announces-an-historic-9-million-enforcement-package.

17. "Kingston—The IBM Years," New York Heritage Digital Collections, nyheritage.org/collections/kingston-ibm-years.

18. "Social Scene and Hangouts, Kingston—The IBM Years," Hudson River Valley Heritage Exhibits, omeka.hrvh.org/exhibits/show/kingston-the-ibm-years/the-workers-of-ibm-kingston/social-scene-and-hangouts.

19. "Kingston, New York, Population 2023," worldpopulationreview.com/us-cities/kingston-ny-population.

20. "Governor Hochul Announces Zinc8 Energy Solutions, a Long-Term Energy Storage Leader, Will Locate Its First Commercial Manufacturing Facility and American Headquarters in Ulster County," NY State, January 26, 2023, www.governor.ny.gov/news/governor-hochul-announces-zinc8-energy-solutions-long-term-energy-storage-leader-will-locate.

21. Michael Wilson et al., "The Monster Buffalo Snowstorm May Have Set a Record. More Is on the Way," *New York Times*, November 20, 2022, www.nytimes.com/2022/11/19/nyregion/buffalo-ny-snowstorm-blizzard.html; Emily Shapiro, "Buffalo Storm Victims: What We Know about the Lives Lost," *ABC News*, December 30, 2022, abcnews.go.com/US/buffalo-storm-victims-lives-lost/story?id=95887294#:~:text=Thirty%2Dnine%20people%20have%20died%20in%20Erie%20County%2C%20New%20York,Erie%20County%20Executive%20Mark%20Poloncarz.

22. "Governor Hochul Announces Zinc8 Energy Solutions."

23. Paul Wellener et al., "Creating Pathways for Tomorrow's Workforce Today," Deloitte Insights, June 2023, www2.deloitte.com/us/en/insights/industry/manufacturing/manufacturing-industry-diversity.html; National Association of Manufacturers: Facts about Manufacturing, Nam.org, https://www.nam.org/facts-about-manufacturing/.

24. "Imperial County, CA," Data USA, datausa.io/profile/geo/imperial-county-ca#:~:text=Poverty%20%26%20Diversity&text=22.5%25%20of%20the%20population%20for,the%20national%20average%20of%2012.8%25.

25. Elizabeth Aguilera, "What Keeps Families in One of the Most Polluted Places in California?" CalMatters, June 23, 2020, calmatters.org/health/2019/01/what-keeps-families-in-one-of-the-most-polluted-places-in-california.

26. Ryan Kennedy, "EV Battery Gigafactory with 54 GWh Output Planned for Southern California," *Pv Magazine USA*, April 20,. 2022, pv-magazine-usa.com/2022/04/19/ev-battery-gigafactory-with-54-gwh-output-planned-for-southern-california; "Lithium Mining in North America," *IER*, September 21, 2022, www.instituteforenergyresearch.org/renewable/lithium-mining-in-north-america/#:~:text=Despite%20the%20United%20States%20having,of%20the%20world's%20annual%20supply.

NOTES

27. "President Biden Hosts a Roundtable on Securing Critical Minerals for a Future Made in America," the White House, YouTube, February 22, 2022, www.youtube.com/watch?v=DYZfC8JNsZ0.

28. "Governor Newsom Visits Lithium Valley to Highlight Momentum on Becoming Global Source for Battery Production," State of California Governor's Office, March 21, 2023, www.gov.ca.gov/2023/03/20/governor-newsom-visits-lithium-valley-to-highlight-momentum-on-becoming-global-source-for-battery-production.

29. "State Budget Commits $80 Million to Bolster STEM Education, Research in Imperial Valley," NewsCenter, SDSU, newscenter.sdsu.edu/sdsu_newscenter/news_story.aspx?sid=78807.

30. "Blue Ribbon Commission on Lithium Extraction in California Submits Final Report to State Legislature," California Energy Commission, www.energy.ca.gov/news/2022-12/blue-ribbon-commission-lithium-extraction-california-submits-final-report-state.

31. "Lithium Carbonate Price 2010–2022," Statista, August 6, 2023, www.statista.com/statistics/606350/battery-grade-lithium-carbonate-price/#:~:text=In%202022%2C%20the%20average%20price,and%20silvery%2Dwhite%20alkali%20metal.

32. "President Biden Hosts a Roundtable."

33. "Stellantis Secures Low Emissions Lithium Supply for North American Electric Vehicle Production From Controlled Thermal Resources," Stellantis.com, www.stellantis.com/en/news/press-releases/2022/june/stellantis-secures-low-emissions-lithium-supply-for-north-american-electric-vehicle-production-from-controlled-thermal-resources

34. "EV Battery Gigafactory with 54 GWh Output Planned for Southern California," *Pv Magazine USA*, April 20, 2022, pv-magazine-usa.com/2022/04/19/ev-battery-gigafactory-with-54-gwh-output-planned-for-southern-california.

35. Ally Muir, "California Governor Gavin Newsom Visits CTR's Hell's Kitchen in Imperial County's 'Lithium Valley,'" C Thermal, March 2023, www.cthermal.com/latest-news/california-governor-gavin-newsom-visits-ctrs-hells-kitchen-in-imperial-countys-lithium-valley.

36. "President Biden Hosts a Roundtable."

37. E2, "How The Clean Economy Is Benefiting Rural America through the Inflation Reduction Act," www.e2.org.

38. Tia Lynn Ivey, "'Rivian Go Away' Demonstrators Flood JDA Meeting in Protest of $5 Billion Plant," Morgan County Citizen, March 3, 2023. https://www.morgancountycitizen.com/news/rivian-go-away-demonstrators-flood-jda-meeting-in-protest-of-5-billion-plant/article_94024642-7e1f-11ec-8cb4-fbdbe1228577.html.

39. https://www.redfin.com/city/17651/GA/Savannah/housing-market

40. https://www.colliers.com/en/research/savannah/2022q4industrial

41. Adam Van Brimmer, "Bracing for Hyundai's Impact: What 8,100 Jobs Paying $20-Plus per Hour Means for Savannah," *Savannah Morning News*, June 1, 2022, www.savannahnow.com/story/opinion/2022/06/01/hyundai-ev-and-battery-factories-transform-savannah-economy/9992369002.

42. "U.S. Department of the Treasury, IRS Release Proposed Guidance to Continue U.S. Clean Energy Manufacturing Boom, Strengthen America's Energy Security | U.S.

Department of the Treasury," 2023, https://home.treasury.gov/news/press-releases/jy1989.

43. "Clean Economy Works," E2, www.e2.org/announcements.

44. Interview with Gina McCarthy, June 16, 2023. "U.S. Department of the Treasury, IRS Release Proposed Guidance to Continue U.S. Clean Energy Manufacturing Boom, Strengthen America's Energy Security | U.S. Department of the Treasury," 2023, https://home.treasury.gov/news/press-releases/jy1989.

45. "Remarks by President Biden on Bidenomics," the White House, July 6, 2023, www.whitehouse.gov/briefing-room/speeches-remarks/2023/07/06/remarks-by-president-biden-on-bidenomics.

46. "Anovion Technologies Announces Plans for $800 Million Initial Investment in New Manufacturing Facility in Southwest Georgia," Anovion Technologies, July 2023, www.anoviontech.com/news/anovion-technologies-announces-plans-for-800-million-initial-investment-in-new-manufacturing-facility-in-southwest-georgia.

47. Trump, "Agenda47."

CHAPTER 12

1. Donald J. Trump, "Agenda 47: Rescuing America's Auto Industry from Joe Biden's Disastrous Job-Killing Policies," *Rumble*, rumble.com/v316b1u-agenda47-saving-americas-auto-industry-from-joe-bidens-job-killing-policies.html.

2. "Foreign Direct Investment in the United States, Preliminary 1st Quarter 2023," Global Business Alliance, June 2023, globalbusiness.org/fdius-q1–23.

3. "Clean Economy Works," E2, https://e2.org/reports/clean-economy-works-2023/.

4. Joshua Huff, "Vitro Enters Agreement with First Solar to Manufacture Glass for Solar Panels," *USGlass Magazine & USGNN Headline News*, April 26, 2023, www.usglassmag.com/2023/04/vitro-enters-agreement-with-first-solar-to-manufacture-glass-for-solar-panels.

5. Makenzie Boucher, "A Company Is Expanding Their Footprint in Shreveport by $28.5 Million," *Shreveport Times*, April 26, 2023, www.shreveporttimes.com/story/money/business/2023/04/26/a-company-is-expanding-their-footprint-in-shreveport-by-28-5-million/70151917007.

6. Nina Korman, "Nextracker, MSS Steel Tubes USA Join Forces on New Factory," *Solar Industry*, May 18, 2023, solarindustrymag.com/nextracker-mss-steel-tubes-usa-join-forces-on-new-factory.

7. Riley Beggin, "Michigan to Get $400 Million Hydrogen Technology Facility from Norwegian Company," *The Detroit News*, May 3, 2023, www.detroitnews.com/story/business/2023/05/03/michigan-to-get-400m-hydrogen-technology-facility-from-norwegian-firm/70179864007.

8. "Whitmer Announces Michigan Wins 400 Million Investment from Nel Hydrogen," www.michigan.gov/whitmer/news/press-releases/whitmer-announces-michigan-wins-400-million-investment-from-nel-hydrogen.

9. Beggin, "Michigan to Get $400 Million Hydrogen Technology Facility from Norwegian Company."

10. "KORE Power Receives Conditional Commitment for $850 Million from the U.S. Department of Energy's Loan Programs Office for the KOREPlex Advanced Battery Manufacturing Facility," korepower.com/media/kore-power-receives-conditional-commitment-for-850-million-from-the-us-department-of-energy-for-the-koreplex.

11. "KORE Power Receives Conditional Commitment."

12. Riley Beggin, "GOP Lawmakers Threaten to Call Ford CEO before Congress over Chinese Battery Tech," *Detroit News*, September 27, 2023. https://www.detroitnews.com/story/business/autos/ford/2023/09/27/gop-lawmakers-threaten-to-call-ford-ceo-before-congress-over-catl-ties/70980088007/.

13. "Financing the Energy Transition Webinar," Resources for the Future, June 20, 2023, https://www.rff.org/events/pls/director-jigar-shah/.

14. "Financing the Energy Transition Webinar."

15. Yohan Min et al., "Effects of Renewable Energy Provisions of the Inflation Reduction Act on Technology Costs, Materials Demand, and Labor," Zenodo (CERN European Organization for Nuclear Research), European Organization for Nuclear Research, June 12, 2023, https://doi.org/10.5281/zenodo.8027939.

16. "Global PV Module Manufacturing Share 2021 by Country," *Statista*, February 8, 2023, www.statista.com/statistics/668749/regional-distribution-of-solar-pv-module-manufacturing

17. Vincent Shaw, "Hounen to Build 1 GW Solar Module Factory in U.S.," *Pv Magazine USA*, March 17, 2023, pv-magazine-usa.com/2023/03/17/hounen-to-build-1-gw-solar-module-factory-in-u-s

18. Will Wade, "First Solar Rejects US Site for New Factory, Eyes Europe or India Instead," *Bloomberg.com*, June 29, 2022, www.bloomberg.com/news/articles/2022-06-29/first-solar-rejects-us-site-for-new-factory-eyes-europe-or-india-instead.

19. https://investor.firstsolar.com/news/press-release-details/2022/First-Solar-Selects-Alabama-for-Fourth-American-Manufacturing-Facility/default.aspx

20. "Energy Technology Perspectives 2023," IEA, https://iea.blob.core.windows.net/assets/a86b480e-2b03-4e25-bae1-da1395e0b620/EnergyTechnologyPerspectives2023.pdf.

21. Ben Holland and Alexandre Tanzi, "Factory Boom Sweeps US with Construction at Record $190 Billion," *Bloomberg.com*, June 1, 2023, www.bloomberg.com/news/articles/2023-06-01/factory-boom-sweeps-us-with-construction-at-record-190-billion; "Unpacking the Boom in U.S. Construction of Manufacturing Facilities," *U.S. Department of The Treasury*, August 16, 2023, home.treasury.gov/news/featured-stories/unpacking-the-boom-in-us-construction-of-manufacturing-facilities.

22. Brooke Sutherland, "Industrial Strength: A 'Bidenomics' Factory Boost, but Maybe Not in Reshoring," *Bloomberg.com*, June 30, 2023, www.bloomberg.com/opinion/articles/2023-06-30/industrial-strength-a-bidenomics-factory-boost-but-maybe-not-in-reshoring.

23. Sutherland, "Industrial Strength."

24. Yellen remarks at PosiGen in New Orleans, Louisiana, June 30, 2023, https://www.prnewswire.com/news-releases/posigen-hosts-treasury-secretary-janet-yellen-at

-its-new-orleans-area-headquarters-301873888.html#:~:text=We%20are%20committed
%20to%20ensuring,and%20lowering%20costs%20for%20consumers.

25. "Energy Technology Perspectives 2023."

26. "Press Corner," *European Commission*, ec.europa.eu/commission/presscorner/
detail/en/ip_23_510; "Europe Unveils $270 Billion Response to US Green Subsidies,"
CNN.com, February 1, 2023. https://www.cnn.com/2023/02/01/business/europe-green
-deal-industrial-plan/index.html.

27. Derek Brower, "Canada Warns US against Waging 'Carbon Subsidy War,'" *Financial
Times*, April 2, 2023, www.ft.com/content/4b102da2-5f3e-4046-8d12-ab9e3ca89332.

28. Alex Ballingall, "Federal Budget's Clean Tax Credits Try to Ensure Joe Biden
Doesn't Outgreen Canada," *Toronto Star*, July 19, 2023, https://www.thestar.com/politics
/federal/2023/03/28/federal-budgets-clean-tax-credits-try-to-ensure-joe-biden-doesnt
-outgreen-canada.html.

29. "Japan's 'GX: Green Transformation Policy' Is a Missed Opportunity to Respond to
the Current Climate and Energy Crises," Renewable Energy Institute, www.renewable-ei
.org/en/activities/reports/20221227.php; Hirata Kimiko, "What Is Green Transformation (GX)?," *Climate Integrate*, July 25, 2023, climateintegrate.org/archives/2700.

30. "Government Allocates 39600 MW of Domestic Solar PV Module Manufacturing Capacity under PLI (Tranche-II)," pib.gov.in/PressReleaseIframe-
Page.aspx?PRID=1911380; "Indian Government Awards Production Linked
Incentives to First Solar's India Manufacturing Facility," First Solar, Inc., inves-
tor.firstsolar.com/news/press-release-details/2023/Indian-Government-Awards-Pro-
duction-Linked-Incentives-to-First-Solars-India-Manufacturing-Facility/
default.aspx.

31. Aditi Shah, "India Approves $3.5 Bln Scheme to Boost Clean Fuel Vehicles,"
Reuters, September 15, 2021, www.reuters.com/world/india/india-approves-35-billion
-incentive-scheme-auto-sector-drones-2021-09-15; "Indian Government Awards
Production Linked Incentives to First Solar's India Manufacturing Facility," First
Solar, Inc., investor.firstsolar.com/news/press-release-details/2023/Indian-Govern-
ment-Awards-Production-Linked-Incentives-to-First-Solars-India-Manufacturing-Fa-
cility/default.aspx; "Energy Technology Perspectives 2023."

32. Jon Emont et al., "Mineral-Rich Developing Nations Demand Bigger Piece of the
EV Pie," *Wall Street Journal*, July 1, 2023, www.wsj.com/articles/mineral-rich-developing
-nations-demand-bigger-piece-of-the-ev-pie-d1421603.

33. "Global Low-Carbon Energy Technology Investment Surges Past $1 Trillion for
the First Time," *BloombergNEF*, January 25, 2023, about.bnef.com/blog/global-low-car-
bon-energy-technology-investment-surges-past-1-trillion-for-the-first-time.

34. Zhou Feng, "China's 14th Five-Year Plans on Renewable Energy Development and Modern Energy System," www.efchina.org/Blog-en/blog-20220905-en#:~:
text=The%20plan%20targets%20a%2050,China's%20incremental%20electricity%20and
%20energy.

35. "Global Low-Carbon Energy Technology Investment."

36. "Global Low-Carbon Energy Technology Investment."

37. "Energy Technology Perspectives 2023."

38. "IFC Study Finds Climate Pact Helped Open Up $23 Trillion in Emerging-Market Opportunities," 2016, IFC Press Releases, https://pressroom.ifc.org/all/pages/PressDetail.aspx?ID=17382.

EPILOGUE

1. Michelin Greenville, SC HNA https://jobs.michelinman.com/recruitment-sites/greenville-sc-hna; Krys Merryman, "Michelin North America CEO Talks EV, Sustainability in South Carolina," GSA Business Report, February 16, 2023, https://gsabusiness.com/news/automotive/83175/.

2. Scooter Doll, "BMW Breaks Ground on New US battery Facility," Electrek, June 27, 2023, https://electrek.co/2023/06/27/bmw-new-us-battery-facility-south-carolina-ev-hub-aesc-woodruff/; BMW, https://www.bmwgroup-werke.com/spartanburg/en.html.

3. Maxine Joselow, "How Dark Money Groups Led Ohio to Redefine Gas as 'Green Energy.'" Washington Post, January 18, 2023, www.washingtonpost.com/climate-environment/2023/01/17/ohio-natural-gas-green-energy.

4. Aaron Cantú, "California Lobbyist Explains How to Skirt Climate Scrutiny in State Legislature," https://capitalandmain.com/california-lobbyist-explains-how-to-skirt-climate-scrutiny-in-state-legislature, June 28, 2023; capitalandmain.com/california-lobbyist-explains-how-to-skirt-climate-scrutiny-in-state-legislature. Accessed August 25, 2023.

5. Heritage Foundation, Project 2025 Mandate for Leadership, Forward: A Promise to America, https://thf_media.s3.amazonaws.com/project2025/2025_MandateForLeadership_FOREWORD.pdf.

INDEX

CAISO. *See* California
Independent System Operator
California, 164–66; Advanced
Clean Cars II standard in, 15,
85–86; carbon capture and
storage in, 121–23; E2 in,
99–100, 106, 216–17; equity
in, 131–47; EVs in, 164–65;
Global Warming Solutions Act
in, 163, 217; greenhouse gas
emissions in, 164; heat pumps
and, 97–99; hybrid vehicles
in, 85, 164, 217; Lithium
Valley in, 192–96; misleading
information in, 215–16; Paris
Climate Accords and, 153–54;
solar energy in, 171; wind
energy in, 71
California Air Resources Board,
85–86, 92, 165
California Global Warming
Solutions Act, 151–52
California Independent System
Operator (CAISO), 69
Calpine Corporation, 122
Campbell, Carroll, 157
Canada, 89, 116, 207
Cantwell, Maria, 156
carbon capture and storage,
117–23; in Canada, 207; DOE
and, 118–19, 120; EPA and,
121; in IRA, 51, 119–20
CarbonCapture Inc., 122–23
Carbon Free Power Project, 111
Carper, Tom, 27

carried interest loophole, 33–34
Carrier, 93, 96
Carson, Jon, 59
CATL. *See* Contemporary
Amperex Technology Co.
cement, 119
Center for Biological
Diversity, 114
CES. *See* Consumer
Electronics Show
Channing Street Copper Co., 106
ChargePoint, 88
ChargerHelp, 90
Cheung, Albert, 209
Chevron Corporation, 150
Chile, 208
China, 26; batteries in, 11–12, 30,
209; semiconductors in, 45;
solar energy/panels in, 204–5,
209. *See also specific companies*
CHIPS and Science Act. *See*
Creating Helpful Incentives to
Produce Semiconductors
CHIPS for America International
Technology Security and
Innovation Fund, 51, *52*
Cirba Solutions, 13, 159
Clark, Jeff, 170
Clean Communities Investment
Accelerator, 142
Clean Power Plan, 183
ClearPath Foundation, 68
Clemson University International
Center for Automative
Research (CU-ICAR), 159–60

clean air standards and, 8–9;
consumer demand for, 7;
Department of Energy Loan
Programs Office and, 145–46;
distorted information on,
178–79, 215; electrical grid and,
67; electricity for, 57; EPA and,
84; equity and, 140; fossil fuels
and, 15; in Georgia, 198–99;
greenhouse gas emissions and,
16, 85; growth of, 85; incentives
for, 49; IRA and, 49, 77, *78–81*;
Jordan and, 20; long-term
storage and, 126; Manchin
and, 30; McConnell and, 20; in
North Carolina, 176; in Ohio,
173–74; projected increases in,
7; sales of, 77; savings from, 49;
semiconductors for, 31, 38; in
South Carolina, 158–59, 179–
80, 181, 212–13; tax credits for,
30, 41, 42, 84; in Texas, 167–67;
in Wyoming, 173. *See also
specific companies*
Ellis, Evette, 90
Empowering Diverse Climate
Talent (EDICT), 141
Energy Dome, 126
Energy Futures Initiative
(EFI), 47
Energy Star, 57, 67, 105, 164
Energy Storage for Social Equity
(ES4SA), 124
Enersystems, Inc., 23–24
EnerWealth Solutions, 138

engines, 75–92; in IRA, 49. *See
also* electronic vehicles
Enphase Energy, 198
Enron, 171
Entergy, 60
Entrek, 184
environmental justice. *See* equity
Environmental Protection Agency
(EPA), 22; auto pollution
standards of, 84, 85, 165;
carbon capture and storage
and, 121; Energy Star of,
67, 105, 164; EVs and, 84;
Greenhouse Gas Reduction
Fund and, 141–44; Volkswagen
and, 82–83; White House
Environmental Justice Advisory
Council in, 133
EnvironSpark, 88
Envision ACSC, 158
Eolian, 124–25
EPA. *See* Environmental
Protection Agency
equity, 131–47; ARRA and,
135; Biden and, 133–36;
Department of Energy Loan
Programs Office and, 136; IRA
and, 136, 139, 141–44; Obama
and, 135; Tesla and, 133
ES4SA. *See* Energy Storage for
Social Equity
Eticitty, Erik, 100
Eubanks, Steve, 100
European Union (EU), 207
Evergreen Action, 162

EVGo, 92
Eviation, 155–56
EVs. *See* electronic vehicles
EVSE. *See* electric vehicle supply
  equipment
Exelon Corp, 90
Exxon Mobil, 114

F-150 Lightning trucks, 15,
  77, 188
FAA, 73
Fan, Ariel, 89–90
FAST-41, 72
Federal-Aid Highway Act of
  1956, 37
Federal Power Act, 72
Fell, Mike, 95
Ferguson, Patrick "Bulldog," 1–2
fiber optic network, 73
First Solar, Inc., 6, 10, 61,
  202, 208
fission, 110–12
Fjord1, 92
Florida, 61, 104, 106, 144, 174;
  climate change and, 182
Floyd, George, 133, 138, 141
Ford, Bill, 82
Ford, Henry, 82, 87–88
Ford Motor Company, 10; battery
  plants of, 77; charging stations
  of, 89; EVs of, 4, 15, 77, 82,
  87–88, 188; F-150 Lightning
  trucks by, 15, 77, 188
Form Energy, 126–27

fossil fuels: in China, 209; EVs
  and, 15; extracted amounts of,
  15; for heating and cooling,
  9; hydrogen and, 114–15;
  Manchin and, 30; PTC and,
  54; solar panels and, 15; tax
  credits for, 55; in Texas, 168,
  169; transition from, 41. *See also*
  coal; natural gas; oil
Foster, Dave, 47
Fox News, 24–25
fracking, 15, 31, 40
France, 210
FREYR Battery, 10
Frito-Lay, 91–92
Frontier Energy, 117
Fusion Industry Association, 110
fusion power, 109–10

Gaetz, Matt, 176
Garcia Richard, Stephanie,
  149–50
Gates, Bill, 27, 127
GE Hitachi Nuclear Energy, 111
General Motors (GM): battery
  factories of, 11; at CES, 75–76;
  charging stations of, 89; EVs of,
  4, 76, 195; in Imperial Valley,
  195; locomotives of, 165
Generate Capital, 128
Georgia, 161–62, 176, 181–89,
  196–99, 213; Hyundai in, 161,
  181–82, 186–87, 196–97
geothermal, 58; in Canada, 207;
  electrical grid and, 67, 70

About the Author

Bob Keefe is executive director of E2 (Environmental Entrepreneurs), a national, nonpartisan group of business owners, investors, and professionals who leverage economic research and their business perspective to advance policies that are good for the environment and good for the economy. He is the author of *Climatenomics: Washington, Wall Street, and the Economic Battle to Save Our Planet* (Rowman & Littlefield, 2022). Previously, Keefe spent nearly twenty-five years as a journalist, reporting for the *Atlanta Journal-Constitution*, the Cox Media Group, the *St. Petersburg Times*, and the *Austin American-Statesman*. He resides in San Diego, California.